THE HISTORY OF TATTOOING

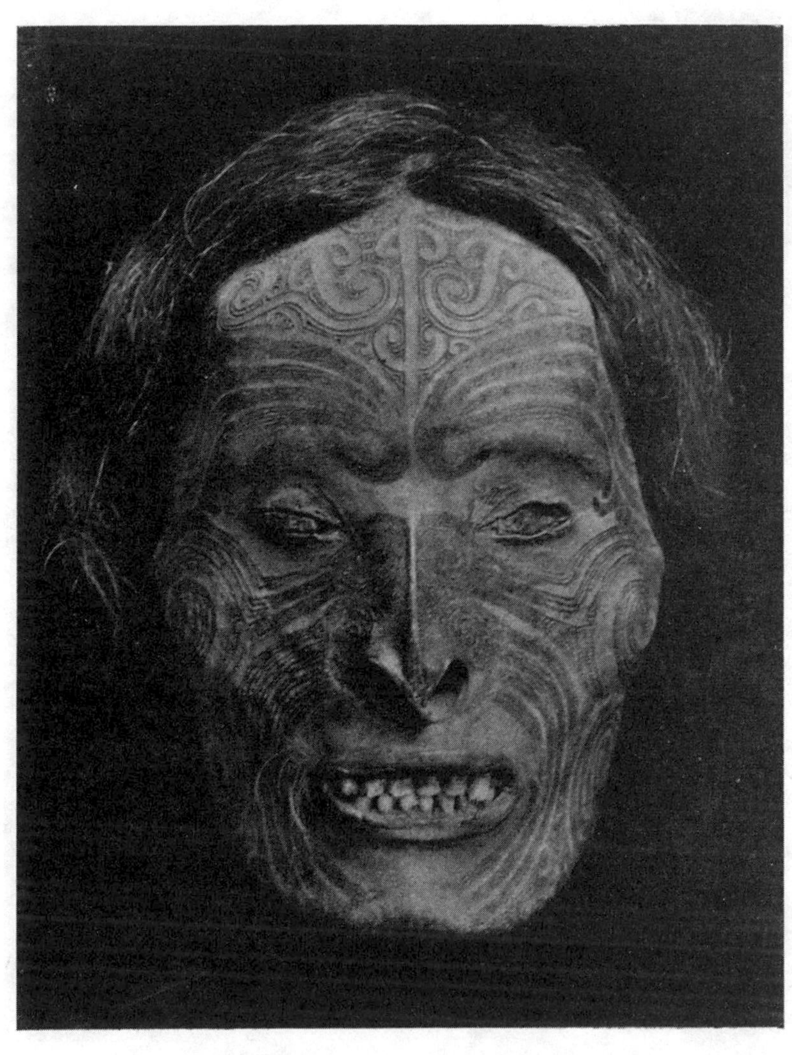

MOKO TATTOO, NEW ZEALAND

THE HISTORY OF TATTOOING

Wilfrid Dyson Hambly

DOVER PUBLICATIONS, INC.
Mineola, New York

Bibliographical Note

This Dover edition, first published in 2009, is an unabridged republication of the work originally published by H. F. & G. Witherby, London, in 1925 under the title *The History of Tattooing and Its Significance.* The original foldout map has been reproduced here as a double-page spread. The present volume also includes twenty-two additional pages of tattoo designs, selected from various sources, inserted between pp. 108 and 109.

Library of Congress Cataloging-in-Publication Data

Hambly, Wilfrid Dyson, 1886–
[History of tattooing and its significance]
The history of tattooing / Wilfrid Dyson Hambly. — Dover ed.
p. cm.
Originally published: The history of tattooing and its significance. London : H.F. & G. Witherby, 1925.
Includes bibliographical references and index.
ISBN-13: 978-0-486-46812-9
ISBN-10: 0-486-46812-7
1. Tattooing—History. 2. Tattooing—Social aspects. I. Title.

GT2345.H35 2009
391.6'5—dc22

2008039140

Manufactured in the United States of America
Dover Publications, Inc., 31 East 2nd Street, Mineola, N.Y. 11501

CONTENTS

LIST OF ILLUSTRATIONS

PLATES

TEXT ILLUSTRATIONS

TEXT ILLUSTRATIONS—continued

MAP

ADDITIONAL ILLUSTRATIONS

[Inserted between pp. 108–109]

INTRODUCTION

To readers who are acquainted with the contents of "Die Tatowirung," published by Joest some forty years ago, an addition to the subject of body marking may on first considerations appear to be a work of supererogation. This, however, is far from being the case, and in this connection it should not be forgotten that "Die Tatowirung" (1887) antedated the advent of modern anthropological inquiry. Consequently Joest has concerned himself chiefly with painting, tattooing and scarification in their technological aspects, and of necessity without reference to the research of the past twenty years, which reveals the existence of taboo, ceremonial and belief, forming the *raison d'être* of body marking in New Guinea, Borneo, Assam and North America.

In view of the publication of data gleaned in the fields of modern ethnological research, and the important connection of body marking with such cognate subjects as head hunting and totemism, there is not merely justification but necessity for publication of a detailed consideration of this subject. Pursuit of the inquiry has followed along psychological, sociological and historical lines. The technological problem of design, motive, colour, perspective and other aspects of technique are discussed in Chapter IV.

Of these main aspects of the problem the psychological, sociological and æsthetic present fewest difficulties, for as a mental and social process body marking forms part of a congruous whole including totemism, exogamy, and the search for immortality. This harmonious entity of magico-religious beliefs, so closely interwoven with body marking, illustrates the view of Rivers[1] that there is a logic of primitive man though his premises may be false owing to absence of a system of natural science.

The historical aspect introduces many difficult, one fears almost insuperable problems, for a review of archæological evidence and artefacts in the way of marked female figures, and use of red ochre in interments, takes the investigator far beyond the narrow confines of 6,000 years of recorded history to the dim recesses of palæolithic times. Consideration of the antiquity of body marking in culture centres of the world, including, of course, Babylon, Egypt, Peru, Mexico and China, brings to light many interesting facts, and in addition gives a reasonable dateable sequence of the migration of tattooing. From the thirteenth to the nineteenth centuries there is no paucity of dated testimony relating to the existence of body marking. But early observers contented themselves with casual references to, or at best a description of technique and *modus operandi.* Not until the last quarter of the nineteenth century was there detailed anthropological field inquiry which

[1] W. H. R. Rivers, " Medicine, Magic, and Religion," 1924. *Hibbert Journal*, 1912, Vol. X, p. 393. " Primitive Conception of Death," " Aims of Ethnology in Psychology and Politics," 1923. Compare with Bruhl, " Les Fonctions Mentales dans les Sociétés Inférieurs," Paris, 1910.

supplied knowledge of taboo, ritual and belief connected with body marking. Ceremonial provides evidence of migration of culture as opposed to the older idea of a psychic unity accounting for the appearance of identical beliefs, taboos, and practices at disparate points all over the globe.

Malinowski,[1] in reviewing recent expositions of the migrations of culture as detailed in "The Children of the Sun,"[2] "Megalithic Culture in Indonesia,"[3] and "The Migrations of Early Culture"[4] thinks a compromise between the historical and ethnological schools possible. In this connection I suggest that there is a helpful sense in which the term "psychic unity" may be legitimately used to express a uniform emotional tendency including curiosity with regard to a future life, self-assertion, sympathy, power of suggestion and suggestibility. All these aspects of mental activity are common to man, and some are noticeable in present-day representatives of his anthropoid precursors.

This common emotional trend accounts for the rapid spread of cultures, especially when these in certain aspects and doctrines satisfy an insistent demand for acquisition or preservation of social status; answer a query respecting survival after physical death; offer a means of escape from demons of pain or sickness; show a safe passage from puberty to maturity; or present some positive means of alluring good luck and avoiding the evil eye. These

[1] "Nature," March 1st, 1924, Vol. CXIII, p. 299.
[2] W. J. Perry, 1923.
[3] *Ibid.*, 1918.
[4] Grafton Elliot Smith, 1915, also "Evolution of the Dragon," 1919.

are a few of the desiderata conferred by systems of body marking which have a world-wide distribution.

There is an objection to the method of taking a universal survey, in that superficial resemblances may lead to hasty generalizations. Detailed work in a restricted area among peoples of kindred cultures has without question a high value in forming the basis of philosophical and historical speculation. But sociological, psychological, and historical inquiry cannot progress satisfactorily without a frequent silhouetting of details against a broad anthropological background. Unless fragments of the pattern are dovetailed, enlightenment is no greater than that derived from sectional pictures on a jigsaw puzzle. It is isolated study that gives rise to unconnected and often conflicting hypotheses and opinions.

Westermarck, while not ignoring magico-religious aspects of tattooing, stresses the connection of body marking with sexual impulse.[1] Joest denies the religious significance of tattooing and argues his point with particular reference to Samoa, disposing somewhat lightly of legends of divine origin and exercise of the craft by priests. He appears to regard painting as an ornament and insecticide.[2] Sinclair, whose researches have been extensive, connects body marking with a play of religious and patriotic sentiments.[3] Lombroso treats tattooing among criminals as atavism.[4] Lacassagne is interested in the medical aspect of body marks and their indication of an

[1] "History of Human Marriage," 1901, Vol. I, p. 516.
[2] "Die Tatowirung," Berlin, 1887, pp. 60-5, etc.
[3] A. T. Sinclair, "American Anthropt.," 1908, Vol. X, etc.
[4] C. Lombroso, "L'Homme Criminel," 1895.

undeveloped emotional temperament.[1] Captain F. R. Barton thinks that tattooing in the Pacific is founded on a religious impulse.[2] Brewster, after twenty years residence in Fiji, attaches extreme importance to tattooing, which he regards as the key to many historical and ethnological problems.[3] Haddon notes the connection between body marking and totemism.[4] H. Wuttke[5] and Waitz Gerland[6] admit the religious impetus for tattooing, but Marquardt[7] would not concede this point for Samoa.

Frazer[8] says: "When we observe how often the custom of tattooing women at puberty exists not merely for ornament, we are led to believe that the savage regards the custom as a charm against dangers which he apprehends at that period of life."

Theories concerning the origin and impetus for tattooing necessarily vary according to the particular area studied. When there has been elimination of taboo and ritual, and peculiar beliefs are not reported, desire for ornament is the facile explanation. There are for the inquirer difficulties of language not wholly overcome by a good interpreter, while reticence and secrecy are the natural safeguards of useful magico-religious observances, whose influence persists vaguely after cessation of the actual rites.

[1] "Les Tatouages," Paris, 1881, and "Le Criminel au point de vuu Anthrop," 1908.

[2] J.A.I., 1918, p. 22.

[3] A. B. Brewster, "Hill Tribes of Fiji," 1922, p. 185.

[4] A. C. Haddon, "Evolution in Art," 1895, pp. 43-5, 252.

[5] "Die Enstehung der Schrift," p. 96. "Abbildungen zur Gesichichte der Schrift," Leipzig, 1873, Band I, pp. 733-40.

[6] "Anthropologie der Naturvolker," Leipzig, 1865, pp. 34-5, Band VI.

[7] "Die Tatowirung in Samoa," 1899, p. 12.

[8] "Totemism and Exogamy," Vol. IV, p. 207.

In 1888 Buckland[1] called attention to the geographical distribution of tattooing, and Elliot Smith[2] has recently noted the coincidence of this distribution with the megalithic track; without over-stressing geographical agreement as an indication of migratory allied cultures. Tattooing by puncture is found over the greater part of the world, and configuration of surface marks out certain lines as an obvious and comparatively easy means of dispersal. Hence the practice of tattooing plotted geographically will give a fairly good coincidence with related and unrelated factors alike, provided these are widely distributed. Useful arts, practices and beliefs suffer local decline. Part of a complex may be abandoned, or custom survives without explanation; but in spite of lacunæ, body marking presents an almost complete story of ritual, taboo, and belief, whose similarity, often identity, distribution, and utilitarian value in primitive society afford material for discussion throughout these pages. Body marking is largely concerned with attempts to secure a place in heaven, to acquire a *rite de passage* from one social status to another, to assist in retention of class privilege, and a varied category of benefits detailed in the summary following Chapter III.

The three main varieties of body marking, namely, painting, tattoo by puncture, and scarification, have been considered simultaneously. Painting certainly was the first form of technique to appear, and this far back in palæolithic times when red ochre was extensively used. Tattoo by puncture was probably

[1] J.A.I., Vol. XVII.

[2] "Migrations of Early Culture," 1915, p. 2.

a deliberate invention of some genius who saw a way of making a magico-religious colouring more permanent. I think with Rivers[1] that scarification was probably therapeutic in origin, but there has been no difficulty in demonstrating the connection of ritual and taboo with this form of marking; possibly the connection arose from contact with tattoo proper, the result being a grafting of ritual, belief, and taboo, from one form of technique to another. On the whole beliefs relating to scarification are less varied, and ceremonial taboo and ritual are less pronounced, than in the case of painting and puncture tattoo.

The basis of classification in succeeding chapters has been the beliefs associated with body marks irrespective of the particular technique employed. And in the similarity of these beliefs, rites, and taboos, is found the strongest evidence of migration of culture. It appears unlikely that the various ideas detailed in Chapters I, II, and III should have arisen again and again in an independent manner at numerous widely-separated points. Of local migration of patterns there is clear evidence.[2]

My own interest in the subject of body marking was aroused by consideration of tribal, therapeutic, and amuletic markings in the Anglo-Egyptian Sudan, also by inspection of a great variety of tattooed designs worn by soldiers and sailors in Gallipoli, Malta, and France.

The following description of several classes and periods of literature may assist the student of body

[1] "Medicine, Magic, Religion," 1924, p. 99.

[2] "Unexplored New Guinea," W. N. Beaver, 1922, p. 169. "In Primitive New Guinea," J. H. Holmes, 1924, p. 84. "Pagan Tribes of Borneo," Hose and McDougall, Vol. I, p. 244.

marking in selecting what is most useful for his particular research from the extensive bibliography available.

References to the occurrences of body marks are numerous from the fourteenth to eighteenth centuries, but early travellers usually made brief mention of outward form without investigating attached belief and ritual. Early Spanish voyagers use the word "pintado" meaning "painted," or "stained," "patterned" or "dappled." The word "tattoo" was not adopted into English until the late eighteenth century, so an investigator may be left in doubt as to the nature of the markings. Henry Ibbot, midshipman of H.M.S. *Dolphin*, 1767, says of Tahitians: "One thing very remarkable, which I never heard of any people before, is that both men and women have their backsides blackened, which is done by pricking it in."[1] Here we know the technique, but ritual connected therewith is not explained. Leichhardt[2] says of natives he met in the York Peninsula: "They had horizontal scars on their chests." Sturt[3] says of natives he met on the Murrumbidge: "They lacerate their bodies, scars being their chief ornament. On the Murray natives were warlike, some with ribs, thigh, and faces marked with white, others daubed with red and yellow ochre. There were white painted women laden with supplies of darts."[4] Hans Stade[5]

[1] "Quest and Occupation of Tahiti," Hakluyt Society, 1919, Vol. II, pp. 460, 471, 478.

[2] "Journal of Overland Expedition in Australia," London, 1847, p. 447. See this work, p. 181.

[3] "Life of Charles Sturt," Mrs. N. G. Sturt, 1899, p. 55.

[4] *Ibid.*, p. 63.

[5] "Captivity of Hans Stade," Hakluyt Society, 1874, pp. 129, 155.

was captive in Brazil 1547-55. He gives brief references to body painting: "They disguise themselves with painting. They paint their captives before dancing round and mocking them." Works of early missionaries, especially Jesuits, are briefly informatory with regard to body markings, and Marquette and La Salle give references. Cranz describes tattooing in Greenland, and Dobrizhoffer gives a full account of tattooing in Paraguay in the middle of the eighteenth century. Symes, an ambassador, says: "The Birmans tattoo their thighs and arms into various fantastic shapes and figures, which they believe operate as a charm against weapons of their enemies." [1]

All such references assist in confirming the importance of body marking which persists even to-day in many places with elaborate ritual. References to works of missionaries of the early nineteenth century are often helpful with regard to belief and ritual as the following examples will show. The Rev. John Williams states that Samoan women blistered the skin to perpetuate the memory of some important event, or beloved and departed relative. Tepo of Raratonga tattooed in consequence of the death of his ninth child.[2] As time progressed interest in ethnology increased with corresponding attention to native beliefs and ritual. John Chalmers gives useful data relating to tattooing in South-East New Guinea in 1878-86.[3] Of ritual in connection with tattoo in Samoa J. B. Stair (1897) renders an interest-

[1] "Embassy to Ava," 1795, p. 312.

[2] "Narrative of Missionary Enterprises in South Sea," 1840, p. 140.

[3] "Pioneering in New Guinea," p. 283.

ing account, which is of special importance because Marquardt (1899), though dealing thoroughly with technique, is not impressed with underlying ritual. Stair describes a special sprinkling ceremony for the tattooed: "The evening before this rite attendants provided themselves with lighted torches and proceeded to the malæ where torches were extinguished simultaneously. A water bottle was brought out and dashed to pieces in front of the newly tattooed. Next day water was sprinkled over each of the party; tattooed and tattooers then separated. This singular custom appears to have been used, as in other cases, to remove what was considered to be a kind of sacredness attaching to the newly tattooed." [1]

The most valuable accounts of body marking in connection with associated ritual and belief are to be found in works of the late nineteenth and early twentieth centuries. During the period 1890 onward the ethnologist has set forth with a specific purpose; questions have been carefully prepared, difficulties of inquiry foreseen, and interpreters judiciously chosen. Consequently Reports of the Smithsonian Institution, "American Anthropologist," Reports of Cambridge Expedition to Torres Strait, "Pagan Tribes of Borneo," Journal of the Royal Anthropological Institute, and "Melanesians of British New Guinea," are a few selected from many examples of the type of modern publications which will best repay the student who is chiefly concerned with body marking in relation to allied social and religious practices. Joest's "Die Tatowirung," 1887, is useful on the side of technology relating to all forms of body marking, but omission of,

[1] "Old Samoa," 1897, p. 164.

and in places almost a disdain of the psychological and historical aspects which are fundamental, detract seriously from an otherwise valuable work.

In these researches I have been advised and encouraged by Dr. R. R. Marett, Henry Balfour, Esq., F.R.S., Mr. W. J. Perry, Mr. T. A. Joyce, Mr. E. T. Leeds, Professors E. H. Parker, Donald A. Mackenzie, Warren R. Dawson, H. R. Hall, Sidney Smith, A. A. Macdonell. Sir Arthur Keith kindly allowed reproduction of photographs taken in the Royal College of Surgeons. Mr. R. W. Williamson and his publishers, Messrs. Seeley Service, generously supplied photographs of tattooing in New Guinea. To the trustees of the British Museum I am indebted for pictures relating to Australian scarification. Mr. J. A. Hammerton, editor of "People of all Nations," kindly permitted use of a photograph showing "Amazonian Snake Dance." Dr. A. C. Haddon readily consented to reproduction of photographs showing scarification in islands of Torres Strait. To my publishers, Messrs. H. F. & G. Witherby, I am grateful for a generous view respecting the scientific importance of numerous illustrations and bibliographical references.

W. D. H.

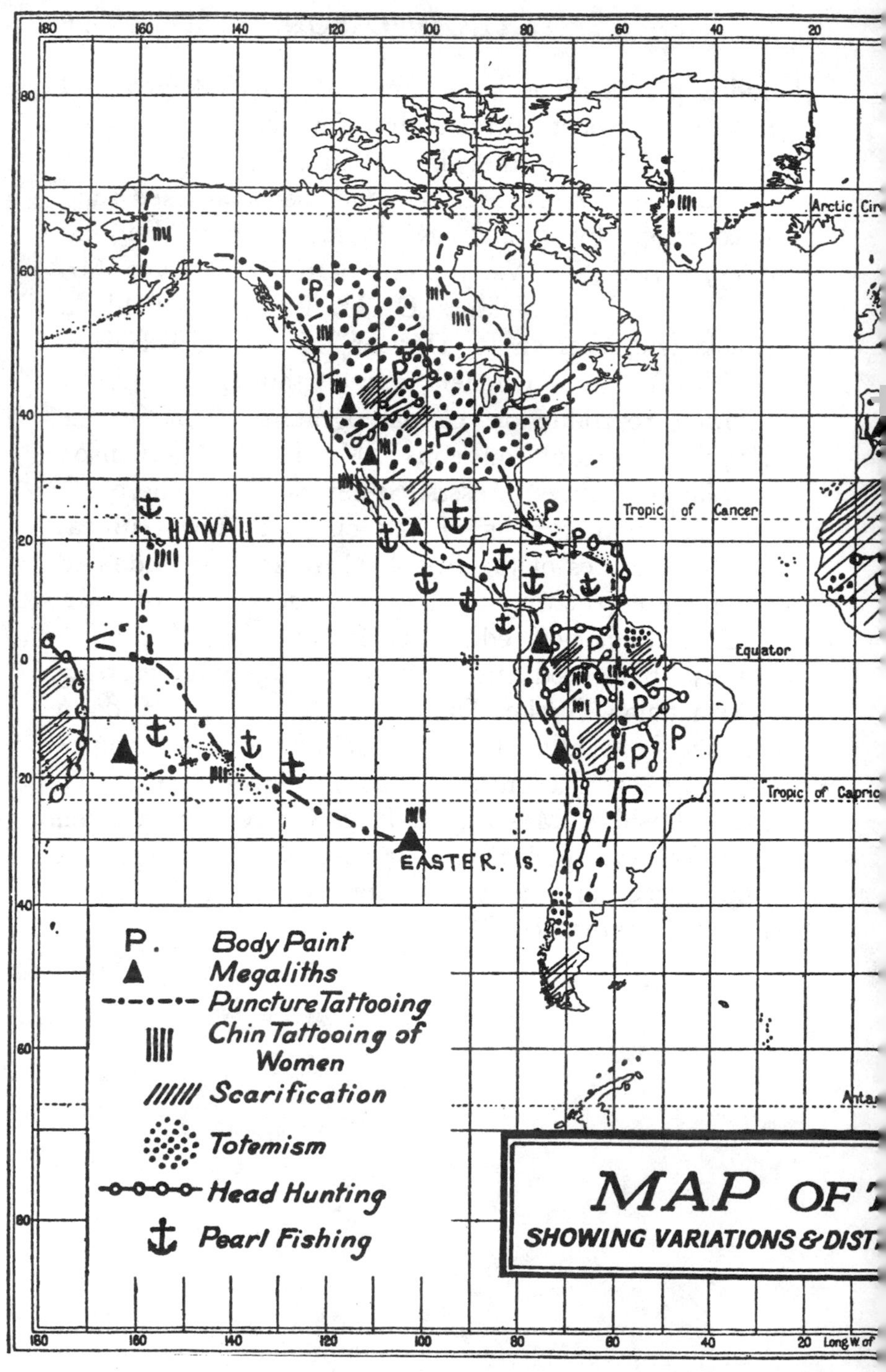

HAWAII
EASTER. Is.
Arctic Cir
Tropic of Cancer
Equator
Tropic of Capric
P. Body Paint
Megaliths
Puncture Tattooing
Chin Tattooing of Women
Scarification
Totemism
Head Hunting
Pearl Fishing
MAP OF
SHOWING VARIATIONS & DIST
Long W. of

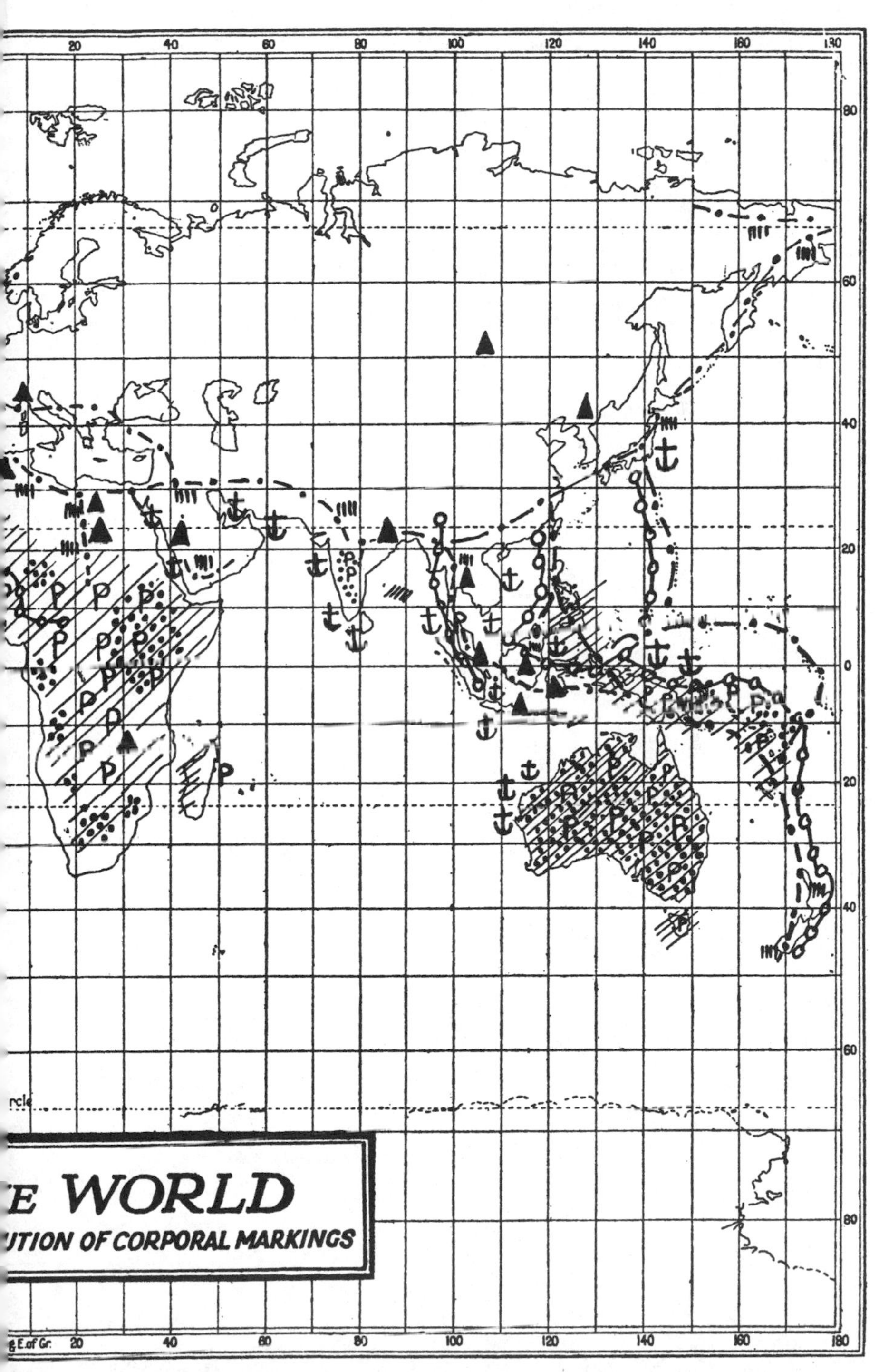

E WORLD
UTION OF CORPORAL MARKINGS
20
40
60
80
100
120
140
160
180
g. E. of Gr.
rcle

CHAPTER I

BODY MARKING IN RELATION TO RELIGIOUS BELIEFS AND PRACTICES

Negative rites or "taboos"—Positive rites or ritual—Considerations of taboo and ritual—Priesthood and the tattooers' craft—Tendency to decline of ceremonial—Tattoo marks and future life—Instances from North America, Assam, Polynesia, Borneo, and West Africa—Body marking and worship—Religious marks of Hindus—Dedication of children to the Sky God—Aztec dedication ceremony—Symbolism of colour Totemic and other animal markings.

In this section an attempt is made to show the bearing of tattooing and other forms of body marking on religious beliefs and practices.

Primitive man approaches non-human forces by positive rites carried out with meticulous accuracy, and at the same time he employs a number of negative rites in the form of prohibitions or "taboos." Association of such ceremonial with body marking is a sure indication of its importance. When, in addition to caution, secrecy, and ritual there are definite beliefs relating to the value of tattoo marks in heaven, dedication to a deity, relegation of the tattooers' craft, to priests, or other clearly expressed concepts of like kind, the evidence for a religious dynamic force in body marking is incontrovertible.

Furthermore, when similar beliefs, restrictions, and

rites, as for example those relating to tattooing of women at puberty, can be collated from widely separated areas inhabited by peoples ethnically diverse, the case for migration, as opposed to that of independent origin, becomes correspondingly impressive.

There is, on account of the disputed connection between magic and religion,[1] a preliminary difficulty in dividing evidence relating to body marking as a religious exercise from that pertaining to magical practices. But for practical purposes instances of body marking deemed to be of religious import are those connected with ideas of a superhuman being, survival after death, prayer, sacrifice, and communion.

Distinct from these definitely religious exercises are those of a magical nature dealing with pain, good luck, love charms, preservation of youth, rain making, trial by ordeal, dangerous enterprises, death, mourning and execution. These important factors, largely in the hands of a specialist, who has an extensive selection of garbs, each for a specific purpose, form the subject matter for a separate chapter.

Tattooing and Precautionary Measures

The tattooing of a Kayan girl is a serious operation which is performed at intervals between the ages of four and eighteen years, and in connection with the practice there are some important positive and negative rites which tend to show the connection between

[1] Sir J. G. Frazer, "The Golden Bough." R. R. Marett, "On the Threshold of Religion."

tattooing and an appreciation of non-human powers.[1] On no account must the operation be performed in seed time, or if a dead person is lying in the house, while the work is interrupted if the operator should dream of floods, such a dream being looked upon as indicating excessive bleeding of the patient. A tattooed woman may not eat of the flesh of the monitor lizard and her husband is under a similar restriction, sharing the taboo with his wife until their first child is born. Much importance is attached to the hereditary office of professional tattooer, and this person's vocation imposes upon her a number of restrictions which illustrate the Kayan's association of the tattooing craft with dangers of an undefined kind. Like the Smiths the professional tattooer is under the guardianship of a tutelary spirit, and as long as the children of the artist are young she may not with safety pursue her avocation.[2] Hence there seems to be the same idea which operates to produce that interesting practice the "Couvade" among the Nagas, Amazonian[3] Indians, and many other peoples, who believe that the tender soul of the child is capable of being injured by any indiscreet action the father may commit. Hence the male parent retires to bed when his child is born and there remains until the infantile nature is less impressionable. Should the professional tattooer fail to observe certain food taboos, her disobedience will be followed by failing health or the fading of the designs which she executes.[4]

[1] "Pagan Tribes of Borneo," Hose and McDougall, Vol. I, p. 252.

[2] J.A.I., 1893, pp. 204, 241.

[3] Ethnographical Guide to British Museum Collections, pp. 100-1, 285.

[4] "Pagan Tribes of Borneo," Vol. I, p. 254, also Vol. I, p. 247.

Misfortune will attend the letting of a friend's blood, and so the operator makes a small present of beads to the patient, whose parents would suffer through general misfortune, and the artist herself would go blind, if such a ceremonial gift was forgotten.

The operation may not be commenced at any time the girl or her parents desire; it must be started on a day named "butit halap," namely the ninth day after new moon. Provided the first instalment of the operation is performed on this particular day, the process may be recommenced on any occasion whatever.[1]

Among the Batang Kayan tattooing may not be done in the communal house, but only in a hut built specially for the purpose, while the males of the family of the girls who are being tattooed must assume a special bark cloth garment and must not venture out of doors until the tattooing operation has been completed. Should any male member of the family be absent the operation must not be commenced until his return.[2] A sacrificial rite is introduced among the Long Glat people who cause a woman who is being tattooed to kill a black fowl for the artist each day.

Evidence concerning the ceremonial observances among Kayan peoples is well authenticated by Hose and McDougall who are intimate with the peoples studied. The facts adduced show that among Kayan peoples there is a definite association of the tattooing operation with possible misfortune and non-human agencies.[3] Not only is the patient in a state of

[1] "Pagan Tribes of Borneo," Vol. I, p. 262.

[2] *Ibid.*, Vol. I, p. 263.

[3] Dr. Hose tells me of the excessive anxiety of women to have the tattoo completed before confinement.

"taboo" or dangerous sanctity during the operation, but the professional worker is at this time peculiarly liable to misfortune. The idea of a non-human power appears to affect all related to the patient, and is likewise a possible source of danger to the children of the artist, who safeguards her offspring by observing certain restrictions of diet.

The offering of a fowl may be mere payment for service rendered, but the stipulations of "a black fowl each day the operation is performed" seems to point to the gift being of a propitiatory nature.

Dr. Frazer has observed that the custom of tattooing women at puberty is possibly not for mere ornament but to guard against mysterious dangers which the savage apprehends at this period of life.[1] This suggests that the taboos are not associated directly with tattooing but only because tattooing is allied with puberty and blood letting, which give danger to any operation taking place at the time.[2] This hypothesis of taboo being indirectly connected with tattooing, because that operation is performed at puberty, does not account for the precautionary measures just quoted from "The Pagan Tribes of Borneo." Why is there considered to be a tutelary spirit of the tattooers' art? Why the precautions of not tattooing in seed time, or after a dream of floods? The last named precaution, also that referring to suspension of operations when a dead body is in the house, seem to indicate that the tattooing is in itself an operation charged with dangers of a vague and ill defined nature. A woman has passed puberty, but on account of her tattoo marks,

[1] "Totemism and Exogamy," Vol. IV, p. 207.
[2] "Blood Covenant," Trumbull, New York, 1885, pp. 236-7.

she may not eat of the monitor lizard. The detailed evidence, not forgetting the clause concerning tattooing beginning on the ninth day after new moon, seems to point to the direct connection between the act of tattooing and some supra-human power which may take offence if not propitiated.

Investigation by Dr. Séligman among the Melanesians of New Guinea brings out very clearly the association of the tattooers' art with superstitions and apprehensions.[1]

The women of the Roro-speaking tribes are all tattooed from head to foot, and the operation is begun when a girl is from five to ten years of age. The work is performed by some skilled old woman, generally a relative who for her services is usually fed but not otherwise remunerated.

The body of every Koita woman is covered with designs which are the same as those used by the Motu from whom the practice has probably been learned. It is worthy of note that there is a ceremonial order in which the parts of the body are treated. Commencing with hands and forearms at the age of five years or thereabouts, the work progresses until the age of ten years, by which time the chin, nose, lower part of the abdomen, and inner region of thighs have all been decorated. Breasts, back and buttocks are tattooed as signs of approaching puberty appear, while the V-shape marks on the chest and on the back of the neck, together with markings on the lower legs, are given when betrothal has taken place. Finally there are markings made between the navel and the

[1] "Melanesians of British New Guinea," pp. 276-7.

GIRLS OF THE MEKEO DISTRICT, BRITISH NEW GUINEA. ON THE RIGHT THE FINAL NECK TATTOO, "GADO" HAS BEEN ADDED. *(The tattoo marks have been blackened.)*

breast when a marriage agreement is eventually ratified.[1]

Among the Roro tribes, when the girl is considered to be of marriageable age, the buttocks, the legs, and last of all the face are tattooed. A small feast is given before the work on the back parts is commenced, and at this time there is ceremonial shaving of the head. On completion of the main part of the tattooing operation, a feast lasting for five days is given by the girl's relations, and on the last day of that banquet a few finishing touches are given to the designs. At the end of this ceremony the girl is considered "nubile" and is termed "waho." The young lady is decked with ornaments of shell and bone, in which finery she parades ceremonially up and down the village, while for five days she is expected to sit on the verandah of her father's house wearing the ornaments given at the time of the five-days' feast. During this period the girl is spoken of as "rove." She may walk down the centre of the village only, and must take care not to do any menial work such as gardening or drawing water. When eating the girl must take care not to touch the food with her hands; she must use a fork wrapped in the handle of a banana leaf. After four or five months, during which her hair has grown, she is considered fit for matrimony.

Again, as in dealing with tattooing among the Kayans, we have to ask the question: How much of this ceremonial relates to puberty, and is a precaution against dangers attendant on an advance from girlhood to womanhood? and how much may be attributed

[1] "Melanesians of British New Guinea," Seligman, pp. 73 *et seq.* "Pioneering in British New Guinea," James Chalmers, p. 283.

directly to the act of tattooing? A ceremonial order for the tattooing of various parts of the body as they come to maturity appears to indicate a belief that the act of tattooing is in some mystical way calculated to stimulate physical development and the attainment of perfection. There are two ceremonial feasts which seem to be very directly connected with the act of body marking, namely, the small feast given before the decoration of the back parts is commenced, and the great feast which marks the conclusion of the tattooing operation. The inadvisability of gardening and drawing water may be connected with fears respecting impaired fertility of the land. With respect to the taboo against touching food with the hands, there is a curious parallel in the case of the Maori warrior who may not touch food with his hands while the Moko operation is being performed.

The warrior is a fully matured person assuming marks, not at puberty, but as a sign of prowess in battle and advanced social status. The taboo is there very closely connected with the act of body marking, and probably the taboo which prevents the Melanesian girl from touching food with her hands immediately after the tattooing is completed is connected with the body marking operation rather than with puberty. If the danger of touching food arose from the condition of puberty, why was the taboo observed only when the finishing touches of the artist were given? and not throughout the period of gradual advance to puberty?

In the absence of definite evidence from the people who perform these rites and observe these precautionary taboos, it is useless to be dogmatic as to whether the sanctity and danger attaches mainly to (1) the tattooing operation or (2) to the state of puberty, or (3) to the tattooing only because it happens to be performed at puberty. The only reliable way is to bring side by side the authentic instances of (1) body marking in connection with taboo and ceremonial obligations, (2) trustworthy evidence of body marking in connection with beliefs in an after life, (3) body marking and magical practices for securing spiritual power. Then looking at the evidence as a whole we may ask: Are we justified in recognizing that body marking, in very many instances, is mere ornament and decoration? *Per contra*—is it very definitely allied, positively and negatively (i.e., by ritual and taboo), with man's beliefs in and attempts to deal with non-human forces?

Major Veten who was employed by the Bengal Government to make investigations among the Abor tribes has something to say on the subject of tattooing among the Nagas, and his reports are confirmed by those of Mr. Hodson,[1] who points out that tattooing is done among the Nagas in instalments during cold weather, the operator being an old woman who uses as pigments the juices from wild indigo pricked in with a splinter of bamboo. The diet of the girls is restricted, though what the exact nature of that restriction is we are not told, but on another form of privation during the operation we have more precise information.[2] The girl who is under treatment may not leave her village until the tattooing is completed,

[1] T. C. Hodson, "Naga Tribes of Manipur," pp. 30, 31.

[2] Restriction of diet may be imposed in order to minimize possibility of blood poisoning.

and in some instances a further precaution is observed by arranging that the patient is tattooed in a village other than her own. This precaution is usually taken when the girl's mother is a native of some village other than that in which the girl herself was born.

Naga tattooing provides an excellent example of the interconnection of various aspects of culture. Mr. Henry Balfour, recently returned from investigation among Naga tribes, tells me how essential is successful head hunting for fertility of land and marriageability. The latter point relates to human fertility so that for both men and women tattooing is indispensable for successful procreation. Mr. Perry speaks of head hunting as a modified human sacrifice originally carried out to fertilize the land. In dealing with the origin and history of tattooing I have been able to show that in Egypt from 4000 to 2000 B.C. tattooing and body painting were definitely connected with certain well developed female figures, generally held to symbolize fecundity. In Naga customs I see plainly the interconnection of body marking, human sacrifice and fertility both of the land and the Naga race. Possibly among Kayans, Nagas, Melanesians, and others who observe taboos during the time of body marking, there is no clearly defined idea of the why and wherefore of the precautions imposed. At one time fertility rites and their sanctity were clearly defined, but now in taboos on food, and restrictions with regard to feet touching the ground, or a newly tattooed girl gardening, or mixing with other people, we are dealing only with a vague superstition and apprehension. Ideas, other than the original union of tattooing with fertility rites, contribute to the preservation of precautionary measures. Possibly cases of blood poisoning during the operation have been attributed to the entry of an evil demon of disease.

The North American Indian cuts himself before taking his sweat bath either to let out what is bad or to provide means of entry for what is good. Among the Amazonian Indians,[1] and widespread among the negroes of Africa is the practice of cutting the body to alleviate pain of any kind, and such action is understandable in the light of Mr. Turner's description of the Samoan doctor making an incision to let out the headache.[2] Now if forces of good and evil may find access to, or egress from the body by means of incisions in the skin, is it not quite possible that the tattooing is looked upon as dangerous partly because numerous punctures are made, through which the evil spirits of disease, misfortune and even death may find a ready entrance? Or does primitive man believe that the soul may escape from the punctures made?

As medical officer among the coloured mine labourers of Johannesburg, Dr. G. A. Turner has had many opportunities of observing tribal marks of the labourers, and has in addition been able to inquire into the methods of operation employed.[3] Among the Mtyopi there are regulations concerning the patterns which a girl may adopt at puberty, for these must differ from designs worn by a man who has killed another in

[1] Sir Everard im Thurn, "Indians of Guiana."

[2] "Samoa," Turner, 1884, pp. 55, 88, 308.

[3] "Anthropological Notes of South African Coloured Mine Labourers," Dr. G. A. Turner, p. 73. Typewritten MSS. of above at offices of R.A. Institute of Great Britain and Ireland.

action, or by a woman whose pregnancy resulted in abortion, the fœtus being a male. On no account must the Mtyopi girl allow any male to watch the operation of making incisions at puberty, and should she do so the father of the patient is liable to a penalty. Dr. Turner does not say to whom such penalty is to be paid, presumably to the community of which the parent is a member, and the reason for such fine may be that the daughter's action of allowing a male to watch this operation has resulted in a danger to the community. How the danger arises is not quite clear unless it be just another phase of that attitude of awe and avoidance which the one sex is inclined to assume toward the other at specified times, namely at puberty, or during periods of menstruation, when the opposite sex is regarded as something uncanny, which must be set apart because there is ill defined danger in contact. Primitive man would naturally be impressed by the rapid physical and mental changes at puberty. He has no physiological or psychological explanation to offer, so the emotion of fear comes into action. The Mtyopi girl must retire to the bush in order to suffer the process of cicatrization, which consists of making a number of nodules "tindorha" on the face, while the abdomen and thighs are scarred until the flesh has the appearance of a crocodile's back. In addition to these markings linear scars are made from near the external auditory meatus to the eye. Although the operation of cicatrization must be carried out with such secrecy the girl may return to camp in the intervals which are necessary between the various periods of the operation. It is important to note that only while the operation is actually being performed is the subject a possible source of danger to the community.

Before missionary influence was strongly felt in the Pacific the tattooing operation performed on young girls at puberty was accompanied by confinement in cages for periods varying from a few months to two or three years, during which time the novice might not put her feet to the ground. Mr. Brown gives information supplied to him by two missionaries, the Rev. R. H. Rickard (1892) and Rev. I. Rooney, both of whom observed this caging operation in New Ireland.[1] The latter says: "I was just in time to witness the caging of one of these girls; the poor thing loaded with necklaces and belts of red, white, and blue beads, looked very frightened, for on the morrow she was to be tattooed after the New Ireland fashion, that is, have all kinds of patterns marked on her body." Here the isolation of the patient appears to have been preparatory for the operation of tattooing, which was regarded as of great ceremonial importance. The precaution of not allowing the feet to touch the ground appears to have been taken in order to prevent contact between the girl in a sacred or tabooed state, and the earth, to which the native looked for sustenance.

An observer after long residence in Fiji obtained from Malakai, headman of the most purely Melanesian clan in Fiji, an account of ritual connected with tattooing of women at puberty. The novice was required to be free from the custom of women, to fast twelve hours, to search all night for prawns, and to secure three lemon thorns for the tattooing instrument. Two women were concerned with the operation: the "wise

[1] "Melanesians and Polynesians," G. Brown, 1910, p. 108.

woman" who blessed the pigment and prayed to the spirits of the dead that pain might be alleviated, and the operator. Tattooing in Fiji is, as elsewhere, strongly associated with sexual feeling, but this very important aspect is not sufficient to account for the wealth of ritual, taboo, and secrecy.[1]

The Chinese historian, Ma-Twan-Lin, states that in his time, twelfth century A.D., there was a custom of tattooing young girls at time of marriage in the island of Hai-Nan. This was practised only among noble families. At the time when the child attained puberty the parents made a feast for all members of the family. The young girls themselves carried the needles and designs. Pictures tattooed on the face represented flowers, butterflies and insects, finely executed, usually by an old woman.[2] Ma-Twan-Lin, to borrow Professor E. H. Parker's words, is "absolutely trustworthy." In 1893 Loi women, an uncivilized tribe of the interior of Hai-Nan, tattooed themselves.[3]

One of the most impressive instances of taboo in connection with body marking is that observed by a Maori Chief who is receiving Moko designs. Disabilities imposed on the Chief relate to his social intercourse and taking of food. With reference to the former he may not have intercourse with those who are "not of the same condition as himself," but whether "condition" is meant to refer to social status, or to the state of being tattooed, is not clear. There is, however, a very definite restriction to the intercourse

[1] "Hill Tribes of Fiji," A. B. Brewster, 1922, p. 185.
[2] Laurent Emile, "Le Criminel," Paris, 1908, p. 109.
[3] Professor E. H. Parker. Personal communication.

which the Chief may have, and the prohibition is a fact of importance in showing a relation of body marking to the original idea of the divine nature of chieftainship. The second part of the disabilities suffered by one who undergoes the Moko operation is to prevent the contamination of food by handling, for the patient may not take his food in his fingers, but must transfer it to his mouth with a fern stalk; "And any man who presumed to raise a finger to his mouth before the tattoo was finished would find his stomach invaded by 'atua' or fiends who would devour him alive."[1] Sometimes the warrior was fed by slaves who poured fluids into a funnel, or the patient might eat from a platter while lying flat on his stomach.[2] Fish was taboo, but might be eaten if first held up to see the tattoo marks. Drinking water was poured directly into the mouth, and any vessel touched by the patient was rendered unfit for further use.

In old times the priest and all people under the Chief's jurisdiction were "taboo," or in a holy state on account of blood letting during the Moko operation, which consists of cutting lines to the depth of an eighth of an inch, the instruments used being a small adze and mallet. An ancient practice in connection with the tattooing of a Chief was the building of three stone ovens, one for the gods, one for the priest, and a third for the tattooed man. One of the stones from the gods' ovens was handled by the priest, and so the "taboo" or sanctity was transferred to the gods' food

[1] "Moko," Major-General Robley, p. 58. "Islanders of the Pacific," Lieut.-Colonel T. R. St. Johnston, 1921, pp. 168, 171.

[2] See illustration from British Museum Guide to Ethnographical Specimens, Fig. 28, p. 31, also Specimen in Pitt River's Museum, Oxford.

which was hung from a tree. After this ceremony all partook of the food which was suspended, and so became "noa" or free, after which they were allowed to receive food from the basket containing the food of the one who was being tattooed.[1]

The case of tattooing a Maori Chief presents one or two points of exceptional interest which appear to show the connection which the Maoris deemed to exist between the body marking operation and supernatural power. Firstly there are the taboos which must be observed because the operation has placed the divine Chief of the community in a state in which he is dangerous to the ordinary man, and no contact, direct or indirect, must be allowed between the "taboo" (sacred), and the "noa" (common). Blood letting during the operation assists in accounting for the attachment of a certain amount of deference to the Moko[2] process, for the world over the shedding of blood, be it from natural process connected with child-birth or puberty, or an artificial process such as circumcision, or opening veins at the totemic ceremonies of the Australian tribes,[3] is regarded as a process of no ordinary nature. Respect for all forms of blood letting are a reflection of original concepts of blood as life, and therefore necessary for fertilizing the land by human sacrifice. In addition to the awe connected with the act of shedding blood, there is something to be said about the feeling of reverence which every savage attaches to a change of state or condition. The primary purpose of this tracing of Moko designs

[1] "Moko," Major-General Robley, p. 62.

[2] "Moko," Major-General Robley.

[3] "Across Australia," Spencer and Gillen, Vol. I, p. 97. Trumbull's "Blood Covenant," New York, 1885, p. 236-37.

is the enhancing of the person's prestige, a *rite de passage* showing transition from one social status to another. Kingship and divinity account largely for the sacredness of a Maori Chief's Moko.[1]

The initiated boy, or more exactly the boy during process of initiation, and possibly for some time after the ceremony, is a person set apart from the community and condemned to isolation in the bush, or in a specially prepared hut.[2] Among the Papuans and "Pagan Tribes of Borneo"[3] the youths retire at puberty to a special hut, in the village in the former case, and in the latter to a forest glade. Initiation means that an age of fertility has been reached. Puberty implies powers of procreation, hence body marking of boys and girls at this period possibly owes its rites and taboos to original ideas of fertility cults.

Dr. Rivers, when among the Todas in 1906, approached the subject of tattooing among women, but from the looks and reticence of the people questioned, and from the warning of his interpreter he came to the conclusion that the question of tattooing women was one which was not to be approached in public, so he reserved his inquiries, and unfortunately forgot to resume them. The process is performed by a Toda woman, who is paid with eight or twelve annas and her food, and any

[1] A. M. Hocart, "Chieftainship in the Pacific," American Anthropologist, 1915, p. 631; "Common Sense of Myth," American Anthropologist, 1916, p. 307. "Polynesian Researches," W. Ellis, Vol. III, pp. 101, 108, 114.

[2] Seligman, "Melanesian of New Guinea," p. 496.

[3] "Pagan Tribes of Borneo," Hose and McDougall, Vol. II, p. 166.

person who has the requisite skill may undertake the operation which, contrary to the general rule, is not to be performed at puberty, but takes place immediately before or after child-birth. In this case the tattooing is very definitely disassociated from puberty; but is clearly allied with birth, the best evidence of fertility.[1]

Dobrizhoffer[2] gives a clear account of tattooing in Paraguay. "At puberty girls are tattooed at intervals, meanwhile they are shut up for several days in their father's hut. Abstinence from meat and fish is enforced, but fruit is allowed. The chin is tattooed with straight lines. The Abipoines think that their daughters are ornamented by being thus mangled and at the same time they are instructed and prepared to bear the pains of parturition in the future. Every Abipoine woman has a different pattern on her face. Those that are most painted and pricked you may know to be of high rank and noble birth. If you meet a woman with but three or four black lines on her face you may be quite certain she is either a captive or of low birth. When Christian discipline was firmly established in Abipoine colonies this vile custom was by our efforts abolished, and the women now retain their natural appearance."

The Abipoine women are not content with marks common to both sexes, and have the face, breast and arms covered with black figures of various shapes so that they present the appearance of a Turkish carpet. The higher their rank, and the greater their beauty the more figures they have; but this

[1] Dr. W. H. R. Rivers, "The Todas," 1906, pp, 313, 576.

[2] "Abipoines of Paraguay," London, 1822, Vol. II, p. 19.

savage ornament is purchased with much blood and many groans. As soon as a young woman is of age to be married she is ordered to be marked according to custom. Her head rests on the lap of an old woman, thorns are used for a pencil, and the pigment is ashes mixed with blood. If the wretched girl does but groan or draw her face away she is loaded with reproach, taunts, and abuse. "No more of such cowardice," exclaims the old woman in a rage. "You are a disgrace to your nation." "You will die single, be assured." "Which of our heroes would think so cowardly a girl worthy to be his wife?"

This evidence of Dobrizhoffer's shows tattooing to have been important in the centre of South America as a puberty rite for girls. In this connection the statements are extremely important in bringing this region into social and psychological union with many other parts of the world where tattooing is indispensable as a sign of marriageability.

Another observer, the Rev. Henri Junod, who has contributed to anthropology a detailed account of the Ba Thonga people of Portuguese East Africa, affirms that there is in connection with the tattooing of young girls, a secrecy and precaution which point to a former deep meaning which has more or less disappeared.[1]

It appears that the custom of tattooing triangles on the shoulders and ornamenting the belly with tattooed designs is most common among the Ba Thonga, while in addition to being a kind of initiatory

[1] "Life of a South African Tribe," Rev. Henri Junod, pp. 179-81.

rite, and an ornament, the arrangement of triangles varies in such a way as to indicate a particular tribe. Girls must prepare for the operation by taking a special diet which is calculated to soften the skin of the abdomen, and after the operation is completed the newly tattooed maiden must hide herself for a period of seven days, a precaution distinctly reminiscent of that observed by the Mtyopi during scarification.[1] The seven days of seclusion having elapsed, the young lady appears before her boy, who sacrifices a fowl and congratulates her on the ornamental nature of the designs by remarking: "It is pretty to tattoo yourself, otherwise your belly would be like the belly of a fish or a white person." No doubt there is some importance to be attached to the question of ornament, but the ceremonial precautions connected with body marking would preclude us from falling in with Joest's view, that ornament is the primary concern of all who undertake to be decorated, and that religious and magical significance is slight.[2] After the sacrifice of the fowl the precautions are not done with, for during the whole process of healing the girl is taboo, as she would be if suffering from a disease, and as a consequence of this restriction she may not put salt in her food, neither may she partake of the food of other people, lastly, like the Naga girl of Assam, who is receiving her tattoo marks, the Ba Thonga maiden may not visit another village.[3] The point of difference between the "village visiting restriction" of the Naga and the Ba Thonga is that

[1] Dr. Turner, "Coloured Mine Labourers of Johannesburg." See MSS. and photographs in the Anthropological Institute.

[2] Joest, "Die Tatowirung," pp. 60-5.

[3] Hodson, "Naga Tribes."

in the former case the taboo operates while the tattooing is being performed, whereas in the latter case the taboo against visiting a neighbouring village is strongest while the process of healing is taking place, namely, for a week after the marking operation.

Even if one could show that at the present day body marking among savages is little more than ornament, there would be no justification for arguing that the operations of tattooing, painting and cicatrization had never had a much deeper significance. The points to which our attention should be directed are: What survivals of positive and negative rites can we find? Do current legends seem to point to the alliance of body marking with the patronage of some supra-normal power?

Among European witches who claimed to have received the symbol of their craft from the devil, a small blue or red puncture, sometimes a larger mark depicting the foot of a hare, or body of a toad, symbolized the connection of the wearer with devil worship.[1]

What present-day evidence is there of the use of body marking for religious, magical, and social purposes? What testimonies and information can be derived from the oldest members of the community with which we are dealing? When such items have been surveyed in a world-wide manner, and instances brought side by side for comparison, it will be time to speculate as to whether, at some remote date in the history of the human race, body marking was

[1] Sir J. Mackenzie, "Laws and Customs of Scotland," Title X, p. 48, edited 1699. Forbes, "Institute of Laws of Scotland," Vol. II, pp. 32-4, edited 1730. "Man," 1918, Art. 81. M. Murray, "Witchcraft in Western Europe."

adopted to enhance sexual charms, or whether we must take the broader view that the whole series of body marking operations are survivals of beliefs and practices relating to fertility of women, preservation of life in the underworld, the sacredness of chieftainship, and other factors of a culture complex.

Decline of Ceremonial in Connection with Tattooing

The Reports of the American Bureau of Ethnology abound with instances of decline of meaning attached to body marking,[1] and with the exception of the Haidas, tattooing proper seems rapidly to be losing its old significance. Notwithstanding this there is, for careful observers, a wealth of meaning still attached to the body marking process. To some people body marking does not seem to come spontaneously, but only by a laborious copying process, as for example in the south-east of Tibet where the Tibetans borrow the general idea and particular designs from the Shans,[2] and in Borneo where Sarawak tribes such as the Si-hops and Lirongs borrow from the warlike Kayan.[3] For a good example of decline of meaning attached to the tattooing process, we may turn to the inquiry of Messrs. Hose and McDougall among the people of the Barito river. In this region the body marking

[1] J. R. Swanton, "Contributions to Ethnology of Haida," Leyden and New York, 1905, p. 141.

[2] Ethnographical Guide to British Museum Collections, p. 68.

[3] "Pagan Tribes of Borneo," Vol. I, p. 267.

process had a very elaborate significance as recently as 1850, but since then the decline of importance has been exceedingly rapid.

One old survivor was able to give an account of the meanings which were identified with certain marks in his younger days. Thus, when the shoulders were tattooed with two interlacing spirals having stars at their extremities, it was to be assumed that the wearer had taken several heads. Two lines meeting each other at an acute angle behind the finger nails signified dexterity in wood-carving, while a star on the temples was the sign that a man so adorned was in love, and that his affections were requited. Originally there seems to have been the adoption of marks to give expression to the complex sentiments of pride, and love, also to the tendency for pugnacious action; but the whole attitude toward these marks is changing, and the decline is expressed in the words of the author who says: "With the borrowing of exogenous designs arises such an alteration in their forms that the original name and signification is lost." [1]

On this account the value of body marking as an index to ethnic affinities and migrations is unreliable,[2] and added to this opinion of observers in Borneo we have that of Dr. Turner, who observes that among the Kaffir tribes there has been so much interchange of cicatrized designs, that these are no longer a clue to the tribal connection of the individual who bears

[1] "Pagan Tribes of Borneo," Vol. I, p. 275. Nieuwenhuis, A. W., "Quer Durch Borneo," Leyden, 1904-7.

[2] My own observations in the Anglo-Egyptian Sudan lead me to believe there is confusion of tribal marks.

them.[1] At the conclusion of the chapter on tattooing in "Pagan Tribes of Borneo" there is a table showing that with some tribes, for example the Kayans, the ceremonial connected with tattooing is still punctiliously observed; in other instances there are easily recognized vestiges of ceremonial performances; a third division is formed of cases in which the only clue to former ceremonies and attached meanings is by oral tradition. For instance, some legend or direct evidence handed down by an elderly member of the tribe. Finally there are in the table several blanks which indicated that the observers were unable to satisfy themselves as to whether ceremonial had, or had not, existed.

The nature of the designs would at times suggest that the scar or tattoo mark was not made merely for ornament, and when we find a peculiar design made on such parts as are frequently covered, the possibility of a meaning of some importance being attached increases. Mr. Wollaston found that tattooing proper is not known among the Mimika Papuans, but many practise cicatrization and scarring, the usual mark being a cross only on the left buttock, while on the right is a cross surrounded by a circle. The back is marked with very irregular cicatrices of straight lines, while on the upper left arm is a design of a snake, scorpion, or cray fish. A usual form of decoration is the painting of the face with bright red earth, or possibly with black intermixed with fat and charcoal, or again with white powdered sago. Unfortunately the remarks concluding the paragraph

[1] "Observations among Coloured Mine Labourers," Anthropological Institute MSS.

on body designs do not bring forward any attached meaning, and the author says that he was unable to discover whether the designs were merely ornamental or not.[1] The position and nature of the buttock marks seem to suggest a kind of charm, the portrayal of animals on the arm might be allied with totemic practices, but these cases of riddles unsolved do seem to impress upon us the necessity of very careful observation without delay, for the meaning and importance declines, and even after such decline there remains in the mind of the individual who marks himself a vague indefinable feeling that some intrinsic value is attached to these processes which are by several authors regarded as ornament. The tattooed person feels that an explanation to the stranger, or even a discussion of the subject, may rob the marks of their power.

The whole problem of native reticence on this subject is well illustrated by a comparison of the results of investigation of the subject of tattooing among the Ainu, firstly by Mr. Savage Landor, who could discover no attached meaning or special significance of designs during his journey through the Kuriles and Sakhalin,[2] and secondly by the Rev. Batchelor, who worked for many years as a missionary among the Ainu, gaining the people's confidence, with the result that he discovered legends showing that the tattooing process is intimately connected with ancient religious ideas, also that special significance is attached to some designs which are of the nature of amulets and cures.[3]

[1] Wollaston's "Pygmies and Papuans," p. 112.

[2] "The Hairy Ainu," S. Landor, p. 253.

[3] "The Ainu and their Folk-Lore," Rev. Batchelor, pp. 23-4 *et seq.*

Although a reference to so many recent pieces of anthropological research are disappointing when one is looking for evidence which will help to form some justifiable conclusions respecting the nature and true significance of body marking, there is much very reliable and positive material which is well worth collating and reviewing.

Tattooing and a Future Life

A question which has been touched upon by Joest, Waitz Gerland, and Sinclair, is that of tattooing in connection with religious thought and feeling.[1] Among the points of evidence which should elucidate such an inquiry, are those relating to direct statements made to investigators who have inquired into the meaning of marks which have attracted attention. The design itself may signify that, originally at any rate, the marking had some reference to a deity, an occult power, or a future state. With reference to the last named, there are on record a number of very similar ideas, of wide geographical distribution, referring to the part which marks of tattooing, painting, and cicatrization play in bringing the individual into relation with some mystic power or future state.

A problem which puzzles the man who speculates as to the conditions of the spirit world is the means of identification of relatives, and the distinguishing of one's lawful wife or wives. In addition to these

[1] "Anthropologie der Naturvolker," pp. 34-5. "Die Tatowirung," Joest, pp. 60-5. Sinclair, "American Anthropologist," Vol. X, p. 361; Vol. XI, p. 362.

difficulties there is the possibility that the spirit, journeying from this world to the next, will be confronted with barriers, one of which may take the form of an imposing person who will challenge the travelling soul and ask for some sign of eligibility for the spirit world. Usually these difficulties are surmounted by the assumption that after death the soul, regarded as a very tangible object, escapes, but retains a spiritual counterpart of the earthly tenement just quitted. So exact a replica of the earthly body is this counterpart that any tattoo or other marks assumed during the lifetime of the individual will identify the celestial body. Tattoo marks will serve as a *rite de passage* from this world to the next.

Commencing with the Sioux Indians we find that at the death of a warrior very elaborate precautions are taken for his safe and comfortable journey to the next world. The tattoo marks assumed during life are an important asset. The ghost warrior mounts his ghostly steed and sets forth on his journey to the "Many Lodges," feeling confident that he will reach there in safety, provided he has during life taken the precaution to have tattooed on his forehead or wrists, possibly also on the point of the chin, any designs which he thinks suitable. Along the path to the Many Lodges there dwells an old woman who examines each ghost as it passes. If she is unable to find the tattoo marks the luckless warrior and his steed are pushed from a cliff or cloud, and falling into this world they become homeless wanderers who go about aimlessly, the warrior whistling, presumably to relieve his melancholy; but there is no further attempt to gain admittance to the spirit world.[1]

Among the Nagas of Assam there appears to be a very definite belief that tattoo marks are useful as a means of identification in the spirit world, and being determined to secure the Naga women who are their lawful wives, the husbands decide that each female shall receive certain tattoo marks. When dealing with this subject Mr. Hodson says that among the more distant and poorer villages occupied by the Tangkhuls women are tattooed in a very simple way, the design consisting of three lines about three-eighths of an inch in width, starting from the point of the chin, passing round the neck, and in some cases being carried down to the navel. The upper arm is tattooed in a similar way, the lines being arranged in diagonal patterns so as to make two crosses which are generally kept separate. The breasts are not tattooed, and as a rule a woman who can afford a necklace does not receive the tattoo mark. The necklace, when buried, accompanies the spirit and serves as a means of identification.[2]

Among the Abor tribes it was customary to tattoo a cross on the forehead, but this was not done if the individual could afford to have certain brass utensils buried with him. So it appears that the Naga woman and the Abor people regard the tattooing as a substitute which is used should the person be too poor to avail himself or herself of those ornaments or objects which would, if buried with the corpse, give prestige among the spirits and serve as a means

[1] American Bureau of Ethnology, 1889-90, pp. 485, 527.

[2] "Naga Tribes," Hodson, pp. 30, 31.

of identification. The tattoo is the poor man's identification mark in heaven.[1]

The term "mander" is intended to cover all payments made to a woman's relations at her death in order that in the next world she shall not remarry, but must await the coming of her earthly husband. The Northern Tangkhuls, whose women are most constant in the practice of tattooing, declare that the marks are assumed so that the husband who has paid "mander" at his wife's death may claim her in the spirit land, and it is held that the woman's ghost is not finally laid to rest until the "mander" has been paid.

This idea of identification after death appears to arise from a very simple process of reasoning by analogy from the conditions of this world. Mr. Hodson quotes from Colonel McCulloch,[2] saying that the women of the north of Assam are much sought after by the Southern men because however fierce the feuds a tattooed woman always goes unharmed, because, should any ill befall her, her Northern relations would be able to identify the body, and vengeance on the murderer would be swift.

There is among the Hindus of Bengal a very widespread idea that the untattooed person will meet with considerable difficulties during a journey from this world to the life beyond.[3] It is thought that tattoo marks survive death, and the authority quoted goes on to say that low caste women believe that if they die without these marks their parents will

[1] "Naga Tribes," Hodson, pp. 30-1.

[2] "Selections from Records of the Bengal Government," No. XXIII.

[3] "Things Indian," Wm. Crooke, p. 462.

not recognize them in heaven. A variation of, or sometimes an addition to this belief, is that the great god Parameshwar will demand an exposure of their tattoo marks as proof that the ghost has lived on earth. If such tangible proofs are wanting the deity causes the woman to be reborn as an evil spirit, or if inclined to be lenient he allows the person to enter heaven, after she has been dragged through thorns which supply the marks which she had refused to assume during her earthly sojourn.

Sir J. C. Scott refers to the tattooing customs of the Li or aboriginal inhabitants of Hainan, who arranged that a woman's face should be tattooed just before marriage according to a pattern prescribed by her husband, who received it from his ancestors. It was not permissible that there should be the slightest deviation from the original pattern lest the husband's ancestors should fail to recognize his wife's spirit at her death.[1]

There are on record for Oceania several examples of body marking and ornament which are deemed to be of service in the next world. According to the beliefs of natives of Maero, an island in the New Hebrides, all whose ears have not been pierced will receive no water in the spirit life, while the untattooed will be deprived of food.[2] The people of Florida Island conceive of the soul as an entity which undertakes a perilous journey in the course of which it meets a "tindālo" (ghost); the meeting usually takes place on the shores of the Island of Souls. If the nose is pierced the soul is admitted to the fellowship

[1] Sir J. C. Scott, "France and Tongking," London, 1885, p. 348.

[2] Leo Frobenius, "Childhood of Man," p. 55.

of the spirits, but if this identification is lacking the one who has failed to adopt the perforation enters upon a period of sorrow and suffering.

People of the Gilbert Islands replace this respect for nose-boring by a belief in the efficacy of tattooing as a passport into the next world, to use the words of Frobenius, "the tattooed alone reach the abode of bliss." [1] In the Hades of the Fijians all whose ears are not bored are treated with the utmost contempt, and women who are not tattooed are at once struck down by the souls of their own sex, and without further ado are served up as food for the gods.[2] The importance attached to this assumption of body marks becomes explicable when we consider the regard of men of all periods and grades of culture for the fate of the soul. Anxiety for preservation of identity and assurance of immortality was the chief object of many ancient Egyptian practices including use of red paint on face and bandages of the mummy.

Lord Avebury in "Prehistoric Times" makes references to the value of tattoo marks after death, saying that a woman of Fiji who was not tattooed in the orthodox manner could not hope for happiness after death,[3] while far away among the Eskimo the women attach very great importance to their tattoo marks, holding that these will, in the next world, be regarded as a sign of goodness.[4] The Reports of the American Bureau of Ethnology make many interesting references to the beliefs which the Eskimo

[1] "Childhood of Man," p. 55.

[2] "Fiji and the Fijians," T. Williams, London, 1860, Vol. I, p. 160. "Islands Far Away," A. G. King, 1920, p. 95.

[3] Page 437, 6th edition.

[4] C. F. Hall, "Life with the Eskimo," Vol. II, p. 315.

associate with their body marking, which appears to be carried out chiefly for magical and social purposes.[1] There is no direct reference which confirms this statement in Hall's "Life with the Eskimo," though no doubt that statement was quite correct at the time of investigation, since which the Eskimo have been much in contact with traders and explorers; hence beliefs and practices have suffered considerable variation and decline. In all probability cicatrization is therapeutic in origin, at a later stage ornamental, with isolated instances of ritual borrowed from painting and tattooing. One would expect that a reference to anthropological literature dealing with the great Bantu family would reveal a large variety of beliefs connected with scarifying if such existed. But it is exceptional to find that in Africa body marks are anything but the indication of membership of a blood clan or secret organization. There are indeed several instances of a belief in the magical use of scars as an inducement for good luck, a pain cure, or propitiation of the ghost of a murdered foe, but we know of only one people who have stated that the scars are of service to them in the spirit world, of service not merely as a passport, but of direct pecuniary or commercial advantage.[2]

Among the Ekoi, women are marked from shoulder to wrist with carefully made round scars; and these, Mrs. Talbot was informed, are made during life, so that after death the ghost may remove and sell them to other spirits in exchange for food.

The people of Borneo, especially the Kayans, have

[1] A.B.E., 1889-90, pp. 207, 485, 527; 1896-7, pp. 50, 322. "Jesup Expedition to North Pacific," Vol. VIII.

[2] P. A. Talbot, "In the Shadow of the Bush," p. 203.

very pronounced and well elaborated beliefs concerning the spiritual significance and value of their tattoo marks. These marks have not only a use as a passport to the land of spirits, but when once the soul has gained admission, the designs may be used as a further qualification for entering upon certain profitable occupations.[1]

Among Kayan women tattooing is universal and among many useful properties of the designs is that of providing torches to the next world, and it is believed that without these tattoo marks the journeying soul would wander for ever in darkness. Professor McDougall was further informed that after death a woman would be recognized by the nature of the tattoo mark and the pigment used.

Among the Long Glat women there is an elaborate system of tattooing which commences at the first menstrual period, the backs of the fingers are marked with concentric circles, and a year later the designs are carried over the backs of the hands to the wrist. The feet also are tattooed during the same periods that the hands are being treated, and about the age of eighteen or twenty the fronts of the thighs are covered with designs. The ladies believe that after death those who have been tattooed with the orthodox designs on hands, feet, and thighs will be able to bathe in the heavenly river, Telang Julan, and in consequence of this they will be able to pick up the pearls which lie in the bed of the river. Partially tattooed women will remain on the banks of the river to watch their more fortunate sisters reap a rich harvest, while the untattooed women will not be allowed to approach

[1] "Pagan Tribes of Borneo," Vol. I, p. 252.

the banks of the mythical treasure stream. These beliefs are not confined to any one tribe, but are universal among the Kenyahs, the Klemantans of the Upper Mahakam, and the Batang Kayan.[1]

These well elaborated beliefs are quite easy to understand and appear natural enough when considered in the light of Bornean concepts concerning heaven. The soul must journey through forests and over mountains, overcoming many difficulties and using the tattoo marks as a right of passage along the heavenly track until the goal is reached. From a lofty eminence the weary soul surveys his heaven which is sharply demarcated into five divisions, one of which he must select according to the manner of his death. For men who have died in battle there is one division, for those drowned there is an allotment beneath the river bed, from which position of advantage they are able to receive jewellery, fish hooks, or any other property which earthly friends may lose in the river. Suicides have a very unhappy time wandering about and existing miserably on sour fruits and berries, while for the souls of stillborn infants there is a reserved compartment. For people who are able to elaborate such a system of beliefs there is no difficulty in constructing the few additional hopes concerning the value of tattoo marks in the next world. The beliefs concerning tattooing seem to be well in keeping with the other ideas concerning the life beyond this.

In dealing with the beliefs of the people of Borneo there seems to be no uncertainty. Again when dealing with inquiry among the Ainu, we realize the great value of anthropological work done by experts who

[1] "Pagan Tribes of Borneo," Vol. I, p. 265.

have lived among the people sufficiently long to gain their confidence in order to lead them out into a discussion of those beliefs, whose sanctity and efficacy depend on secrecy.

The whole series of remarks dealing with the beliefs of Sioux, Eskimo, Nagas, Hindus, Polynesians, Ekoi and Borneans concerning the value of body marks in the spirit world provide a very apt illustration of primitive man's logic, though adoption of false premises may induce readiness to argue by a process of false analogy. On this earth I wish to be decorated, food is required and when travelling it is necessary to show some mark which is a guarantee that my tribe is friendly with the people through whose territory I am passing.

Then comes the assumption that this necessity for food, purchasing power, distinction and passport will be extended to the life beyond and there is the very practical problem of facing the next life with some provision for these exigencies. On the side of those who advocate the connection of tattooing and body marking with religious beliefs, there is overwhelming positive evidence, easily correlated with, and forming a logical division of a more general system of ideas relating to immortality and the perilous journey of a soul.

Continuity between this life and the one beyond; natural law in the spiritual world, are the great principles fundamental to the whole fabric of primitive religious ideas and thoughts concerning heaven. With this complex fabric of ideas, the conceptions referring to the parts played by body marks are readily fused. One might even go further and say that they form a necessary part of the views concerning a future life.

Beliefs in an after life usually form an integral part of any system of ideas of a religious nature; but an examination of the connection between body marking and conceptions of a world to come does not form the only means of testing whether there is a tendency to associate the skin marking process with religious ideas in general. If there does exist such a tendency we might hope to find in the mythology and folk-lore of people who practise tattooing some references to a deity or occult force presiding over the tattooers' craft. It is possible that ideas of a deity might have been brought to such a focus that the people impressed upon their bodies a representation of their god or some object closely associated with him, feeling no doubt that such a practice brought them into very close touch with their divinity, their mark being just the outward and visible sign of a spiritual unity between the human individual and the god or power he worships. A further pursuit of the inquiry into an association of religious ideas and body marking might be carried out by collecting a number of instances having reference to corporal decoration at times of spiritual revival, as for example during dedication ceremonies of adults or children, or at times when the religious sentiments are aroused and expressed by a pilgrimage. Then in addition to these points there are the questions of the operation being performed by priests, sorcerers, and the like, under conditions which suggest that there is some association of the tattooers' art with magical and religious rites. "In Fiji tattooing was carried out by priestesses in secret recesses of the forests."[1] Many Marquesan signs have a decisive and

[1] "The Hill Tribes of Fiji," A. B. Brewster, 1922, p. 185.

arbitrary character highly suggestive of a hieroglyphic system, the interpretation of which is confined to the Tuhunas or priests, now very few in number.[1] Among Taiyals and Paiwan of Formosa tattooing is always done by priestesses. A newly married couple

Tattooing of Marquesan Islanders.

on return from their honeymoon build a hut where the bride has her face tattooed with the insignia of matronhood. The design, which extends from lips to ears, is always pricked in by a priestess who also unites

[1] "Eastern Pacific Islands," F. W. Christian, 1910, p. 93.

the blood of bride and bridegroom at the wedding ceremony.[1] The weight of evidence reviewed as a whole is in opposition to the view of Marquardt, who says: "Ich bin mit Joest der Ansicht dass die Priester zunächst mit der Sache (i.e., tattooing in Samoa) garnichts zu thun hatten."[2] But Joest wrote on tattooing in 1886, before anthropological method was developed, and his work is concerned more with details of technique than psychological and sociological considerations.[3]

Turner speaks of two patron goddesses of the tattooers' craft, namely, Taema and Tilafanga, who set out to swim from Fiji in order to introduce their art into Samoa, repeating as they swam a formula inviting the inhabitants of Samoa to tattoo the women but not the men. The fatiguing journey caused the goddesses to muddle the formula, and they arrived chanting "tattoo the men but not the women."[4] Mr. Brown's version of the story is more elaborate for, after remarking that Taema and Tilafanga were worshipped as deities presiding over the tattooers' art, he gives legends concerning the origin of these deities, and concludes by relating the story of the swim from Fiji to Samoa, during which the two goddesses became interested in diving for clam shells and so arrived at a reversion of their message.[5]

Dr. Tylor has a similar story, relating to the

[1] "Among Head Hunters of Formosa," J. B. M. McGovern, 1922, p. 189.

[2] "Die Tatowirung bider Geschlecter in Samoa," 1899, p. 17.

[3] "Tatowirung," Joest Wilhelm, 1887, pp. 60-5.

[4] Turner's "Samoa" and "Nineteen Years in Polynesia," 1861, p. 192.

[5] "Melanesians and Polynesians," G. Brown, 1910, pp. 96, 101, 108.

mythical origin of tattooing, which is quoted to explain why some people tattoo their women, while others mark only their menfolk. A messenger was sent from Fiji, where the women are most generally tattooed, to Tonga, where the practice of tattooing men was most common until a few years ago. The messenger landed safely in Tonga repeating, "tattoo the women but not the men." After accomplishing his long swim without mishap he stumbled over a tree-stump when landing, and was so disturbed that he inverted his message, arriving at the chief's house repeating, "tattoo the men but not the women." A work recently published in Germany deals in detail with the subject of tattooing in Samoa, where, contrary to expectations, Marquardt found that the ancient art is still flourishing.[1] Even now, all the men, and from sixty to seventy per cent. of the women are tattooed most elaborately in the ancient manner.[2] This persistence of habit and exact reproduction of design is very remarkable when one considers the civilizing influences which have been brought to bear on the Samoan people, and the admixture with races for whom tattooing would have very little attraction. The illustrations given in Marquardt's recent work show that the most elaborate designs of the artist are inscribed on the thighs and buttocks which are usually covered.[3] If ornament only was the object of the body marking, it seems natural to suppose that after years of contact with Europeans and Asiatics, the Samoans would have discarded the tattooed designs in favour of some of the highly-ornamented

[1] "Die Tatowirung in Samoa," Carl Marquardt, p. 15, etc.

[2] See illustrations. This work, Ch. IV, pp. 260, 265.

[3] "Die Tatowirung in Samoa," Carl Marquardt, p. 15, etc.

Manchester prints which are so easily obtained. Hawaiians had divine patrons of tattooing whose images were kept in the temples of those who practised the art professionally, and every application of their skill was preceded by a prayer addressed to them that the operation might not occasion death, that the wounds might soon heal, and that the designs might be handsome.[1]

There is certainly a most interesting variety of opinion concerning the significance of tattooing, and amongst many writers we have Joest, who denies the religious significance of the tattooers' art, or at any rate claims that it is slight compared with the promptings of the æsthetic sense.[2] Westermarck favours the hypothesis that body marking is a means of artificially aiding the process of natural selection; simply a means adopted by one sex for the purpose of attracting the other.[3] Dr. Frazer is more inclined to the idea that tattooing is a survival of the ancient rites of blood letting, and certainly the taboos observed in connection with body marking processes seem to favour the idea that there is in connection with the marking itself some special degree of sanctity which requires precautionary measures.[4]

Messrs. Sinclair,[5] Swanton, and especially Herr Wuttke,[6] might be taken together as representing those who believe that the "ornamental" hypothesis will in no wise account for the facts brought to light

[1] W. Ellis, "Polyn. Res.," Vol. I, p. 262.
[2] Joest, "Die Tatowirung," pp. 60, 65.
[3] "History of Human Marriage," p. 541.
[4] "Totemism and Exogamy."
[5] "American Anthropologist," Vols. X and XI.
[6] "Die Enstehung Derschrift," p. 96.

in connection with body marking. Wuttke says: "No one would be willing to assert that the custom of tattooing is something natural and evolved of its own accord. Its origin was in the oldest times of the human race before the wide dispersal of man." Another theory would emphasize the importance of a wild and primitive people who had subdivisions, possibly hostile, who therefore required some means of readily recognizing friends and foes.[1]

With the relative merits of these theories we will not at present attempt to deal, but will go forward collecting such evidence as is available concerning any connection between body marking and religious ideas.

In the "Living Races of Mankind" there is a reference to the maid of the Solomon Islands who is not sought in marriage until the tattooing operation has been performed by a specialist who is regarded as a sorceress, sometimes as a "tindālo" or ghost whose services are handsomely rewarded.[2]

Frobenius, whose inquiries have been made personally, states that in the central islands of Polynesia it is customary to have the tutelary deity tattooed on the person, or maybe the deity is replaced by the form of a sacred animal. The reference is given for what it is worth, but it is far too vague to add much weight to a hypothesis of religious origins.[3]

The Maoris,[4] who are of Polynesian origin, attach great importance to the tattooers' art, and the

[1] H. Spencer, "Principles of Sociology," Vol. II, p. 59.

[2] "Living Races of Mankind," Hutchinson, Gregory and Lydekker, p. 37.

[3] "Childhood of Man," Frobenius, p. 36.

[4] "Moko," Major-General Robley, p. 62.

professional operator was at one time highly respected and well remunerated, but there is no reference to his being regarded as a divinity or anything approaching that status. When, however, we come to consider the "taboo" and ceremonies connected with the Moko operation we find the priesthood in great evidence, for at such times the priestly function is the transfer of the sanctity from the chief to the gods.[1]

The practice of painting the body is freely resorted to by the Andaman Islanders, who vary the colour of the paint with their varying emotional states, having olive clay to express the complex sentiment of grief, while the opposite sentiments of joy and general exuberance are denoted by the application of white. Mr. E. H. Man states very definitely that the Andaman Islanders claim a divine origin for their knowledge of pigments and the proper application of these to denote the emotional state of the wearer. The tradition asserts that very early ancestors were instructed in the use of pigments by "Puluga," but unfortunately the art was lost before the great deluge, and no revival took place until the practice was resuscitated after the floods had subsided, by an accidental discovery of the necessary pigments. Among the Andaman Islanders this use of pigments to express emotions and complex sentiments has been well elaborated, but most of the instances concerning the use of body paint are most appropriately dealt with under the heading of "body marking in connection with magic."[2]

Researches into the question of tattooing among

[1] *Op. cit.*, pp. 39, 40.

[2] Journal of Anthropological Institute, 1882, pp. 331-3.

the Ainu have not resulted in extracting from the people a clear and vigorous statement concerning the origin of the custom or the reason for its continuation. In spite of this, there are legends and occasional statements which tend to throw some light on the ideas which the Ainu associate with the body marking art. One legend says that many years ago the Ainu captured a number of small folk, and in order to distinguish the strange women from their own they caused the latter to assume a particular arm and facial tattoo. Other statements are to the effect that the tattooing is a form of blood letting which makes the body strong, a process analogous to the ancient medical "bleeding" treatment, a panacea for all ailments. Another suggestion worth dwelling upon is that there is in women a great deal of bad blood which it is advisable to allow to escape. Among all these statements have we anything which points to the divine origin of tattooing? The Rev. Batchelor narrates a story concerning the introduction of tattooing among the Ainu by "Aioina" and her sister, both of whom are regarded as divinities. Thus the Ainu women are able to assume to some extent the appearance of their goddesses, and the tattoo marks are made on the lips and chin so that evil demons of disease will have every chance of observing them, and mistaking the Ainu women for the goddesses, from whom the art was derived, will flee away without giving further trouble.[1] The superstitious regard for this body marking is very great, and all women carefully instruct their daughters in the practice and its associated beliefs, saying: "The Divine Sister,

[1] "Ainu and their Folk-Lore," Rev. Batchelor, p. 20 *et seq.*

the sister of Aioina, has taught us that if any woman marries a man without first being tattooed in proper manner she commits a great sin, and when she dies will go straight to Gehenna. Upon arrival there the demons will take very large knives and will do all the tattooing at one sitting." This frightens the girls very much indeed, for tattooing is a painful process. Men say that an untattooed woman may not take part in any feast, for to do so is dishonouring both to gods and men alike, and what is more the untattooed women at the feast would bring down the wrath of heaven upon all assembled. The Rev. Batchelor refers to a lapsed custom of observing taboos during the body marking operation, and he is of opinion that such precautions indicated that the Ainus attached very great importance and some sanctity to the body marking process.

The following folk-lore stories show that the mythology of the Ainus makes an occasional reference to the spiritual importance of tattoo markings. In most of the marshes frogs are plentiful, and in connection with those creatures two interesting features have been observed. Firstly, the darker bands on the limbs bear a resemblance to the tattoo marks that the Ainu women make from the wrist to the elbow.[1] In the second place there is the phenomenon of hibernation and reappearance in springtime. The working hypothesis intended to cover the facts is to the effect that untold ages ago an Ainu woman, tattooed in the approved manner, had developed a tendency to murder, and so slyly were the dark deeds accomplished that the woman

[1] "Ainu and their Folk-Lore," J. Batchelor, pp. 20-5.

had removed six husbands before the gods interfered.

At last the day of reckoning came and the wicked woman was metamorphosed into a frog, and so complete was the transition that only her tattoo marks remained. The deity who brought about this abrupt transition said: "Oh thou wicked woman, I indeed made thee good in the beginning, but thou hast lived an abominable and iniquitous life." Then to be more impressive the god delivers a little homily on the inconvenience of having to hop about in the slimy marshes. Hibernation is explained on the ground that the female ancestors of the frogs are in Japan marketing in winter, but by spring they have returned and there is the croaking or gossiping.

The sparrow has at the base of the upper bill a tuft of dark brown feathers which are said to be his tattoo marks, given when God made the world and He was being entertained on earth at a feast given by the birds. The sparrow is sacred, and when killed for food the spirit is propitiated with "inao," that is by a magical formula or a practice which may consist of placing charmed wands in the ground near the house.[1]

Religious Markings of India

India, of course, furnishes a great many examples of body marking in connection with religious ideas. There are innumerable sub-castes among the Brahmins, and each has its own particular body

[1] "Ainu and their Folk-Lore," J. Batchelor, pp. 20-5.

paint, usually an arrangement of lines, dashes, or circles, on forehead, cheeks, and chest, the details of which may be observed in Dr. Thurston's "Tribes and Castes of Southern India," Volume I. Perhaps it would be more correct to describe these Brahmanical markings as giving social distinction, or more exactly as a means of indicating and preserving social status. The Brahmins, of course, form one great caste which is the head of the social scale, on account of its function as an intermediary between the people and the great world soul Brahma. Inasmuch as a mark denotes that a man is employed in serving the gods, it may be considered as body marking as a religious rite, but at the same time there is a very definite social function of the Brahmanical body paint. With respect to the people who distinguish themselves as followers of Siva or of Vishnu (two aspects or manifestations of Brahma), there are marks on the forehead which may definitely be regarded as religious symbols, for unlike the Brahmanical paint they do not emphasize social status, but rather tend to advertise the fact that the wearer is an adherent of Vishnu if a V-shaped design is worn, and of Siva if three parallel lines ≡ are painted on the forehead.

In addition to these Brahmanical and sect markings, there are several instances of body marking being carried out with the very definite aim of indicating an alliance between the human individual and some deity, whose property the individual henceforth becomes.

Dr. Thurston, whose position as head of the Madras Government Museum has afforded ample opportunity for observation, bases his statements concerning body marking on information obtained first-hand from professional female tattooers belonging to the Koravas, a vagrant tribe found throughout the Madras Presidency. The greater part of the body marking is magical and ornamental, but along with the evidence concerning these forms of skin impression there are instances of markings which are no doubt definitely allied with religious feeling.[1]

Many of the Roman Catholic Eurasians of the Malabar coast have a bird tattooed on the forearm as an emblem of the Holy Ghost, and in similar manner the Servian Christians are tattooed with the sign of the cross. Sometimes in case of pain there is an appeal to some god for relief, the appeal being made by tattooing a portrait of the god over the affected part. Dr. Thurston refers to having seen a Bedar of the Bellary district, who had dislocated his shoulder when a lad, tattooed over the deltoid muscle with the figure of the monkey god Hanuman,[2] in the hope that suffering would be alleviated by an appeal to that deity.

In the Bellary district and elsewhere are a class of girls known as "basivis" who are dedicated to the service of the Hindu temples. Substantially they are dedicated prostitutes whose marriage has been contracted with some sacred dagger or other object, and henceforth they are occupied in or about the temple. Their occupations are sweeping, strewing flowers when the idol is drawn along the road, dancing morning and evening before the idol, and

[1] "Ethnographical Notes in Southern India," pp. 376-85.

[2] *Ibid.*, p. 383.

making an offering of rice or other food before the holy shrine. At the time of dedication to temple service the village priest, or "Jangain," draws a lingām on the deltoid muscle of the upper arm, using the juice of the cashew nut. The process of branding a "basivi" with the "chakra" (wheel of the law), and the "chank," shell of mollusc, *Turbinella rapa*, of which the right-handed variety is held very sacred, is becoming a mere pretence, but formerly each dedicated girl was branded on the right shoulder with the "chakra" and on the left with the "chank." Over the right breast another impression of the "chakra" was given, and over the left the "chank" was imprinted.[1]

Among the castes Boyas and Kurumbas, who make basivis of their girls, a few men are branded on both shoulders with the "chank" and the "chakra," believing that this stamping with the sacred symbols gives them a closer communion with the deity Vishnu, so securing their salvation. The stamping with sacred emblems is looked upon as a meritorious action and some deference is paid to those who receive the "chank" and "chakra." For example, they claim the first gift of betel for chewing at a wedding ceremony, and at death the mark of respect is interment with the face downward.[1]

Mr. K. Rangachari, of the Madras Museum, states that this body marking for religious purposes is confined chiefly to two sections of the Vishnavites, namely the "Sri" and the "Madhvas." All Brahmins of these sects must undergo the ordeal at least once during

[1] Thurston, "Ethnographical Notes," pp. 399-400.
[2] *Ibid.*, p. 403.

life, and among the Madhvas there is a regulation to the effect that marking with the sacred symbol must take place each time a subordinate visits the head Brahmin of his sect. In such marking lies much merit, but there is now a tendency to leave the process to the option of the visitor. Vishnavite worshippers are branded with the "chakra" on the right shoulder and the "chank" on the left, and during the operation there are communicated to the devotee a number of sacred words and syllables.[1] A person who has not been initiated and sanctified by marking in this way is looked upon as unfit to take part in ceremonies which are administered by Brahmins. In other words, failure to ally oneself with the divinity by a process of body marking results in a loss of social status.

Naturally enough the sanctity conveyed to the individual by the first application of the sacred symbols is gradually lost by contact with the world and sin, therefore the sacred Madhvas undergo a further stamping process from time to time in order to rid themselves of the accumulating pollution of the world, and further to cause a renewal of spiritual vitality. It is on record that among some of the less resolute tribes the person to be branded hopes that he will receive a luke-warm application, but failure to pay in advance a fee which varies from one to three months' income, usually results in an extra hot application of the "chank" and "chakra" designs. At the first application of the religious symbols thc marking is not confined to the male who agrees to accept the symbols. Similar stamps are applied to his wife and children. A Brahmin who fails to pay for his initial or subsequent

[1] Thurston, "Ethnographical Notes," p. 405.

markings is excommunicated from the Madhvas' sect.

Other authors make reference to Hindu facial marks which appear to be connected with religious ceremonial bathing and fasting.[1]

To keep the forehead quite bare is a breach of etiquette unless the individual is in mourning. If, on the contrary, the forehead paint is absent the usual assumption is, that ceremonial ablutions have not been performed, hence the person is still fasting and in a state of impurity. The forehead mark appears to be a sign of respectability, for another author states from independent observation that in Bengal a respectable Hindu will not take water from the hand of a girl who does not bear the mark of paint on her forehead.

Religious Sanction for Tattooing

An advance of education and civilization generally would naturally tend to drive out such a crude form of affiliating oneself with a divine power. In spite of the evolution of religious ideas and ideals there is no lack of instances to show that the modern devotees of Christianity or Muhammadanism, in spite of Biblical and Koranical veto, are backward in applying to their bodies designs which seem to be regarded as a means of linking the worshipper more closely to the deity whom he serves. Strangely enough among the criminal classes there is a very strong tendency to

[1] "Hindu Manners, Customs, and Ceremonies," 1899, Dubois and Beauchamp, p. 271. "Things Indian," W. Crooke, p. 461.

revert very extensively to the ancient practices of body marking, and the designs frequently include a religious symbol.[1]

In attempting a rapid survey of body marking in connection with religion and its attached beliefs which may border on the magical, it would be difficult to do better than commence with the observations of Mr. Sinclair who has left a record of prolonged personal research, in an article entitled "Tattooing, Oriental and Gipsy."[2]

Armenian Christians who make the pilgrimage to Jerusalem are in the habit of tattooing themselves with the date of the journey, also their name and initials. The Armenian word for a pilgrim is "māhdēsī" (mah = death, and desi = I saw), and the mark with which the pilgrim distinguishes himself is also called "māhdēsī." Mr. Sinclair states that he has examined more than a hundred such devices which the individuals always display with great pride, as it is thought a very great honour to be a "māhdēsī." The tattooing is of the nature of a religious marking as it allies the possessor with a sacred journey for devotional purposes. At the same time there is a tendency to claim social distinction for an act of religious devotion, and the body mark, though primarily of a religious character, will tend to degenerate to an honorific social token according to the egotism of the wearer.

The Koran forbids body marking just as the book of Leviticus forbade the Jews to cicatrize for the dead,[3]

[1] Lombroso's "L'Homme Criminel," 1895, Vol. I, pp. 268, 273, 281-5.

[2] "American Anthropologist," 1908, p. 361.

[3] "Koran," "Muhammadanism" by Margaliouth, Home University Library Series. Leviticus, ch. 19, v. 28.

or imprint any marks upon their bodies. Nevertheless body marking is still in favour with Muhammadan pilgrims who have journeyed to Mecca or Medina. Those who give way to this little weakness for social distinction on the ground of religious devotion, excuse themselves by saying that before entering Paradise they will be purified by fire and all markings will be removed.[1]

In the Sudan, where Muhammadanism is advancing rapidly, there are dark-skinned people on whom a tattoo mark would be invisible, but these overcome the difficulty by giving themselves three gashes on each cheek, a form of marking which the great leader Mahomet himself adopted. Among the designs mentioned as favourites with Christian pilgrims are mentioned those of St. George on horseback, holding a long spear, while before him lies the vanquished dragon; Christ on the cross, the Virgin Mary holding the infant Jesus, Peter and the crowing cock. Annually there is a religious festival at Ancona, Italy, and at this it is customary for visitors to tattoo themselves with pious symbols, while in Bosnia and Herzegovina, Roman Catholic girls are in the habit of gathering in churchyards on Sundays, on which occasions they are tattooed with sacred symbols which they regard with reverence because of the magical protection afforded.[2]

Cocheris has a few remarks to make with reference to body marking for religious purposes, and so that the meaning and value may not suffer in translation perhaps it is advisable to give the original. "Les

[1] Compare with beliefs of "Naga Tribes of Borneo," Sioux Indians.

[2] Sinclair, "American Anthropologist," 1908, p. 380.

anciens Egyptiennes nés de la famille orientale gravaient sur leur peau d'un façon indélébile des emblèmes empruntés aux rites d'Osiris et d'Isis. Ils communiquèrent ce gôut aux peuples africains avec lequels ils furent en rapport."[1] This statement is followed by one having reference to the tattooing of Arabs, and mention is made of the marks being considered by some as the mark of the devil,[2] while others who find satisfaction in tattooing with sacred symbols trust to the passage through fire to remove these before Paradise is gained.

"Les premières chrétiens de l'orient selon Procope etaient tatoues. Loin de s'elever contre le tatouage, le catholicism semble l'avoir encourage." "En Italie la coutume du tatouage s'est perpetuée par suite de l'intensite du sentiment pieux. Aux environs de Naples, les catholiques portent surtout les images du saint, sacrement, du crucifix ou d'une tête de mort. On prefere le monogramme du Christ surmonté d'une croix."[3] From this we find the same evidence as that supplied so much more recently by Mr. Sinclair after personal investigation over a prolonged period; the whole aim and object of these markings, carried out by modern Christians, appears to be a closer communion with, and a desire to gain greater protection from the person worshipped.

Cocheris makes interesting reference to the Russian belief that tattooing is in some way allied with black magic. "Les Russe qui considerent le tatouage

[1] "Les Parures Primitives" by Cocheris, pp. 35-7, 38, etc.

[2] Compare with previous references to tattooing of witches in England, p. 45 of this work. See also "Man," 1918 (81). Article by Miss M. A. Murray, "The Devil's Mark."

[3] "Les Parures Primitives" by Cocheris, p. 39.

comme une alliance avec les mauvais esprits." One has become accustomed to the thought that among the Fuegians there is little conception of a god and few thoughts on a life beyond, probably not much more than a belief in an old man who lives in the woods for the purpose of devouring stray travellers.[1] Nevertheless, in spite of the general belief that the Fuegians are more than any other people devoid of religious conceptions, Cocheris refers to the Fuegians tattooing the fingers, the corners of the mouth and the thighs. She concludes by saying that their religion enforces this practice. The statement is doubtful, as the Fuegians exhibit little idea of a future state.

"Les Fuegiennes se tatouaient les doigts, les coins de la bouche et le haut des jambes; leur religion les y forcait,"[2] a statement we must not be ready to accept until more recent and accurate information concerning the Fuegians is forthcoming.

When referring to the tattooing on people drowned at sea or in flooded rivers, Cocheris speaks of a corpse found in the Seine; on the body were many tattoo marks including one which represented a bishop holding up the sacerdotal cross.

The researches of M. Lombroso into the subject of tattooing among criminals, a practice which he treats as atavism or reversion to incidents in the lives of remote ancestors, reveal the fact that the criminals of France, Spain, Portugal, and Italy, frequently include among the tattooed designs on their bodies, something which has reference to the Christian religion. "Venant aux veritables symboles representes par les

[1] "Voyage in Beagle," Darwin, 1860, p. 214.
[2] Cocheris, "Les Parures Primitives," p. 59.

tatouages, y'ai vu pouvoir les classe en signes d'amour, de religion, de guerre et en signes professionnels."[1]

Out of a hundred and two criminals examined, thirty-one bore religious marks, usually a cross made on the nose; in one case the mark was rendered exceptionally noticeable by an attempt to efface it with acid. It is rather remarkable that thirty per cent. of criminals, the majority of a desperate character, should resort to the use of a religious symbol, and for this strange custom M. Lombroso advances no explanation, save that of an emotional atavism.[2] Perhaps one is to be found in the fact that the Roman Catholic religion seems to be capable of division into two well-defined parts, one polished, intellectual, and highly ornate to suit the æsthetic taste of the well educated worshippers, and at the other end of the scale may be found a number of practices bordering on the magical. For example, those in connection with the sacred healing handkerchief of St. Veronica, the saint's blood in a phial, and fragments of the true cross. Possibly the tattooed sacred symbol is regarded as a charm to ward off punishment for wrong committed.

The criminals dealt with by Lombroso are all from the Roman Catholic countries of Italy, Spain, France, and Portugal, where the peasantry and lower classes generally are extremely superstitious in their religious beliefs, which are barely distinguishable from magic. It seems quite possible that the criminals adopting a religious mark do so, not because of any wish to show an alliance with a spiritual life, but rather as a device for gaining magical protection from

[1] Lombroso, 1895, "L'Homme Criminel," Book I, p. 268.
[2] *Ibid.*, p. 288.

spiritual forces. The religious device imprinted on the body of the European criminal is perhaps comparable to the articles carried by a thief of Northern Nigeria. One charm to make the stolen load light, another to make him invisible, a third to make him tread softly like a leopard, a fourth to make him fleet of foot; and as a last resource a charm which shall make the stick break if the thief is caught and flogged.[1] In place of these numerous and cumbersome charms the modern, up-to-date thief may assume the sign of the cross in order to gain spiritual aid which shall help in his nefarious business.

Religious Markings of North American Indians

We have not, up to the present, considered the body marking of the North American Indians in connection with the evolution of religious ideas, but no doubt the great continent of America would, under careful survey, yield many examples of the use of paint and tattoo marks in connection with, and as a direct expression of religious ideas.

At a Sioux ceremonial performance known as the ghost dance, the body marking is carried out with ceremonial exactness after the manner dictated to the individual in a trance vision, during which he sees a relative wearing the pattern which he is about to adopt. In case the wearer of the paint has not been in a state of trance the details of the design are suggested by

[1] Pitt Rivers' Museum, Oxford.

one who is accustomed to do the ceremonial painting for these performances.

When making his request the dancer lays his hands on the head of the painter and says: "My father, I have come to be painted, so that I may see my friends, have pity on me and paint me." In response to the appeal, which implies that the operator has a high social status, the artist paints a design which serves the double purpose of improving the health of the recipient and stimulating his spiritual vision.[1]

The painting consists of elaborate designs in red, yellow, green and blue upon the face, with a red or yellow line along the parting of the hair. Other favourite marks are suns, crescents, stars, crosses and crows; and it is worthy of note that these designs, along with those of the eagle, magpie and hen, are popular with the youths who are about to assume the sacred body marks before entering the "sweat bath" when approaching puberty.

The dedication of a young child to a particular deity, as for example the offspring of the Pawnee infant to Tira-wa-atius, giver of all life and ruler of all things, who dwells in the sky, must be regarded as a religious ceremony, and the forms of the markings, also the nature and colour of the pigments used, provide striking examples of the importance which the North American Indians attach to the symbolism of body marking.

The child is first anointed with red clay mixed with fat from the buffalo or deer, whose parts were set aside as sacred at the time when the animal was slain. Such anointing applies not only to infantile consecra-

[1] American Bureau of Ethnology, 1892-3, Part II, p. 919.

tion, but also to the devotions of an adult Pawnee who may take no part in a religious ceremony before he has been anointed with the sacred substance. Blue paint represents the sky; and throughout the ceremony red paint, buffalo fat, blue pigment and holy water are all in use.[1]

The ceremony is capable of division into three main parts, the first of which is the touching of the child's forehead with holy water purporting to have been given for this occasion by the sky god. Water is recognized as the chief means of sustaining life and the gift is held to come direct from "Tira," who has also blessed the liquid with cleansing and health-giving power.

A new life is now opening up for the child on the occasion of his spiritual rebirth, and as the reddening clouds of the morning give promise of a new day, so the red paint symbolizes the advent of a new and fuller life for the one who is consecrated to Tira-wa-atius. The Shaman, carrying a shell containing the red pigment, approaches the infant to the accompaniment of music and song which speaks of the life-giving power of the rising sun. Here and there the face of the child is touched with red paint, and the spots are one by one smeared over so that the entire face is covered. During this part of the ceremony the song describes the gradual rise of the sun in the heavens and consequent gaining of strength by the rays.

Marking with the blue pigment, which of course symbolizes the blue vault of the heavens, where the sky god dwells, is carried out with much the same ceremonial approach of the medicine man who carries

[1] Bureau of Ethnology, 1900-1, 22nd report, pp. 222, 233, etc.

the pigment in a shell, while various stanzas are sung from time to time.

The mark made on the forehead with holy water is a symbol of the sky god whose usual sign is a semicircle representing the arch of sky above, and from the zenith a perpendicular line is drawn. During the marking with red paint, a brush of grass, symbolizing food, was used in order to paint over the signs previously outlined with holy water. Then in the third stage of the sacred marking the blue line, which has been painted over the red perpendicular, was continued down the centre of the nose, over the neck and chest to the heart. So the goodness from the sky god enters the forehead and flows downward until the whole being is permeated.

Among the Osages there are sacred pipes, the gifts of god, which are given into the charge of a chief who must never allow them to touch the ground if he wishes to have visions and long life for his children. The Osage Chieftain decorates his chest and neck with a design, on each side of which is tattooed one of the sacred pipes with which he has been entrusted.[1]

The sanctity of the body marking operation among the North American Indians is exemplified by the elaborate ceremonials associated with the tattooing of girls among the Omaha. The mark itself is a badge of honour to be dealt with more fully in a section of this work concerning body marking as a social distinction, but the conditions under which the operation is carried out testify to the sacredness of

[1] Bureau of Ethnology, 1905-6, 27th report, p. 503; 1897, p. 233, "Account of War Customs of the Osages."

the act, and its general connection with religious thought. A special scaffold is erected, and on this are displayed the fees of the tattooer, along with a hundred awls and a hundred knives.[1] There are male and female instruments brought together to symbolize fertility. The girl must face the west during the operation which takes place in the morning, her position appearing to indicate that her young life is rising with the orb of day and journeying in the same direction, namely, toward the west. As additional items of ceremonial two heralds stand at the door of the lodge and announce the names of those who are to sing during the performance, and no person is accepted as a vocalist unless he has received war honours in public.

The mark itself is a disc, representing the sun, tattooed in the centre of the girl's forehead, while an ancient song is rendered. The chant refers to the sun rising to its zenith, and when that point is reached the orb speaks as its symbol descends upon the maid with the promise of life-giving power. On the chest is tattooed a star which is emblematic of night giving way before the rising sun. Each of the points of the star symbolizes one of the four life-giving winds. There seems to be a deification of the forces of day and night, the former symbolized by the sun is the male cosmic force, the latter symbolized by a star is the female cosmic force, and both these are represented on the body of the girl. It is notable, too, that the sun speaks when the zenith has been attained, and the spiritual forces, of which day and night are the outward manifestations, have the power of

[1] Bureau of American Ethnology, 1905-6, 27th report, p. 503.

retarding healing of the tattoo if the girl has been unchaste. Here is an attempt to acquire life-power and fertility by body marking at a sun-worshipping ceremony; an impressive example of the linkage of culture factors. Incidentally, the operation is a kind of trial by ordeal, during which a non-human arbiter is called upon to pronounce upon the chastity of the one receiving the symbols.

Among the sanguinary rites of Aztec civilization there was consecration of a youth, ultimately sacrificed to the god Tezcatlipoca. Painting of this youth red and black to symbolize aspects of the deity was part of an elaborate ceremonial.[1] On the day of sacrifice to Uitzilopochtli the priests made little marks on children, cutting them with their stone knives in breast, stomach, wrists, and fleshy part of the arms.[2] There was a special incision made on the breast of a boy, in the second year of his novitiate in service to Quetzalcoatl, as a mark of dedication,[3] and further evidence of the Aztec regard for body marking as a religious rite is to be found in accounts of striped face painting in honour of Xipe, god of seed time and planting.[4]

[1] "Gods of Mexico," Lewis Spence, 1923, p. 96
[2] *Ibid.*, p. 102.
[3] *Ibid.*, p. 137.
[4] *Ibid.*, p. 205.

Body Marking with Animal Designs, which in many instances are of a totemic and religious nature

A regional survey of the world shows that the practice of applying to the body certain more or less accurate copies of animal forms is very common. The point of difficulty is to decide on the significance of these markings, and to gauge the extent to which they represent an alliance between the individual and totemic beliefs.

Dr. Frazer's "Totemism and Exogamy" makes a world-wide survey of the very common practice of selecting an animal or plant as the badge or emblem of a particular social group, whose members are linked together by spiritual and social ties. A specific case by way of illustration may be found in Australia, where thorough-going totemism is the order of the day. The Urabunna are a very small tribe, but their system is simple and serves well to illustrate the significance of totemism.[1] The tribe is divided into two phratries, "A" and "B," and each of these divisions possesses a number of groups or totemic clans, each of which has an identity preserved by the selection of some animal as a badge or emblem. For instance, within the "A" phratry there might be the wild duck, black swan, and water-hen, totemic clans. Among the "B" phratry the clans might be the snake, owl, and lizard, etc. Such an arrangement has an important bearing on the social system, for not only must a man of the "A" group select a wife from

[1] "Across Australia," Spencer and Gillen, pp. 13 *et seq.*, 19.

" B," it is actually arranged that the wild duck people of " A " shall marry only people of the lizard totem of " B," and in addition there are age groups within the totems, so that a man is very limited in his choice of a partner.

The subject of totemism has two very distinct aspects, namely, social and religious, and as to the relative importance of these it is difficult to decide, so closely are the two blended in the life of the people. On the religious side we have to note that the people who claim the kangaroo as their totemic animal regard the creature as something more than an ordinary animal which they may hunt and kill at pleasure. It is believed that long ago there were semi-human ancestors who entered into the kangaroos, therefore any disrespect to the animal is substantially a disregard for the sanctity of one's ancestors. Among the Arunta the kangaroo may be hunted annually by the men of the kangaroo totem, who eat of the flesh in a strictly sacramental way, the whole ceremony being undertaken to ensure a future supply of kangaroos.[1] The living animal is very useful to the men of the kangaroo totem, for when danger is near it is good enough to warn them by hopping in a particular manner.

On the religious side this deference for an animal really amounts to a form of ancestor worship, and there is always the possibility of a totemic animal developing into an anthropomorphic deity. On the social side the totemites become " all one flesh " with the animal, and so with one another, consequently there must be unity and reciprocal assistance among

[1] " Across Australia," Spencer and Gillen, p. 255.

the members of the totemic group. As a further consequence of being " all one flesh " with the animal and one another, there arises the necessity for each individual to avoid incest, which would occur if he married within his own totem group. It is but natural that a man should seek a closer affinity with his totem animal and ancestor spirits. This he does by marking designs representing that animal, and frequently such marks are applied to the skin, also to houses, weapons, clothing, and special totem poles, all of which practices will be mentioned later in our survey of magical markings.

It appears that although the social side of totemism is extremely important in determining marriage laws and disposal of property, the religious aspect is the basis on which the main structure of totemism depends. The starting point appears to be a conception of half-human mythical ancestors whose spiritual parts reside in present-day animals; hence a crude form of ancestor worship is set up, and from this the social system and restrictions in marriage are evolved.[1] Totemic markings must be distinguished from the mere application of animal designs which may be adopted for a great variety of purposes, including good luck, a charm against the bite of an animal, or merely to get the agility and cunning of some creature.[2] Such animal markings are not necessarily totemic, but may be regarded as interesting examples of body marking for magical purposes.

The numerous tribes of North American Indians

[1] "Totemism and Exogamy," Sir G. Frazer. Aspects of totemism dealt with throughout several volumes.

[2] "Cambridge Expedition to Torres Strait," Vol. V. Whole volume devoted to totemism.

provide a variety of examples showing the relation of body marks to religious ideas concerning the spirit parts of some animal. Mr. C. Hill Tout, referring to facial tattoo marks among the Dené, says that these designs are usually conventionalized outline figures of birds, fishes, or plants; radiating straight lines are also usual. On the forearms are designs symbolizing the totem or possibly the "Manitu." (That is the sacred animal which the individual saw in his trance vision at puberty, and decided to adopt as his tutelary spirit.) In some cases the forearm designs have become vaguely amuletic, but in other instances there is still clear evidence to show that the marks are made to bring the wearer into a close and mysterious relationship with his spiritual guardian. Occasionally a man's breast is tattooed, usually with the symbol of the grizzly bear, whose spirit appears to be held in great veneration. The tattooing of this design involves great expense and outlay in the way of gifts and ceremonial banquets, and naturally enough those who can display the tattooed symbol which brings them *en rapport* with the grizzly bears are much envied.[1]

There appears to be a widespread veneration for the grizzly bear even when he is not the totemic animal. Dr. Tylor speaks of the Indian explaining to the bear that the killing was very necessary, or perhaps accidental, and further the hunter sits down by the dead creature and smokes the pipe of peace with him, occasionally placing the pipe in the mouth of the bear. Dr. Tylor expresses the opinion that there is fear of the bear spirits, and frequently mauling by a bear is looked upon as a punishment for killing

[1] "British North America," C. Hill Tout, 1907, p. 84.

one of the animal's friends. Mr. James Teit, speaking of the Thompson Indians, says that two men who have killed a bear will paint their faces with alternate stripes of black and red, meanwhile chanting the bear song. If this propitiatory painting was not carried out the bear spirits would be offended, so it is believed, and the hunters would have no more success.[1]

Among the Baganda people there is a similar regard for the kindred spirits of the slain animal, usually a leopard or buffalo, but among these people there is a very definite fear of the leopard's ghost. The Baganda make a more elaborate propitiatory ceremony than that mentioned for the Thompson Indians. Each man who assisted in the hunt has spotted the left side of his body until he assumes the appearance of the dead animal; all members of the village steal about acting like leopards. A food taboo which limits them to the flesh of warm-blooded animals is observed. The point of special interest in this ceremony is the painting in order to resemble a dead animal; there is involved the idea of animals having spirit counterparts, with which the natives desire to be on good terms.[2]

The Sioux have a number of symbolical colours,[3] which are employed in the decoration of men who have had visions of bears. As a rule there is a broad blue band representing the earth; and sometimes the bear is represented as issuing from this.

Undoubtedly there is a rapid decline in North

[1] "Thompson Indians," April, 1900, J.E.N.P., p. 347.
[2] Rev. J. Roscoe, "Baganda," London, 1911, p. 447.
[3] American Bureau of Ethnology, 1889-90, p. 527.

America, as elsewhere, in the number and clearly defined significance of body marks. But for the Haida of Queen Charlotte Islands much evidence is still obtainable at the present day, and with this Mr. Swanton has concerned himself. The totemic markings are held to be of double service to the wearer. Firstly, they give a spiritual alliance with the animal selected as an emblem, and after that they may be looked upon as socially useful in uniting individuals. Mr. Swanton remarks that of the designs he examined two hundred were of a theistic nature, and the object of adoration was usually an animal. Mr. Swanton has noted that among the Haida the tattooed marks include family crests, such as designs of the bear, wolf, eagle, or any family of fishes.[1]

Some of the older accounts make reference to these animal markings among the North American Indians, but unfortunately there is much minute observation without interpretation. From the general evidence, extended through the Reports of the Bureau of Ethnology, there is justification for believing that these animal tattoo or paint marks are the outward signs made to signify that there is a good understanding between the wearer and the spirit parts of the animals represented.

Captain John Smith says that among the Virginians: "Some have their legs, hands, breasts and faces cunningly embroidered with divers marks, such as beasts and serpents artificially wrought into their flesh with black spots." He does not speculate on the meaning of these.[2]

[1] Swanton's article, Bureau of American Ethnology, 1888-9, p. 388.

[2] "Hakluyt," 1593, Vol. I, p. 230.

A missionary of Pennsylvania and Ohio, the Rev. John Heckewelder, describes the Indians of these districts as being very elaborately tattooed, and in 1762 he examined a veteran warrior who bore, among many designs, those of the water lizard, a large snake on the right cheek and temple, and on the lower jaw the head of a wild boar. Probably the animal designs are those of the chiefs slain by the strong arm of this warrior who appropriated their marks in order that he might have all the hidden power which would accrue from being in touch with the spirit counterparts of the lizard, the snake and wild boar. These tattoo marks of animals might be expected to confer on him the qualities of agility, subtlety and ferocity.[1]

M. Bossu gives an account of his adoption by the Indians of Arkansas who tattooed a roe buck on his thigh to make him one of them, an incident which illustrates the social rather than the religious side of totemic marking.[2] Among the Arkansas was a chief who had slain a monstrous serpent, and the great event had been suitably recognized by tattooing the design of the snake upon his body. This instance shows that animal marking may be merely commemorative; a sign of social distinction rather than an acknowledgment of a totemic animal.

The Eskimo of Behring Strait tattoo their women freely, and in addition to the designs adopted by women at puberty and marriage, there are marks which indicate the totem to which a man belongs. At Plover Bay Mr. Powell noticed a boy who had the mark of

[1] "Memoirs of Historical Society of Paris," 1876, Vol. XII (Philadelphia).

[2] Bossu, "Travels through Louisiana," 1750, Vol. I, pp. 107, 163. A.B.E., 3rd report, p. 245.

the raven totem over each eye. From Kus Kokwin River to the shores of Behring Strait, also at Kotzebue Sound the Eskimo have a regular system of totem marks. The writer speaks of the difficulty of obtaining information, but is confident in saying that there is sufficient evidence to prove the employment of signs for gentes and totems. It must be admitted, however, that these signs are usually confined to personal property, such as arrows, paddles, or clothing, and with such markings we are not here specially interested.[1] When the evidence is uncertain we take encouragement from Mr. Sinclair who says: "To-day there is still an interesting and fruitful field for study among the Eskimo and along the North Pacific. Much still can be learned among the Indians in the West, and perhaps in Mexico and Central America. There are great difficulties in obtaining such information; one must understand the subject, know the Indians well and obtain their confidence. Many things they do not like to speak of or disclose, and they find it hard to explain and describe even when willing."[2]

Marking with Animal Designs in Africa

Although there are very few African tribes who do not use some form of mark for purposes of indicating the clan or secret society to which they belong, the patterns employed are almost entirely geometrical. True enough there is among the Xosa a form of

[1] Bureau of American Ethnology, 1896-7, Part I, pp. 60, 322.
[2] A. T. Sinclair, "American Anthropologist," Vol. XI, 1909, p. 362.

marking at the initiation of women which gives the individual the appearance of a crocodile, but there is no reference to the resemblance being designed; probably it is only a chance likeness produced by the particular form of the rugæ on the thighs.[1] The case of the Baganda marking themselves like leopards in order to propitiate the ghost of the slain animals has already been quoted, and in addition to these instances there is from Nigeria one example of marking with the lizard. Major A. T. Tremearne gives a record of about one hundred and seventy cases of body marking examined, and in these there is the solitary instance of a lizard design, which, however, has no totemic significance, but is a mark applied to each side of the neck in order to attract prostitutes. The translation of the name of the mark is "Sleeping with the one desired"—"Kawanche da Masoye."[2]

Animal Markings in India

In India there are traces of totemism, but examples of body marking with animal designs are rare, and even when found they appear to refer to a charm rather than to any form of spiritual alliance with animal life. Some of the Dômbs of Jeypur mark themselves with the scorpion and others apply a design which, they say, represents an insect cut through the middle in order to render it powerless to harm them. This is simply a case of protective magic, or possibly a transference

[1] Dr. Turner, "Reports on South African Coloured Mine Labourers."

[2] J.A.I., 1911, pp. 102, 171, Major Tremearne.

to the individual, of any useful qualities the creature may possess. Sir H. H. Risley compares the marking of the Dômbs with other similar practices, as for example the one employed by Bechuanas, who wear a mutilated but living insect. This they do because the creature's tenacity for life is thought to be transferred to the wearer; hence it will be difficult to kill him.[1]

In the Malay area there is a widespread belief that an individual who rubs the joints of his fingers with the ash of a roasted spider will make them lithe and nimble for playing the lute. Tattooing with the design of a poisonous insect, such as the scorpion, may be in one respect compared with the tattooing of a totemic design, for in each case the wearer desires to show some amount of respect and fear for the animal represented. Dr. Thurston gives a general account of tattooing in India,[2] remarking on the number and variety of designs applied to the skin of Tamil-speaking Muhammadans. The patterns include pictures of birds, scorpions and fishes, but no case of tattooing the form of a man-eating animal has been recorded by Dr. Thurston.

A result of visits to Burma, where tattooing is a fine art, is the covering of the body with many elaborate designs. Dr. Thurston gives a detailed account of the marks met with on one hundred and thirty men who stripped for measurement. The animals mentioned as represented in excellent tattoo designs are the scorpion, the elephant, and the lizard. It is not surprising that men visiting Burma

[1] "Man," H. H. Risley, July, 1902.
[2] Ethnographical Notes in Southern India," pp. 376, 385.

should desire to bring away with them some permanent impression of the artistic skill of a Burmese tattooer, whose dexterity has been the admiration of many Europeans who themselves have received tattoo designs. Of examples of animal markings among the Burmese there is no lack, but the designs are merely ornamental and have no special significance. It is quite possible that although the æsthetic impulses account for the bulk of tattooing done in Burma, there is a special significance attached to marking with a portrait of the cat or tiger.

On the subject of tattoo designs in Burma, Mr. Sinclair wrote to Sir H. H. Risley, who, among much interesting information, stated that a Burmese who adopts the picture of a cat or tiger as his body design does so in order to secure the stealth and agility of that animal.[1]

Animal Markings in the Pacific

The last few years have witnessed much inquiry in the Pacific area, and none is more worthy of attention than that carried out by the Cambridge Expedition to Torres Strait, undertaken in 1898.[2] Among the islands in this area are many plant, animal, and geometric designs which are classified as social, commemorative, mourning, magical, and decorative. From some of the information given to Drs. Rivers and Haddon it appears that the animal

[1] "American Anthropologist," 1908, Vol. X, p. 361.

[2] "Cambridge Expedition to Torres Strait," Vol. IV, pp. 13, 29; Vol. V, Plates IX and X.

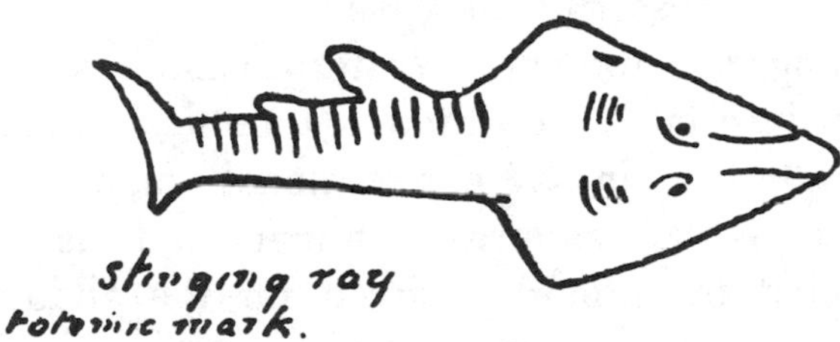

Totemic Animal Designs used as Property and Body Marks by the Islanders of Torres Strait.

emblems are evidence of a decadent totemism, though this is not necessarily the case.[1]

Among the totemic Western islanders some of the cicatrized marks represent a totemic animal, either realistically or in a conventional manner. The crocodile is a favourite animal and is usually represented by a mark scarred on the abdomen in imitation of the creature's scaly covering. Most of the islanders of Torres Strait have a neatly constructed oval and slightly raised scar on the right shoulder, and judging from the shape of the design, and information given, the scar represents a turtle.

The Miriam women cicatrized on the upper arm a figure of the centipede, while the Sam people employed the badge of the cassowary totem. The people desiring to show connection with this bird marked the calves of their legs with a symbolical design representing the print left by the foot of the cassowary. This marking was employed chiefly by women of the cassowary totem. The men claimed very distinct advantages from their alliance with the bird mentioned, and as subsidiary totems they had the snake and dugong. Men of the cassowary totem were reputed to be very fast runners, who prided themselves on their long, thin legs, which they likened to those of a cassowary. When a fight was imminent a Sam man would say to himself: "My legs are long and thin, I can run and not feel tired, my legs will go quickly, and the grass will not entangle them."[2]

The Tabu people liken themselves to their

[1] D. Jenness and A. Ballantyne, "The Northern D'Entrecasteaux," 1920, p. 54.

[2] "Cambridge Expedition," p. 166.

totemic animal, the snake, by making two small holes at the tip of the nose to represent that animal, and among the Mabuiag men there is reported to be a marking of a coiled snake on the calf of the leg. This design is employed only by the Tabu clan, who claim the snake as a totemic animal, seeking, as before stated, to ally themselves with the creature by making two holes at the tip of the nose, and wagging their protruding tongues in battle.[1]

In Kiwai Island, at the mouth of the Fly River, New Guinea, the favourite totems include the cat sign, the cassowary, bamboo and crab, and out of a total of thirty-six totems observed, thirty-one were animals, two plants, and three inanimate objects. Of the fifteen totems in Kiwai, four are animals, ten are plants, and one is an inanimate object, but in all cases of representation on the body the designs were so conventionalized as to be recognized only with difficulty.[2]

The Torres Strait Islander has a very definite idea of his alliance with the totem animal, and a man is supposed to live up to the character of the creature whose design is cicatrized on him. "Augud (i.e., totemic animal), all same as relation, he belong same family," and so the cassowary men are of uncertain temper and kick with extreme violence. A Kodal man belonging to the crocodile totem would be cruel and relentless, and if a member of this totem killed a crocodile his fellows would inflict the death penalty on him, but a member of any other clan might kill a crocodile without having to suffer; the Kodal men

[1] "Cambridge Expedition," p. 168.
[2] *Ibid.*, Vol. V, p. 154.

would mourn for their relative, but no violence would take place. If a Umai man killed a dog his fellow clansmen would fight him, but if the dog was killed by a member of another clan they would merely feel sorry. An Umai man, when going to fight, secures good luck and makes himself distinguishable from his enemies by painting his totem on his back and chest. He has, however, no permanent totemic mark.[1]

The centipede was a favourite design of the Daudai women, who carried it upon their legs, but there is no evidence of a centipede totem, and probably the mark, like the similar one of the Dômbs of India,[2] is a magical protection against the bites of these creatures. A very good instance of body marking with a botanical totemic design was found on a young woman of the cocoanut tree totem, at Mauwata, New Guinea.

According to Mr. Somerville's statement the men of New Georgia mark themselves with a raised cicatrix in the form of a frigate bird or porpoise, and some individuals employ the two markings.[3] The shoulder blade, breast, and thigh are most frequently marked, the thigh being the favourite part for an impression of the porpoise, and the shoulder blade for the sign of the frigate bird. This convention seems to be for the purpose of giving to the marked limb the qualities possessed by the animal whose form is represented. Thus, the shoulders are impressed with the marking of the frigate bird in the hope that the man will have in his arms the enormous wing strength of this bird.

[1] "Cambridge Expedition," Vol. V, pp. 183-5, 188.
[2] "Man," 1902.
[3] J.A.I., 1897, Vol. XXVI, p. 365.

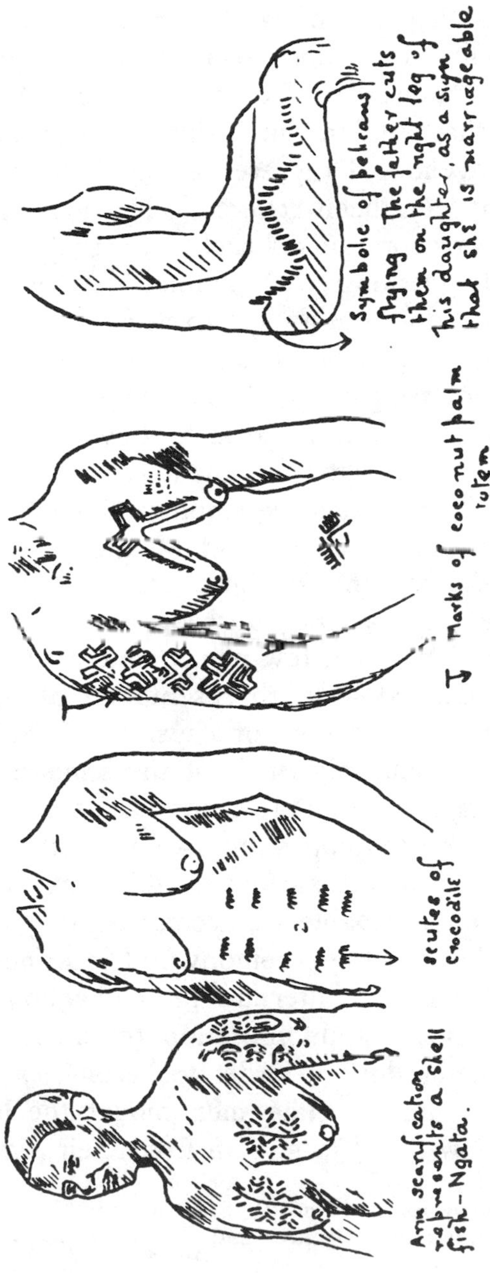

Scarification, Islanders of Torres Strait.

Similarly the legs are marked with the representation of a porpoise in order to make them strong in swimming. Marquardt discusses Von Luschan's suggestion that the Samoan design is of totemic origin, being a conventional representation of the sea eagle which might have been revered. He does not, however, find corroboration of such a theory.[1]

Of body marking with animal designs in New Zealand there does not appear to be any trace, and the geometric devices applied are to be considered as a means of conferring a social distinction.

For Australia there is no lack of evidence to show that totemic markings are made on the body at "intichiuma" and other ceremonies, but the photos appearing in the recent work of Messrs. Spencer and Gillen show that the designs are so highly conventionalized as to be unrecognizable, with the exception perhaps of a few men painted with a mark evidently intended as a representation of the sun.[2] At the annual ceremony for causing the kangaroos to flourish and multiply, men of the kangaroo totem of the Arunta tribe resort to a water hole where there is a huge rock, standing some twenty feet out of the ground, and on to the surface of this rock there is a projecting ledge capable of accommodating three or four men who lead the ceremony. These individuals paint their bodies with alternate red and yellow stripes, which are a very crude imitation of the kangaroo's form; this being done in order to become *en rapport* with the kangaroos. The men mount the ledge of rock and allow blood to stream from their arms down

[1] "Die Tatowirung in Samoa," 1899, pp. 17-19.

[2] "Across Australia," Spencer and Gillen, pp. 288 *et seq.*

the surface of the cliff, while their companions below sing of the proposed increase of kangaroos.

There is a hunt, a sacrificial meal, a second hunt, a second meal and more singing, after which all disperse. In this instance the body marking is made in order to assimilate the wearers with the kangaroo spirits who are the mythical human ancestors of the totemites. What is more important, these semi-human, semi-kangaroo spirits are responsible for the fecundity of the animal in question, and it is thought that their power will not be exerted unless the totemite appeals to and propitiates them by body marking, singing, and elaborate ceremonial.[1]

Spencer and Gillen give a very interesting case of the young men of many totems assembling for the purpose of exchanging designs, and although no explanation is given it seems very probable that this "give and take" arrangement is intended to secure for each man the sum total of spiritual force hidden in the totems taken collectively.

A has the goodness from his totem, then hands it on to B who repays his kindness in like manner, and so each receives the greatest possible amount of spiritual force. In addition the men show by this employment of totemic designs that there may be differences of clans and their accompanying totems, but in reality the people meeting together are united in a larger social unit.[2]

[1] "Across Australia," Spencer and Gillen, p. 97.

[2] *Ibid.*, p. 288.

Classical Reference to Animal Marks

The last few years have witnessed an application of the methods of anthropological inquiry to the solution of problems of life in ancient Greece and Italy. Had the people of classic antiquity systems of magic, primitive religion, votive offerings, sacrifice, and totemic ceremonies, in any way comparable to those which are to-day so abundant among people whose culture is rudimentary? With regard to totemism, Miss Harrison adduces evidence from the works of Homer, Hesoid, Aristophanes and Xenophon, to show what regard was paid to the animals of the time, especially in the case of sacrifice. In the instance of sacrificing an ox to Zeus, the axe was blamed for the deed and the priest who had delivered the blow had to flee for a time as if he was a murderer. With this question of totemism in classic lands we are concerned only in so far as it affects the subject of body marking.

In dealing with the social origins of Greek religion, Miss Harrison mentions totemism,[1] and amongst much interesting evidence for and against the idea of totemic practices, refers to tattooing on the arm of a Thracian woman. It appears that the Thracians were worshippers of Dionysos and the original of the illustration of a worshipper shown in "Themis" is to be found in the National Museum, Athens, in the form of a cylix with a white ground. Male worshippers of Dionysos were stamped with the ivy leaf, which became the emblem of the undying totem soul, for while other plants decay, the ivy keeps its freshness all the year

[1] "Themis," p. 132.

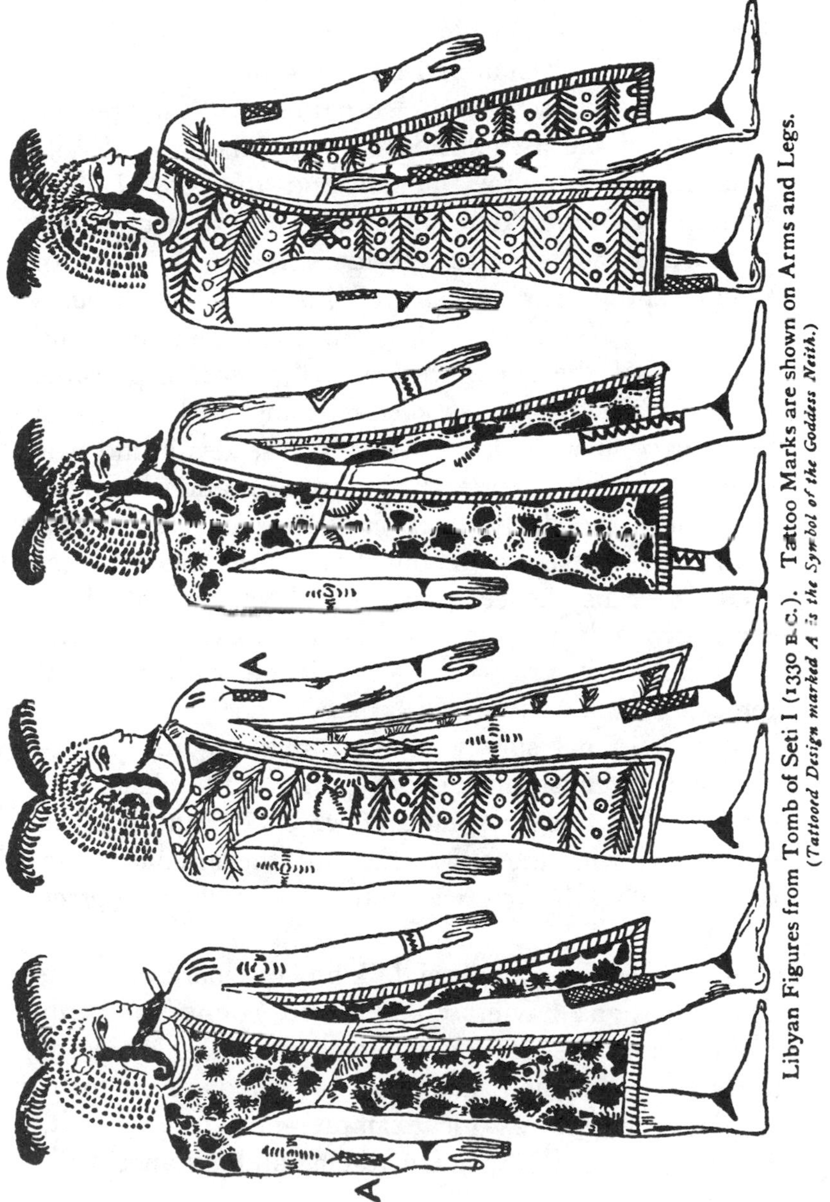

Libyan Figures from Tomb of Seti I (1330 B.C.). Tattoo Marks are shown on Arms and Legs.
(Tattooed Design marked A is the Symbol of the Goddess Neith.)

round. The Bacchante wore faun-skin sandals on her feet, and was further identified with the animal by the design of a faun stamped on her arm.

Egyptian archæology provides an interesting example of the assumption of body marks to denote alliance between the human and divine. Libyan figures from the tomb of Seti I (1330 B.C.) show tattooed symbols of the goddess Neith,[1] a deity of remote antiquity who was well known by the Fourth Dynasty. Neith was thought to be mother and daughter of the sun god Re. She was responsible for the rebirth of the sun each morning, had a function in connection with the dressing of the dead, and was concerned with their immortal preservation. Budge states that the doctrine of parthenogenesis was well known in Egypt in connection with the goddess Neith of Sais, hence there would appear to be an early, probably the earliest, historical example of the tattooers' craft providing an alliance with spiritual forces.

Our regional survey of body marking in connection with totemism makes two points quite clear:

(1) That there is marking which definitely allies the wearer with the spirit parts of the animal, as in Australia, North America, and the islands of Torres Strait.

(2) There is a special kind of marking with animal designs having no apparent connection with the religious beliefs of totemic peoples. Many of the marks assumed must be regarded as magico-religious designs, as for example, in Torres Strait, where there is a cassowary totem, and alliance with

[1] This work, p. 105.

the bird is obtained by applying a device to the body. In every instance of body marking in the Torres Strait the idea of using magical means of obtaining animal qualities seems to be uppermost. So it is in Burma with men who employ the tiger mark, or in New Georgia where the signs of porpoise and frigate bird are the favourites, or again, in India where the marking with animals is magical and ornamental. There is, however, in spite of the confusion of reasons for applying plant and animal marking, very good ground for believing that in Australia, and not long ago in North America, these body designs had a significance which was something more than vaguely magical. They were perhaps akin to an expression of religious feeling, which in North America and Australia is characterized by ideas connecting the spirit life of tribal ancestors and animals. This evidence adduced with regard to various types of body marking relates to acts and thought processes usually associated with the word religion. In the instances detailed body marking relates to a divine personality, or to a future life with preservation of identity. Taboos and ritual, legends of divine origin, and a tendency for the tattooer's craft to be in sacerdotal hands, prove a strong religious impulse of the kind necessary to disperse and preserve body marking processes throughout the world.

As a general proposition it may be truly said that body marking has played a most important part in the evolution, stabilization, and migration of religious concepts. Probably these had their inception in far-off palæolithic days when red ochre was used to symbolize life-giving blood, the token of vitality and immortality.

There is positive archæological evidence to show that body marking by paint and tattoo was applied to female figurines and human beings in Egypt between 4000 and 2000 B.C.[1] Clearly from the evidence discussed in the historical section of this book Egyptian body marking was related to fertility of women, social status, and survival after physical death; all of which points are of fundamental importance in the instances of body marking brought forward in this chapter.

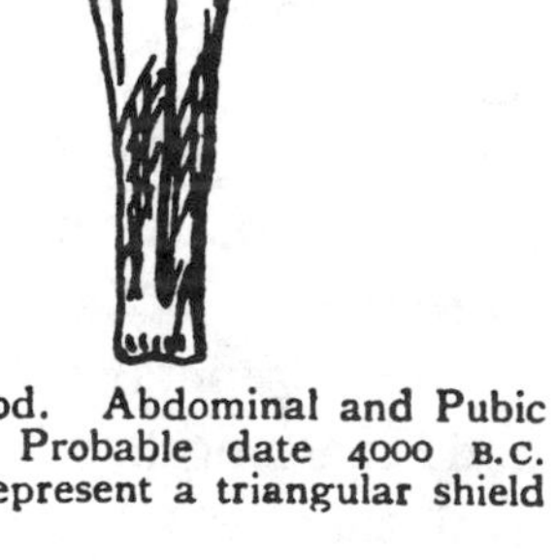

Egyptian Bone Figures of the Archaic Period. Abdominal and Pubic Marks may be Painted or Tattooed. Probable date 4000 B.C. Dr. C. Hose thinks the pubic marks represent a triangular shield such as is worn by young Bornean girls.

[1] This work, p. 325, for summary of body marking in ancient Egypt.

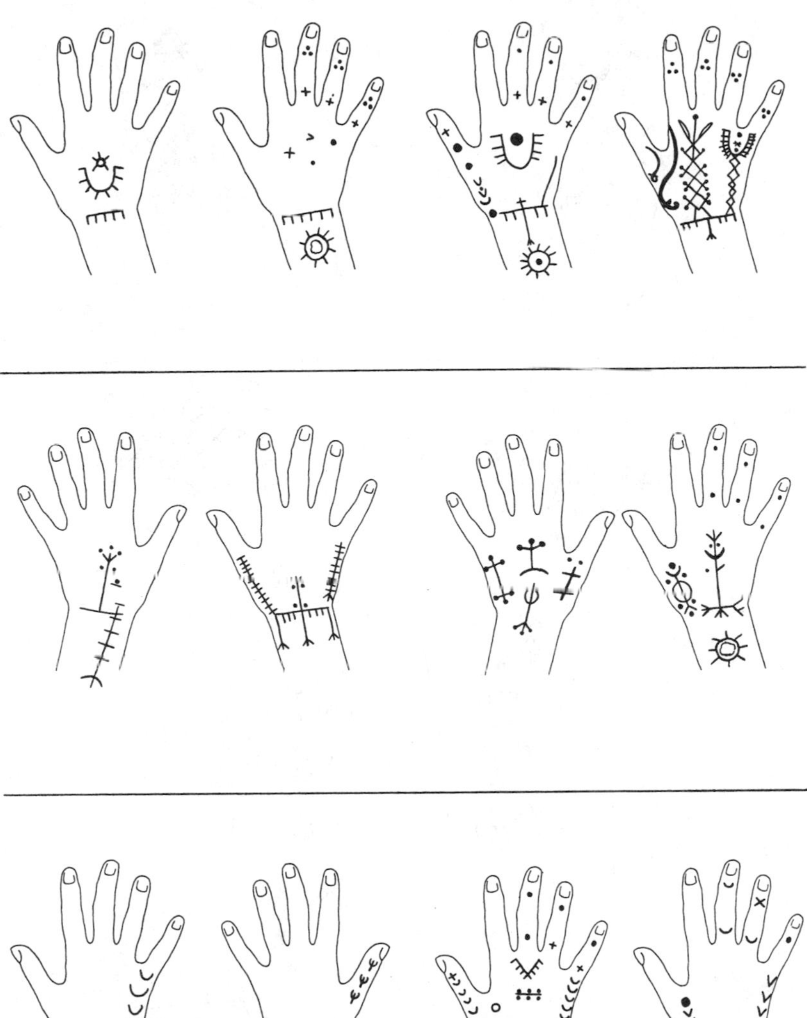

Figure 1. Hand designs of Yezidi and Shammar males.

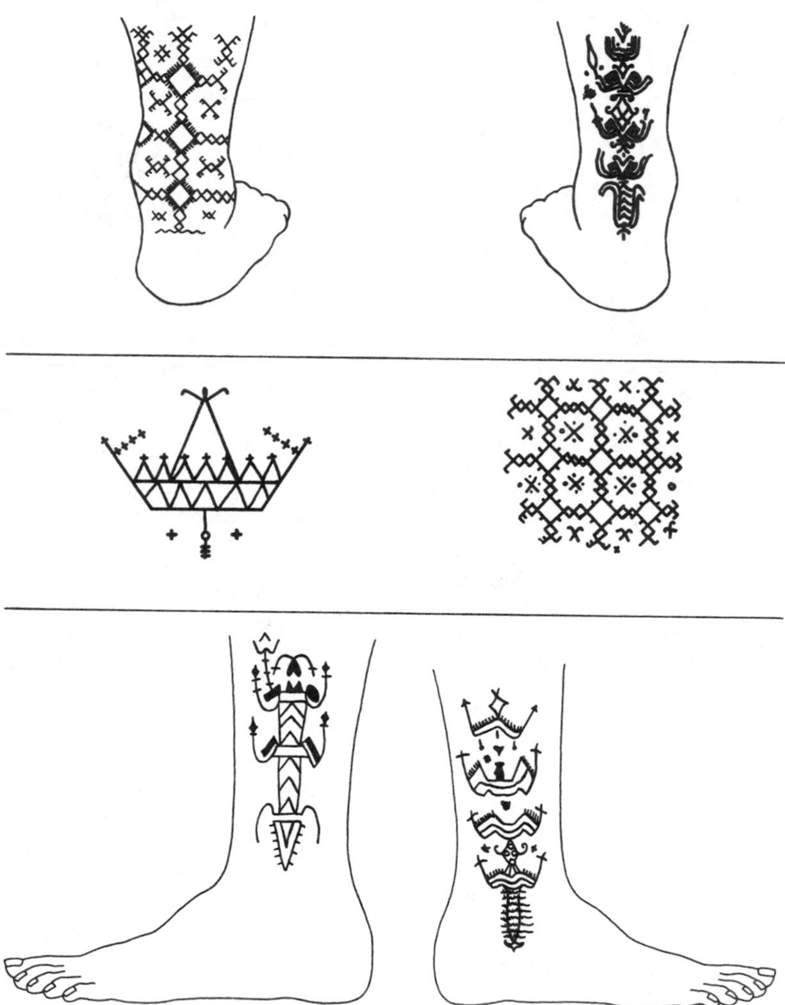

Figure 2. North African designs and patterns.

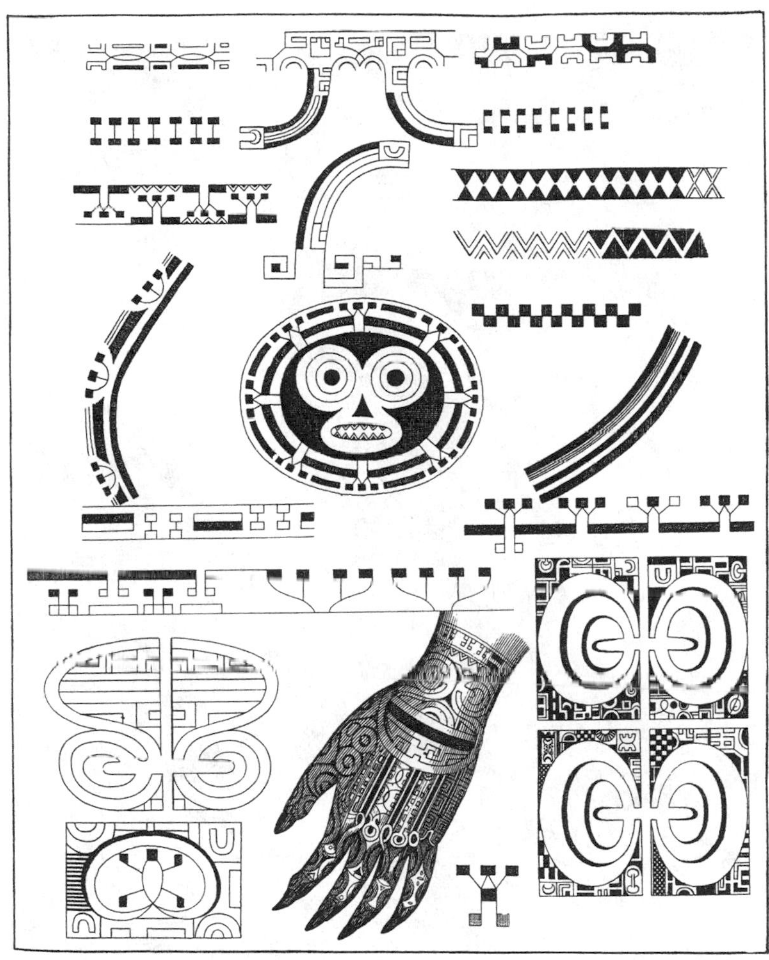

Figure 3. Marquesan designs.

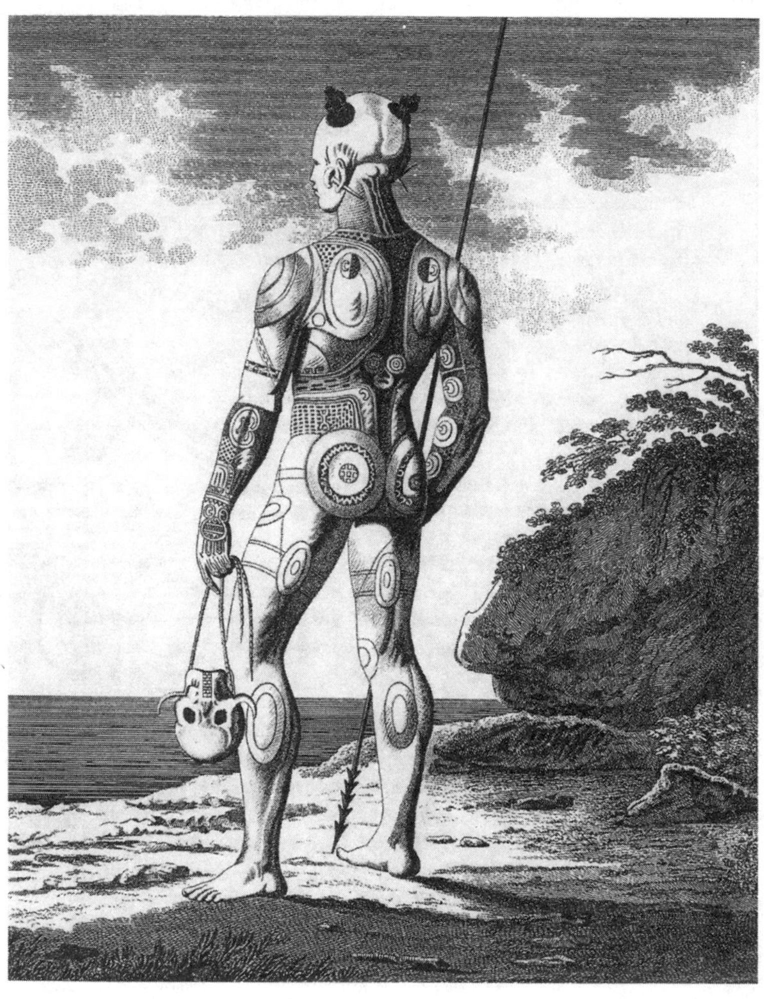

Figure 4. Marquesan warrior, from G. H. Von Langsdorff's Russian voyage of exploration (London, 1813).

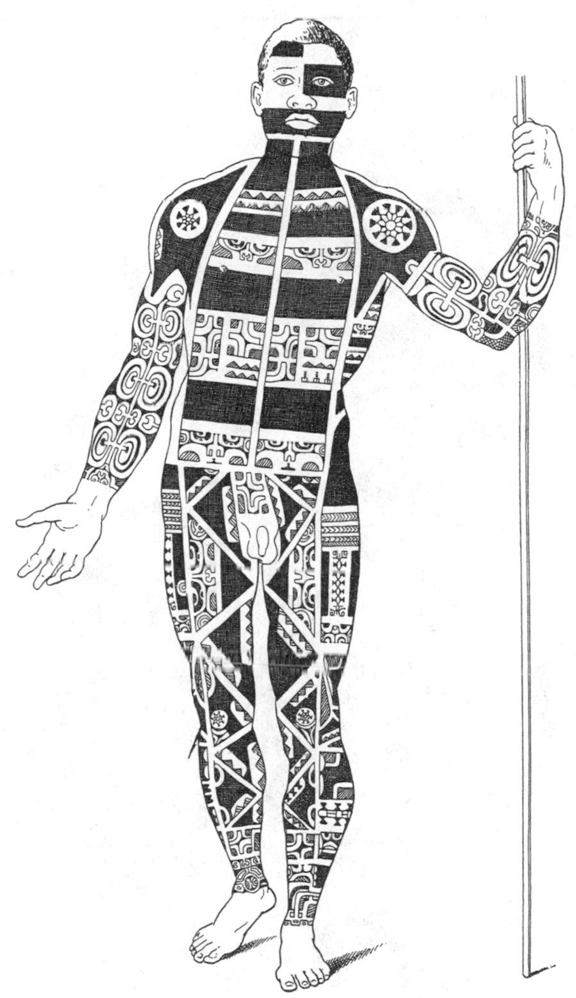

Figure 5. Male tattoo designs, from Karl von den Steinen, *Die Marquesaner und ihre Kunst* (Germany, 1925).

Figure 6. A New Zealand chief, engraved after a drawing by Sydney Parkinson, 1770.

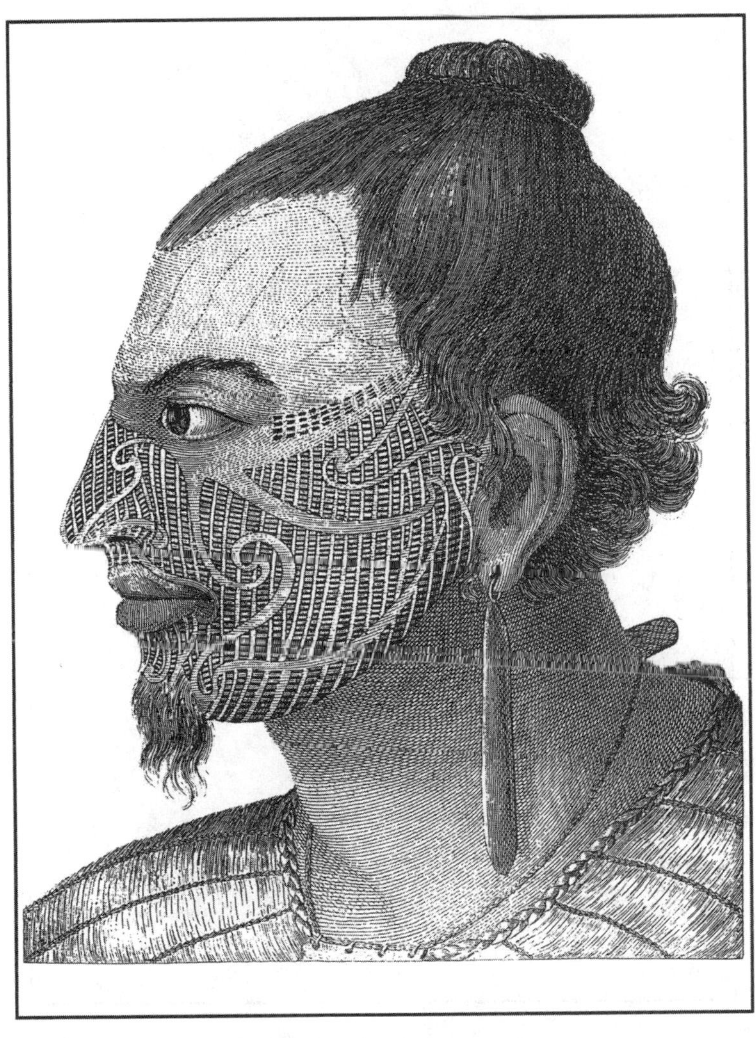

Figure 7. A New Zealand warrior, engraved after a drawing by Sydney Parkinson, 1770.

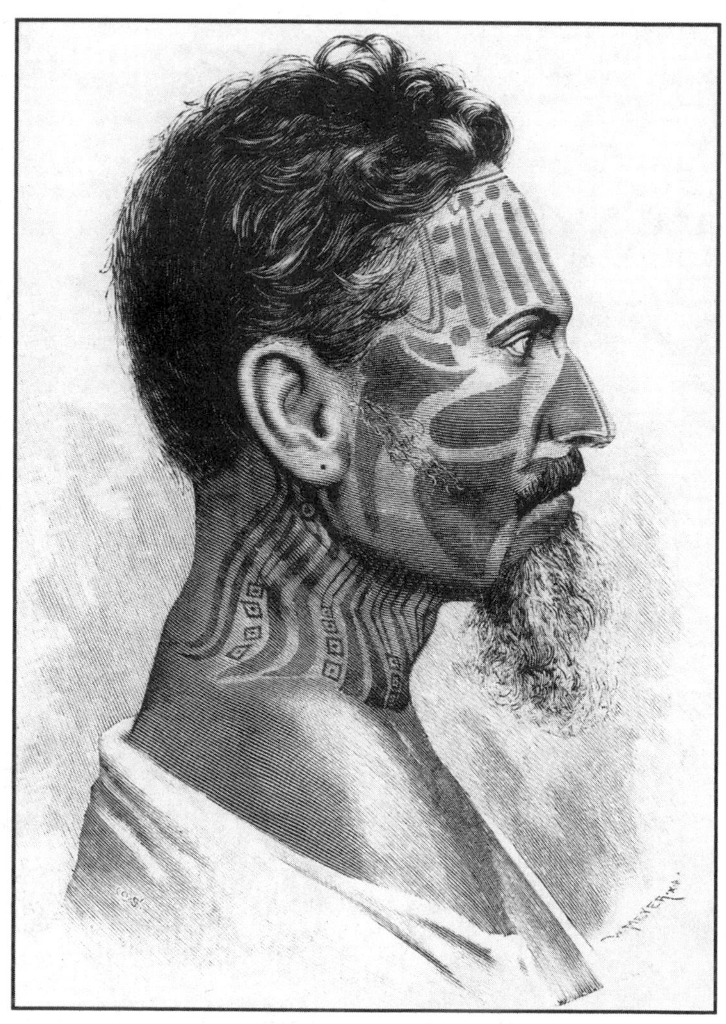

Figure 8. Easter Island facial tattoo.

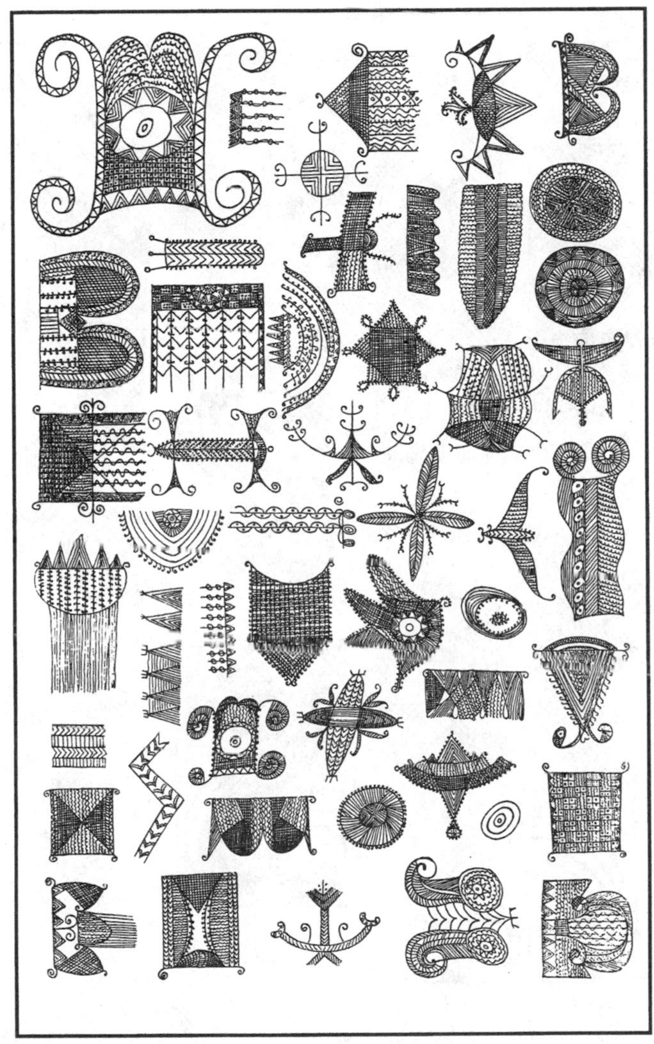

Figure 9. Borneo tattoo designs.

Figure 10. Borneo tattoo designs.

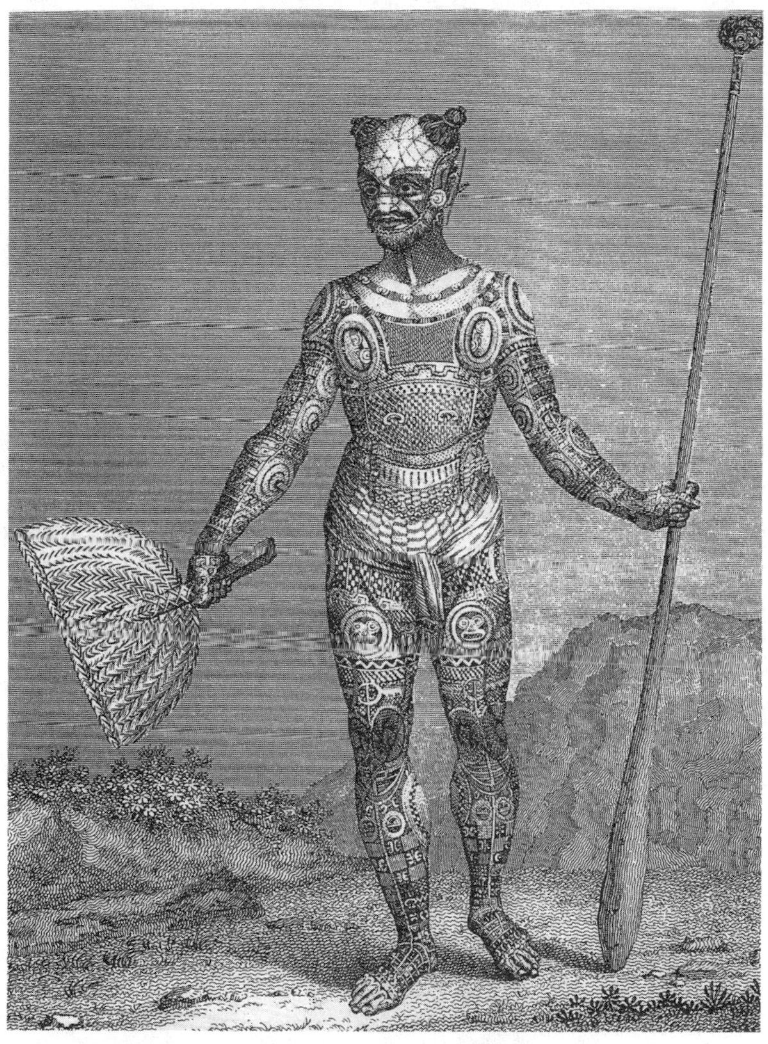

Figure 11. Engraving entitled "An inhabitant of the island of Nukahiva," from G. H. Von Langsdorff's Russian voyage of exploration (London, 1813).

Figure 12. Marquesan leg tattoos for men, from *Tattooing in the Marquesas* by Willowdean Chatterson Handy (Bishop Museum, 1921).

Figure 13. Marquesan leg tattoos for women, from *Tattooing in the Marquesas* by Willowdean Chatterson Handy (Bishop Museum, 1921).

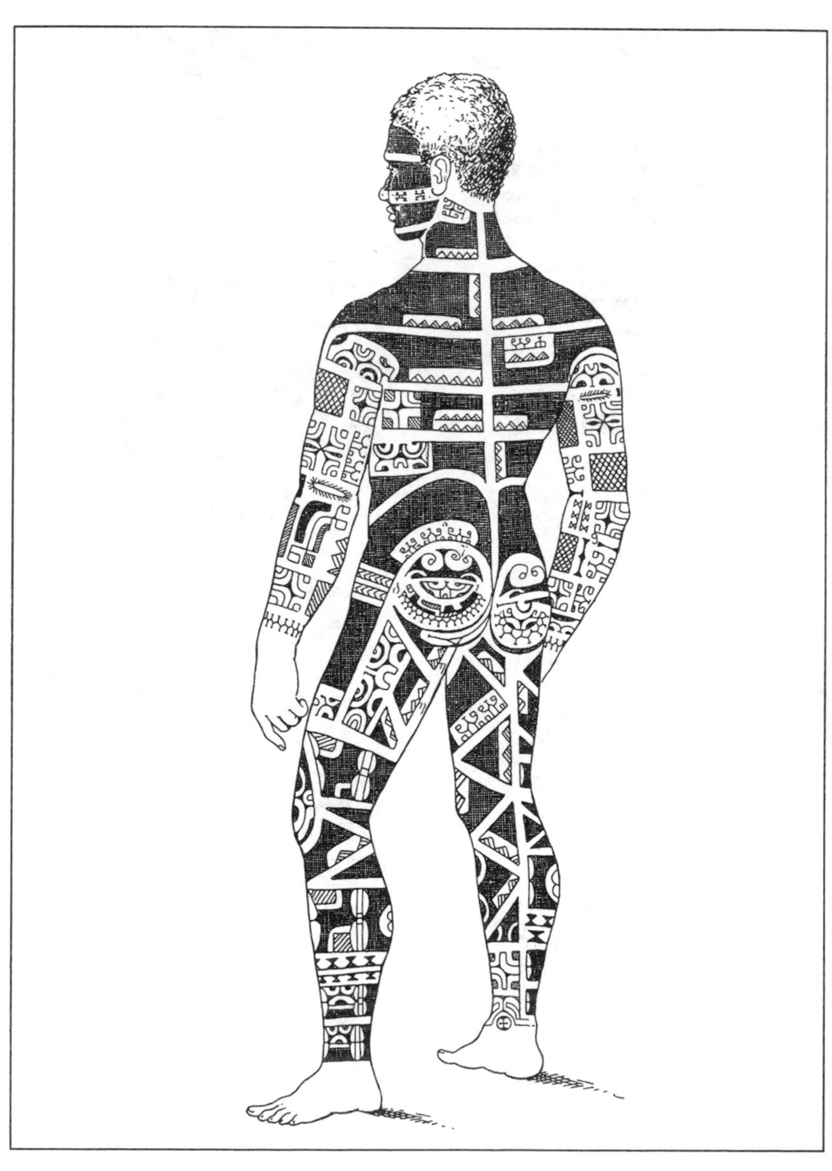

Figure 14. Male tattoo designs, from Karl von den Steinen, *Die Marquesaner und ihre Kunst* (Germany, 1925).

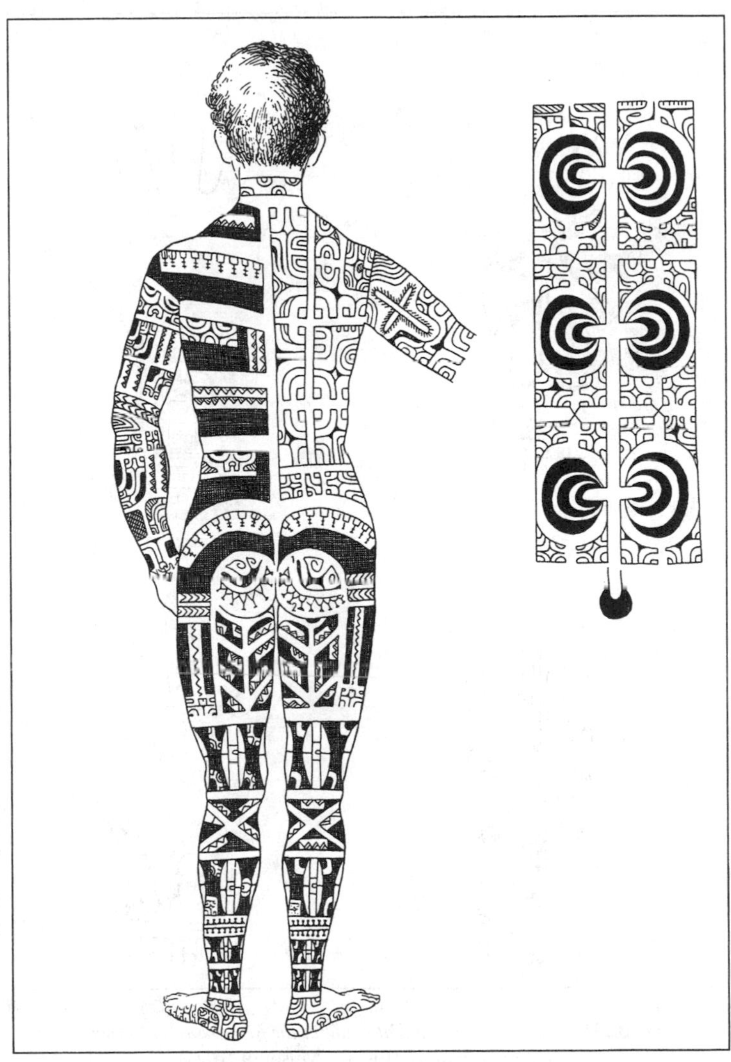

Figure 15. Male tattoo designs, from Karl von den Steinen, *Die Marquesaner und ihre Kunst* (Germany, 1925).

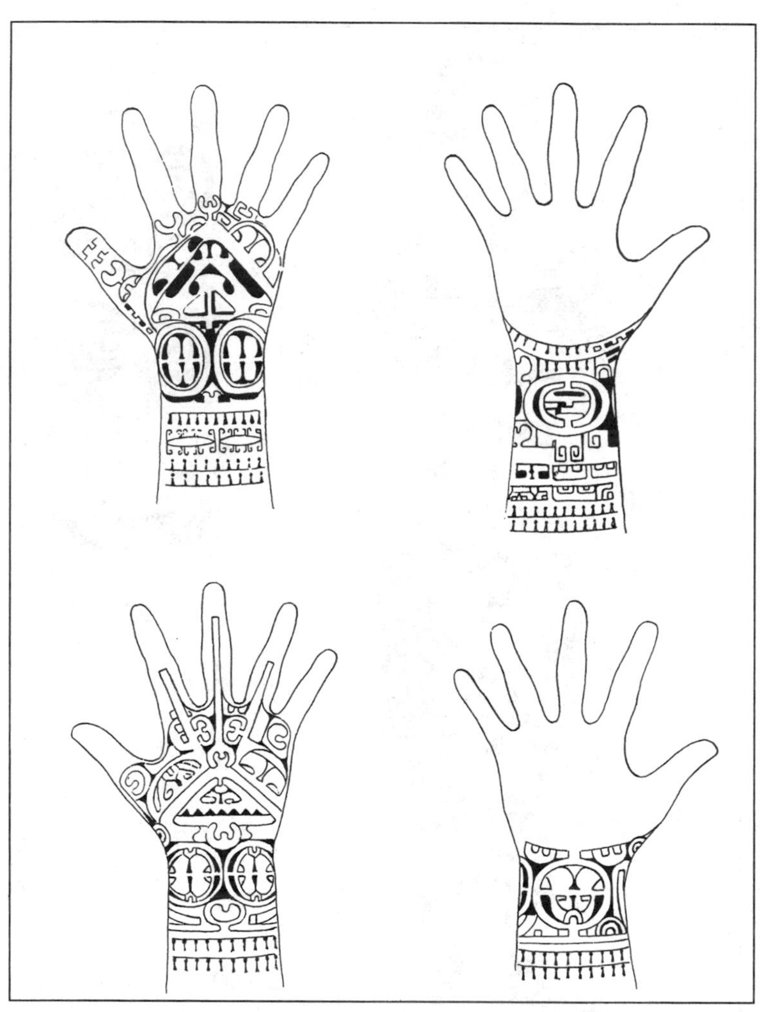

Figure 16. Hand patterns, from *Tattooing in the Marquesas* by Willowdean Chatterson Handy (Bishop Museum, 1921).

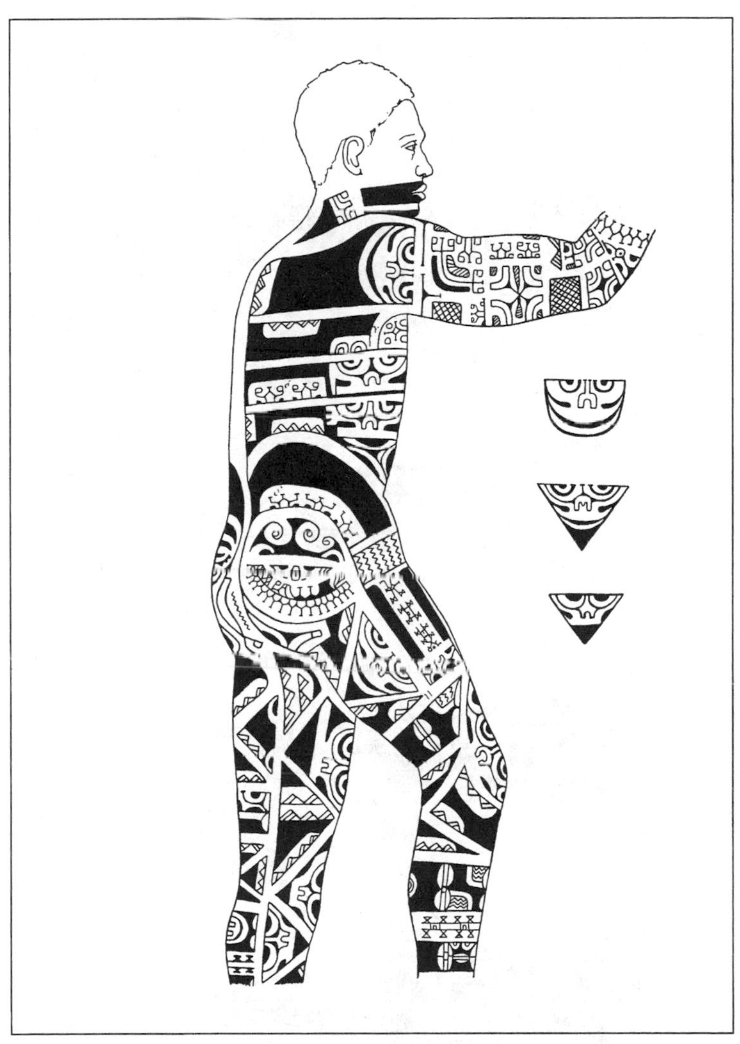

Figure 17. Male tattoo designs, from Karl von den Steinen, *Die Marquesaner und ihre Kunst* (Germany, 1925).

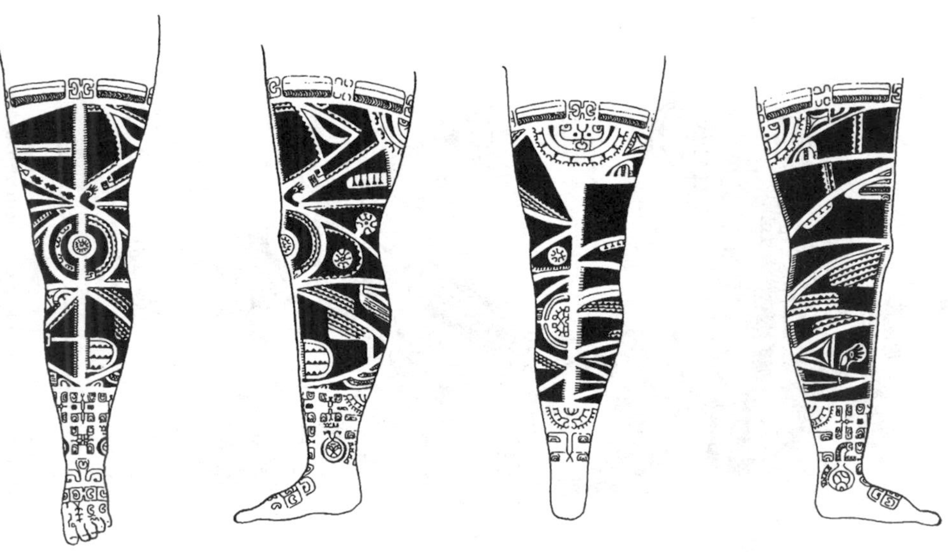

Figure 18. Marquesan leg tattoos, from *Tattooing in the Marquesas* by Willowdean Chatterson Handy (Bishop Museum, 1921).

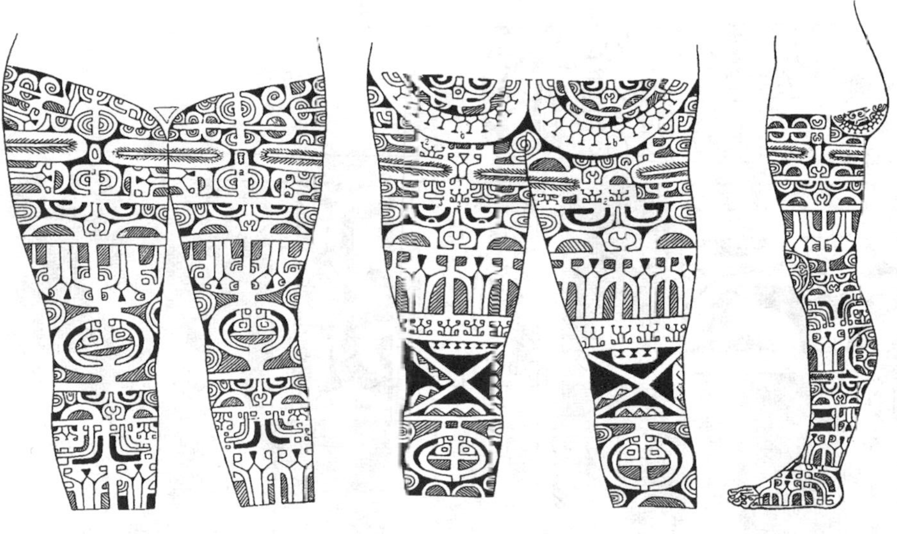

Figure 19. Female tattoo designs, from Karl von den Steinen, *Die Marquesaner und ihre Kunst* (Germany, 1925).

Figure 20. Male tattoo designs, from Karl von den Steinen, *Die Marquesaner und ihre Kunst* (Germany, 1925).

Figure 21. Male tattoo designs, from Karl von den Steinen, *Die Marquesaner und ihre Kunst* (Germany, 1925).

Figure 22. Facial tattoo, self-portrait by Te Phei Kupe.

CHAPTER II

BODY MARKING AND MAGIC

Body marking to cure sickness and pain—To give good luck—As a love charm—To preserve youth—Body marking and rain-making, etc.—Before trial by ordeal—Sacredness of paint and symbolism of colour—Body marking and death, mourning, and execution—Body marks connected with magic and religion—Psychic factors and the body marking process.

NEVER do we find that primitive man has explained sickness and pain as the outcome of natural causes, as for example, his own uncleanly habits and want of precaution in eating and drinking. There is an explanation which appeals to him as being the most satisfactory, and that is the one which attributes disease and pain to the machinations of an enemy, or to the special intervention of some demon spirit.

In addition to these hypotheses he puts forward the theory that the soul is always trying to leave the body, and that medical skill must be directed toward binding this truant soul.[1] Such views are all logical within primitive man's eminence of discourse, and Rivers has given them detailed attention.[2]

[1] "Pagan Tribes of Borneo," Hose and McDougall, Vol. I, p. 248.

[2] "Medicine, Magic, and Religion," Rivers, 1924, p. 52, and "Primitive Conception of Death," *Hibbert Journal*, 1912, Vol. X, p. 393.

So tangible a substance is the soul that it can be caught in a trap consisting of loops attached to a central stick, an apparatus employed by professional soul catchers of Borneo and Polynesia.[1]

Naturally enough the great problems of the medicine men are the exorcising of demons of disease, the detection of the individual who has caused illness by working black magic, and the devising of a means of keeping the soul within the body.

A geographical method of survey would reveal the reasons for body marking and magic, but perhaps the instances have more force when grouped not geographically, but with reference to the particular kind of magical art in which the tattooing or other marking is employed.

Commencing, then, with body marking as a cure for sickness or pain we find in India many interesting examples of a belief that certain marks, usually made by branding, will give relief from suffering.

Reference has already been made to the Bedar of the Bellary district, who tattooed over the deltoid muscle of his shoulder a figure of the monkey god Hanuman, in order to relieve the pain caused by dislocation. Dr. Thurston[2] refers to the Toda boys receiving cicatrices as a means of magically relieving or dispelling the aching which results from early efforts in milking buffaloes. Keloids are usually made on the right shoulder, the burns being inflicted with sacred fire sticks. The Todas believe that branding with sacred sticks enables them to milk the

[1] Fig. 32, British Museum Guide to Ethnographical Collections.

[2] "Ethnographical Notes in Southern India," Dr. Thurston, pp. 383 *et seq.*, 398-9.

buffaloes with perfect ease, and this is confirmed by a recent investigator, Dr. W. H. R. Rivers, who made inquiry in 1906. According to Dr. Rivers' account the only mark made by the male Toda is a cicatrix on the right shoulder, or less commonly on the elbow, the burn being inflicted with a stick made hot by fire produced by the drill method, which is, of course, the ancient ceremonial way of producing ignition. There is, however, no ceremonial added to the use of a fire stick in order to show that an increased sanctity is given to the operation.[1]

The marks may be made by anyone when the boy is about twelve years of age, at which time he begins milking operations. If one application of the hot stick is insufficient to give the boy immunity from pain when milking, other applications are given until the desired result is attained, and in one instance a man had three keloids, one on the shoulder and two on the elbow, the final mark having been given at the age of sixteen because he still suffered from aching arms when milking. The greatest number of scars observed was four, and on the other hand some men went without any mark, because they were members of large families, and therefore had not to do long spells of milking. Similar small scars are made on the wrist to cure pain, and ceremonial keloids are made on the wrists of women at pregnancy, but whether to alleviate pain is not quite clear, the elaborate ceremonial rather indicates that cicatrizing of women at pregnancy is a way of warding off a variety of vague indefinable evils which are always supposed to be active during any crisis of life, such as child-birth

[1] Rivers, "The Todas," 1906, p. 576.

or puberty.[1] Dr. Thurston adds that a cicatrix is made when people are in a state of collapse, say from high fever; the marks usually being made between the eyebrows, toes, or on the nape of the neck.[2]

In the Kistna district babies are branded on forehead, chest, or neck to cure convulsions, and men of the Mala and other castes are branded in the pubic region to cure colic. Another instance of body marking is provided by a man of the Kaikolan people who, when a baby, was cured of his sickness by being marked on chest and abdomen with a number of large and small discs. Some Lingayat children are branded with a hot needle on the stomach, not as a cure, but as an evidence of belief in the maxim that prevention is better than cure. Children who are subject to fits are branded with a heated twig or a glass bangle. In the absence of direct evidence it is possible only to conjecture as to the meaning of, or reason for this marking.[3] The offering of rice or other small gifts to placate the demons of disease is common, and taking as a basis these ideas of disease demons, it is reasonable to suppose that a demon who is in the habit of exacting from each individual a certain toll of pain, would be propitiated if that pain was self-inflicted, and given in such a way that the individual carried for life some evidence, in the shape of scars, which prove that tribute to the pain demon had been paid.

[1] Rivers, "The Todas," pp. 313, 576.

[2] "Ethnographical Notes," p. 398.

[3] *Ibid.*, p. 399, *op. cit.*, Introduction, p. 19. Reference to cicatrizing abdomen amongst Sudanese.

Sir J. G. Scott, who has had prolonged and intimate contact with the Burman, can speak with certainty concerning Burmese beliefs in the efficacy of tattooing as a charm.[1] Most of the men who tattoo charms and cabalistic signs are Shans, who, while performing, mutter spells and incantations. Generally there is for the tattooer of charm designs considerable respect and a profound belief in the efficacy of the work.[2]

One particular design is for the prevention of pain, and a schoolboy who has taken the precaution of having himself marked with the "A-hpee" charm will court a flogging to test the efficacy of the tattooer's work; whether or no the youth is satisfied with the result of his venture does not appear. Sir J. G. Scott naïvely observes that whatever the efficiency of the tattoo charm may be, the youth is notably quiet for some time after the adventure. There is also the "Mooy Say" charm against snake bite, and a very gruesome tattooing which takes place while the patient holds human flesh between his teeth.

This last mentioned, "Baw-dee-mah-da" tattoo charm, is supposed to give to the recipient a supernatural strength, and judging from the instance cited by Mr. Shway Yoe[3] the wearer is not disappointed. In one of the monasteries was a boy who gave assistance to a destitute Shan tattooer, who requited the kindness by tattooing a strength charm on the boy, in order to confer on his benefactor a charmed life.

[1] "The Burman, his Life and Notions," ch. V, pp. 39-47.
[2] *Ibid.*, pp. 41, 43.
[3] Pseudonym for Sir J. G. Scott.

In a month's time there were unmistakable signs that the supernormal strength was about to exert itself, for the lad leaped enormous heights in the air, jumped and ran at random, and carried with ease things which no one else could move.[1]

The youth escaped from a strong box in which he was confined and took refuge on the top of the monastery, a distance of forty feet from the ground, from which point he leaped to earth without injury. So the story proceeds, getting taller and taller until we hear of the youth walking across the river in such a way that the water did not reach his waist. Finally he was cured by a holy ascetic who took out the tattoo charm. Accustomed as one is to the effect of mind over body, and noting the enormous power of a belief in magic among people who dabble with the black art, it is not surprising that a youth tattooed with a charm in which he has extraordinary faith should develop some unusual strength and proclivities. When there had been anything in the way of an extraordinary demonstration the imagination of the brother monks would embellish the narrative until it attained the dimensions given by Mr. Shway Yoe. The loss of power too is easy to account for; the tattoo charm was dug out, faith and subconscious stimulus were gone, and the youth had no further incentive to eccentric conduct.

In the year 1881 at Rangoon there was a young man who received the tattoo design of a young egret because of its efficacy in preventing the wearer from drowning. So great was the faith in this charm that the wearer allowed himself to be thrown into the

[1] "The Burman, his Life and Notions," p. 44.

river, tied hand and foot, which, of course, resulted in a fatality.[1] The men who had assisted in this experiment were charged with murder and were eventually convicted on an indictment of manslaughter, much to the annoyance of many Burmese, who thought that the treatment was harsh, and that the fatality was due to the working of black magic to prevent the tattooed egret having the proper saving power.

A parallel instance comes to mind from far away in Vancouver Island where a woman of the Haida people had a tattooed halibut right across her face, and on the tail of the fish was the head of her Chief. She said that such a design would prevent her from being drowned at sea, and that her relations would enjoy a similar immunity.[2] Such examples might be included under various headings, and one of the difficulties of treating the information is to determine with what group some of the examples of body marking shall fall.

Our immediate interest is not so much the prevention of accident by tattoo charms, as the relief or prevention of sickness by such devices, and among the Sakai there is a magical ceremony for the exorcising of the cholera demon.[3] This demon is driven away by a medicine man assuming a coat of black paint to which he adds broad white stripes down the front of his person. He then goes forward with a ceremony consisting for the main part of dances and

[1] "The Burman, his Life and Notions," p. 47.

[2] "American Anthropologist," 1909, p. 377, from "Queen Charlotte Islands," Francis Poole, London, 1872, p. 321.

[3] "Pagan Races of the Malay Peninsula," Skeat and Blagden, p. 288.

incantations. Painting among the Semang, Sakai, and Jakun for magical ceremonies is common; the favourite pigments being black, white, and red, with yellow on some occasions.[1] These pigments are all used in various magical ceremonies, but primary importance is attached to the yellow and red which appear to be of equal potence.[2]

Among the Semang body painting is indulged in more for magical than ornamental purposes, while among the Sakai the ornamental uses are more frequent. Combs and quiver cases used by the Semang are works of art, and the designs impressed on these articles are said to have a magical power of protecting the wearer; thus a hunter whose quiver displays the correct markings will be immune from falling trees or from the flash of lightning. In Kedah a woman said that the designs on combs were for repelling evil, and that similar marks were sometimes painted on the body. Information concerning the Semang is to be accepted with reservation. Vaughan Stevens gives much that is interesting, but is so vague with regard to places, people, technique, and forms of body marks employed that subsequent explorers found a difficulty in checking the statements. The difficulty of corroboration results largely from the seclusion of the Semang in dense jungle where they wander over wide areas. Tattooing proper is said to be unknown among the Semang, but there is some evidence to show that charcoal is employed for magical body marking when pain is

[1] "Pagan Races of the Malay Peninsula," p. 31, and J. A. G. Campbell, "Sakis of Selangor," *Selangor Journal*, 1895, Vol. III, No. 15, p. 240.

[2] "Pagan Races of the Malay Peninsula," p. 36.

felt.[1] For the Sakai there is something to be said about use of magical paint at the birth of a child, but whether the pigment is used to alleviate the pain of delivery is not quite clear; more probably the instance should be used as an example of magical markings to ward off vague indefinable evils which lurk round during a crisis. In short the instance seems to be very like Dr. Rivers' account of the marking of Toda women with keloids about the time of their delivery.

There seems to be little room for doubt that the Sakai have a very clear distinction between ordinary decorative paint and pigment of magical potence.[2] When in office the medicine man may assume his magical pigment, but this he must discard when he becomes a lay member of the community. The magicians and midwives use a tortoise-shell implement for applying magical white paint, and any other person using this colouring or means of application, will be struck by lightning. Other points of interest are to the effect that the dead must never retain their paint, which appears to be a flat contradiction of all savage parallels whether from primitive men of to-day or cave men of the old stone age.

Until marriage, boys and girls wear red streaks of paint to which no special significance is attached.[3] But when, at a later period, black streaks or white dots are assumed, the individual must take care that he does not carry out the decoration of his own body. An article on the magical use of paint among the

[1] "Pagan Races of the Malay Peninsula," p. 38, and "Zeitschrift für Ethnologie," Vol. XXVI, pp. 150-7.

[2] "Pagan Races of the Malay Peninsula," p. 47.

[3] *Ibid.*, p. 48.

Jakun of the Besisi concludes with an instance similar to one recorded for Burma by Sir H. H. Risley, who says that the Burman desiring to hunt successfully gained the qualities of the tiger or cat by tattooing a picture of these animals on his body. The Jakun who wishes to have power to kill a tiger takes the leaf "tiger chind weh," and after mashing it to a pulp smears it on his body, giving to the chest a most liberal dose.

Among the Nigerian body marks is one given as a cure for pain. Major Tremearne says that an individual named Baba had what he called "babba goro," a series of short parallel cuts on the left side of the body below the waist. He said the marks were made to relieve stomach ache.[1] No doubt there are many scars which are the result of primitive surgical operations; such scars are mentioned by Sir Everard im Thurn in "The Indians of Guiana," and by G. Turner, who speaks of the people of Samoa cutting the head to let the headache out.[2] Henry O. Forbes, writing in 1885, says that the people of Timor Laut mark their arms and shoulders with red-hot sticks in order to ward off disease. The marks made resemble those of smallpox, which is a complaint the people dread.[3]

For the Andaman Islands[4] E. H. Man says that there are three pigments in common use, and from the mode of application it can at once be ascertained

[1] J.A.I., 1911, pp. 162-71.

[2] Compare with "Ainus and their Folk-Lore," London, 1901, Batchelor, p. 21, and "Samoa," Turner, 1884, p. 339.

[3] "A Naturalist's Wanderings in the Eastern Archipelago," London, 1885, p. 313.

[4] J.A.I., 1882, pp. 331-3.

whether the individual be sick or sorry, or whether he has taken or is about to take part in a merry-making. The unmarried may not paint their necks either for ornamental purposes or to relieve pain. Burnt yellow ochre is sometimes applied as a remedy for sickness, and another interesting example of the application of pigment for magical purposes is the use of olive clay on the body when the individual has made a meal from turtle. It is held that evil spirits would be attracted by the good smell of the turtle, so the aroma is prevented by applying clay to the hands and face.[1]

From the Sarawak Kayan of Borneo we learn the art or science of keeping the soul within the body, a condition which is quite rightly regarded as a fundamental of health and activity.[2] Some one is ill, and the "dayong" is called in to diagnose the case, which he will probably declare to be the result of the soul leaving the body; and the cure is of course to be effected by causing the truant soul to return. The "dayong" accordingly throws himself into a trance so that his soul may be liberated in order to pursue the runaway soul of the patient and persuade it to return. The ceremony is usually performed by torchlight in the presence of a circle of anxious relatives, who have made the necessary payment to this skilled soul catcher. Sometimes a blow-pipe is put to the patient's ear and the words "come back," "come back," are shouted. The medicine man continues, "This is your home, here we have food ready for you," to which the soul may reply, "I am far from home following a 'toh' (spirit) and don't know the

[1] J.A.I., 1882, p. 333.
[2] "Pagan Tribes of Borneo," Vol. I, p. 248.

way back." Usually the ceremony ends by the "dayong" producing some small animal or stone from the palm of his hand, and as the runaway soul is in this object the restoration to the patient is made by placing it near his head. The further escape of the soul is prevented by placing a strip of palm leaf round the patient's wrist and making an offering of a fowl, or, in cases of severe illness, a pig to the demon of disease. The palm leaf was easily lost, and now the custom is to tattoo round the patient's wrist an imitation of the former bond. This tattoo mark acts not only as a means of keeping the soul in the body, but as a preventative of sickness from other causes.

There is a clear distinction to be drawn between the pain cure body markings of Africa, of Guiana, of Samoa, and the Australian tribes on the one hand; and on the other hand the pain cure markings of the Hindus, Burmese, Kayans, and Andaman Islanders. In the first group mentioned there is no reason for believing that the cure lies in the mark itself, but the probability seems that the mark is merely incidental to the cure. Now in the second group of instances, namely those pertaining to Hindus, Burmese, Kayans, and Andaman Islanders, the body mark itself, be it a tattoo, cicatrix or paint, is regarded as the essential part of the magical cure, which appears to be effected by a prominent appeal to the demon of disease. In case of Timor Laut, and the marking with representations of the smallpox scars, there is very likely the idea that the demon will go away satisfied that the people have already been the objects of his attentions. Or it may be that, like the Ainu, who consider that their marks cause the demon to flee because he sees they are like their divine protectors, the people who assume the smallpox cicatrix feel safe because their marks show affinity with the demon of smallpox.[1] This demon will, of course, refuse to harm those who are identified with himself, which is suggested as congruous with primitive logic. A third hypothesis is the one suggested to account for the brandings mentioned by Dr. Thurston. It is to the effect that people believe that the demon of pain will exact, in some form or other, from each individual, a given amount of suffering, and that a man may escape by inflicting on himself, early in life, some mild substitute which will be sufficient to appease the pain demon.

The connection between painting, scarification and puncture tattoo is difficult to unravel. The problem of a possible monogenesis with subsequent trifurcation during the prehistoric period, and consequent specialization, is of great interest. Rivers, noting the common distribution of therapeutic and religious blood letting in the Pacific, suggests a definite connection between the two. Probably the religious practice of scarifying is evolved from the therapeutic operation.[2]

Body Marking to Give Good Luck

Body marking for the purpose of giving good luck is a fairly common practice, carried out apparently not with any intention of making an appeal to any supernatural being, but because there is a subconscious feeling that without the traditional mark evil fortune will result. Perhaps a consideration of

[1] Rev. Batchelor, "Ainus and their Folk-Lore," p. 21.
[2] Rivers, "Medicine, Magic, Religion," pp. 98, 99.

a few specific cases in detail will make clear whether the individual has in mind the appeal to some power, person, demon, or spirit capable of protecting him.

Customs of Burma have been referred to as proof that certain tattoo marks are used as charms for some very specialized form of protection, such as securing immunity from death by drowning, gunshot, or spear-thrust.[1] In addition to these cases there is among the Siamese, near neighbours of the Burmese, a custom, widespread among the lower classes, of tattooing certain devices which are regarded as general charms to secure good fortune. Frequently the device consists of a scroll representing Buddha in the attitude of meditation, and the device is usually placed on the points of the shoulder blades, or on the breast or wrist. The example seems to be almost of a religious kind since a deity is represented. The scroll must be right-handed for a boy, left-handed for a girl.

The religious elements in this instance are the reproduction of the figure of a deity, and the carrying out of the operation by a monk. The magical part includes a belief in the efficacy of such a material thing as a body mark, also a repetition of magical syllables and blowing over the design. Both these processes are necessary incidents at the completion of the marking.

The Burman desiring general good luck and favour with princes will have a parrot tattooed on the arm, and while the operation is in progress he must repeat at intervals the words, " A parrot tattooed on

[1] " Lotus Land," P. A. Thompson, p. 141.

the arm will give great favour with princes." [1] The words evidently serve as a mild kind of spell or incantation; no doubt faith comes in and the man goes forth with that confidence and elasticity of spirit which render him master of the situations he has to meet. All Shan boys are tattooed as a test of endurance, and after the regulation work is done on the thighs, designs are added from time to time on the back and arms. These latter markings are charms to ward off wounds or accidents.[2]

Among the Arunta of Central Australia, in Burma, with the Pima of North America, and among the Sakai, there are instances of body marking of children at birth, and although there is no doubt a social significance attached to the marking, we have decided to treat all such instances in the chapter on body marking for magical purposes. It is just a fine point as to whether the magical or the social element predominates, and the best method is to allow the examples to be their own evidence.

From birth to death almost every action of a native of Central Australia is in some way allied with magic, and as soon as the Arunta child is born a black line is painted over the eyebrows to ward off sickness. Should this charm prove ineffective it is assumed that someone has worked counter-magic.[3] Among the Pima of North America it is customary to paint the face of a baby immediately after birth with a mixture of red ochre and his mother's milk. It is now held that this is to improve the child's skin, but the use

[1] "The Burman, his Life and Notions," Mr. Shway Yoe (Sir J. G. Scott), ch. V, p. 47.

[2] "The Shans at Home" by Mrs. Leslie Milne, 1910, p. 67.

[3] "Across Australia," Spencer and Gillen, p. 342.

of the red ochre, which is almost universally held to possess magical properties, was in all probability intended as a protective charm.[1] For Central America there is Bancroft's statement that newly-born children are tattooed round the eyelids.[2]

Among the Sakai the newly-born child has the face painted every day until twenty-eight days, one lunar month, have passed. Should the moon be invisible on the night of any period of twenty-four hours, such a period is not counted. That is to say, the painting of the child's face must be performed on twenty-eight days for which the moon has been visible.[3] The only other case of body marking being carried out with any reference to the moon is found among the Kayans, who do not commence the tattooing of a girl until the "butit halap," the ninth day from new moon.[4] Such ceremonial observances as these indicate the importance of body marking for magical purposes. Not only is the child among the Sakai painted, but during her three or five days of office the midwife assumes facial paint; so also does the mother.

A very common procedure in Burma is the making of a scroll representing Buddha between the eyes of the child, the ceremony being carried out along with the tonsure to which young children are submitted.[5] This process is reminiscent of the Hindu belief that each person's destiny is written on his brow, although invisible to the human eye. Probably the sutures of

[1] A.B.E., 1904-5, p. 161.

[2] "Native Races of North America," Bancroft, Vol. I, p. 532.

[3] "Pagan Races of the Malay Peninsula," Skeat and Blagden, p. 46.

[4] "Pagan Tribes of Borneo," Vol. I, p. 255.

[5] "Lotus Land," P. A. Thompson, p. 141.

the skull, which are not unlike some of the characters in Indian alphabets, gave rise to this belief. Nowadays writing materials are placed beside the new-born babe in the lying-in room in order that Vidhatr may write the child's destiny on the forehead.[1]

It is an interesting speculation as to whether marking round the eye bears any reference to "giving the evil eye," against which a special mark might be a safeguard. In many remote parts of the highlands of Scotland, and in our own counties of Cornwall and Somerset, many country people still believe in the possibility of an animal or young child being "overlooked." The Greeks, who received many ideas from Egypt, had a special word to express this mysterious power, Baokavia, meaning a giving of the evil eye, and in "Polish Folk-Lore," by Woyciki,[2] there is a story of a Slav peasant who had this evil eye, and in order that his children should not be "overlooked" he blinded himself.

It is usually held that the person overlooked pines away from sickness which no medical man can diagnose, and as the evil is from an eye, or from the glance of an eye, it is possible that the black magic is thought to enter by the eye of the one overlooked. Perhaps the painting is carried out in order to prevent this.

Sir Alexander Mackenzie, speaking of the Crees, refers to several interesting examples of body marking, which include scarring of the belly and breast by burning to cure disease, or to show courage.[3] For the

[1] Shib Chunder Bose, "The Hindus as they are," 2nd edition, p. 25.

[2] English translation by Lewestein, p. 25.

[3] "Voyages in North America," Sir Alexander Mackenzie, 1789-93, p. 241.

Western Denés, Father Maurice refers to one or two transverse lines tattooed on the forearms as a charm against "wakun," an omnipresent magical force which may be exerted for good or evil.[1]

Tattooing as a Love Charm

No wonder that magical practices are so dear to the heart of primitive man, for apparently there is no emergency, circumstance, or crisis of life with which magical ceremonies and devices are not capable of dealing. Among the many and varied uses of body marking, we find instances of the art being employed to attract the opposite sex, not by adding artificial ornament to enhance the natural charms, but because there is faith in the magical potence of particular designs and substances, especially if these are applied in ceremonial manner.

The Burmese have such strong faith in tattooed charms that it would be strange if they did not make use of cabalistic marks during the love-making epoch of life. The cabalistic signs adopted include birds, mystic words, squares, rings, images of Buddha, dots between the eyes, over the ears and on the chin. The usual colour is vermilion which is pricked in with the tattooing needle. Along with the colouring matter is mixed a drug which varies with the object of the tattooing, and in the instances we are considering, the "drug of tenderness" is the medicine added.[2]

[1] A. T. Sinclair in "American Anthropologist," 1909, p. 379.

[2] "Things Indian," Wm. Crooke, p. 462, and "The Burman, his Life and Notions," Shway Yoe, p. 41.

The tattooing mixture is evidently a compound of vermilion and a magic drug, which for love purposes is composed of material from the skin of the trout, and the spotted lizard which frequents houses; certain herbs form the vegetable ingredients. So valuable is the magic medicine, that the desired result may be obtained by the tattooing of a small triangle containing a few dots. Perhaps the Sayah recommends that the mark be made between the eyes, on the lips, or even on the tongue, and usually his advice is followed, though one can quite believe Mr. Crooke who says that the maid will ask for the charm in some place covered by clothing, as the girl very modestly does not wish to leave the impression that she is an old maid looking for a husband. According to Shway Yoe this tattoo design has a special significance in Rangoon where a lady adopts the mark when desiring an Englishman for a husband.

Some instances show the use of an unguent for smearing the body of one who is in love. Among such instances is that of the Negritos of Kedah, who burn a plant and extract oil which is smeared on breast and forehead, while a mystical formula is repeated; the gist of the incantation being: "Look, look, comrade, as the oil drips alone by yourself, approach towards me, yearn toward me," an imperfect translation in all probability, but the nearest we can get with our limited knowledge of the language.[1]

A similar device is adopted by the love-sick youth of Mabuiag (Torres Strait),[2] for here it is customary

[1] "Pagan Races of the Malay Peninsula," Skeat and Blagden, Vol. II, p. 232.

[2] "Cambridge Expedition to Torres Strait," Vol. V, p. 216.

for the boy to rub the milky juice of a plant on his knees and shoulder, while charcoal is smeared on the back of the neck. Mr. W. N. Beaver notes cases of arm scarification denoting success in love.[1] A fortnight goes by and then "puti," a magical substance, is burned, and charcoal is rubbed over the boy's face; this second stage is reputed to be very powerful love magic for it makes the girl fall in love very quickly.

From the Sioux and Cheyennes there comes an interesting example of use of paint for expression of the tender emotion. A Siouan or Cheyenne warrior desiring to be alone takes lamp black, or black paint, and smears his face, after which he uses his finger nail for drawing zigzag lines from the hair to the chin, as a sign that he is trapping, melancholy or in love.[2]

Examples of body marking in reference to dealings with the opposite sex are not far to seek, and among those whose intelligence might be expected to suppress any natural tendency toward body marking, there is considerable evidence to show that this means of expressing a complex sentiment is adopted.

M. Lombroso speaks of many designs marked on the bodies of criminals he has examined, and of these he remarks that patterns referring to love are the least numerous. They are to be found chiefly among the Lombards and Piedmontese, who prick into the skin the initials of the lady; sometimes the date of falling in love is added; or maybe several hearts

[1] W. N. Beaver, "Unexplored New Guinea," p. 169.

[2] G. P. Belden, "Twelve Years Among the Wild Indians of the Plains," 1870, p. 144.

transfixed with arrows.[1] In one instance the artist had represented a woman in peasant dress holding in her hand a flower. Given in M. Lombroso's words the account runs: "Les signes d'amour sont les moins nombreux; ils se trouvent presque exclusivement parmi les Lombards et les Piedmontais. Ce sont d'ordinaire le nom ou les initiales de la femme aimée, tracées en lettres majuscules; la date du premier amour, un ou pleusieurs cœurs transpercès par une flèche; deux mains entrelacées. J'ai vu la figure entière d'une femme, vêtue en paysanne, avec un fleur à la main." One instance is mentioned in which the criminal had tattooed himself with a heart to represent his former mistress from whom he had parted, the separation being indicated by an arrow which pierced the heart. Their two little children were symbolized by two small hearts.[2]

Instances of tattooing the body with epithets, proverbs, and epigrams are numerous, and among the short phrases quoted by M. Lombroso is one referring to the sentiment of love. "Louise Chère amante mon unique consolation."[3]

Seamen usually show a leaning toward tattooing as a means of decoration, and the clasped hands are a favourite device to indicate some friendship which, if one may judge by the relative sizes of the hands, exists between the sailor and some lady or ladies. Frequently the head and shoulders, or perhaps the entire figure of a woman is represented on the arms of a sailor, and the habit of tattooing dancing girls on

[1] "L'Homme Criminel," Lombroso, 1895, Vol. I, p. 268.
[2] *Ibid.*, p. 283.
[3] *Ibid.*, p. 281.

the arms is very widespread among Tamil-speaking men of Southern India.[1]

The foregoing instances appear to be an illustration of a spontaneous reversion to very old practices. Emotions arise and there has to be some form of expression, which will, of course, vary according to racial qualities, individual temperament, and education. The emotions are combined to form a complex sentiment of love, which finds expression in body marking with designs calculated to assimilate the wearer with the person desired. The tattoo is an emblem of the unity of two personalities, and of course in cases of degeneration of the passion of love into mere animal sexual instinct, there is a degeneration in the pictorial expression, which as M. Lombroso shows, lapses into obscenity.

Tattoo Marks to Preserve Youth

The quest after perpetual youth has been one of the concerns of mankind from very remote times, and in our own day the quack doctor is ready to supply something cheap which will add years to the life, and give a perpetual bloom of youth. Maori girls solved the problem in their own way, and sought to retain their youth by tattooing the lips and chin, and in reply to the remonstrances of a missionary they said: "We really must have a few lines on our lips, else when we grow up our lips will shrivel and we shall grow old and ugly." Untattooed lips and white teeth were regarded as the type of what is ugly and

[1] Dr. Thurston, "Ethnographical Notes," p. 378.

unwomanly, and any woman who failed to adopt the usual ornament was said to have red lips and white teeth, just like a dog.[1] The distribution of chin tattooing of women is world-wide and suggests definite migration of ideas.

The Ainus have great faith in re-tattooing as a means of restoring youth, and when the eyes of an old lady are becoming dim she re-tattooes her mouth and hands so that she may see better. The Rev. Batchelor says: "I am well acquainted with an old lady who tattooes herself quite frequently in order to strengthen her eyesight."[2] As far away as North America there is a parallel for this belief, and among the Pima a few lines are tattooed on the faces both of men and women who believe that these marks are magically potent in retaining youth.[3] There appears to be some distinction between tattoo marks for retaining youth, as used by Maori women on the one hand, and Ainus and Pimas on the other, for whereas in New Zealand the mark is an artificial aid, rather ornamental than magical, it is among the Ainus and Pima a magical device for prolonging youth.

Body Marking to Assist Magical Ceremonies

The position of the medicine man or magician is of such importance among primitive people that it would be extremely surprising if there were not some magical assistance to be derived from the use of body mark-

[1] "Moko," Major-General Robley, p. 33. Buckland, J.A.I., 1883, p. 325.

[2] "Ainus and their Folk-Lore," Rev. Batchelor, 1901, p. 21.

[3] A.B.E., 1904-5, p. 162.

ing. Among North Americans, Australians, Papuans and many others the medicine man calls body marking to his aid in performing his magico-religious rites. In Dr. Howitt's account of the initiation of a boy of the Yuin tribe[1] to the position of medicine man there are two instances of the use of red ochre, which appears to be indispensable to the ceremony. Among many wonderful experiences through which the boy passed, when in a state of trance, was that of witnessing his father disappear into the ground and come up covered with red dust, and in a further account a boy speaks of being in the midst of old men who were rubbed all over with red ochre.

Figures representing guardian spirits are much in favour with the Lillooit and Thompson Indians, and not only are such devices freely used on all material belongings, but they are frequently tattooed on face and body.[2] Shamans, or medicine men, tattoo themselves with the ghost, deer, bat, frog, rattle-snake, fish, and morning star, while the thunderbolt, canoe, and arrow are sometimes used. The ghost is the guardian spirit of the Shamans, the magic symbol of the medicine man's art. The frog design was tattooed on the middle of the chest and on the front of each forearm. The shoulder blade carried the thunderbolt design, usually in blue, or perhaps in red ochre. The marks employed form a permanent sign of the Shaman's art, but it appears that the ordinary individual is not precluded from adopting one of

[1] "Native Tribes of South-East Australia," A. W. Howitt, London, 1904, p. 406.

[2] "Jesup Expedition to North Pacific," Vol. V, Part II, pp. 298-9.

these magical symbols, among which the bat, frog, and thunderbolt are old friends of witchcraft. These two animals are chosen possibly on account of their winter hibernation, which must be somewhat of a mystery to primitive people.

Rain-making among the Shuswap is practised by a special medicine man who had rain as his guardian spirit. After painting his face with red stripes, or dots, possibly both, probably in imitation of rain-drops, he goes out of the house, and walking round in a circle with the sun sings: "My guardian spirit will go round the world till it meets rain, and will bring it here."[1] This is a very clear instance of the use which a medicine man attaches to his paint; clearly the value of such decoration is not merely to impress the audience, but to gain recognition by the friendly spirit who can send the rainfall. The instance provides a connecting link in a series of examples of body marking which might be classified in evolutionary series to illustrate the passage from what is very vaguely magical to something approaching a religious cult.

Like so many of the Australian tribes, the Dieri practise rain-making, and among them there is a belief that cicatrization is an aid to rainfall. It appears that after the official rain-making ceremonies, carried out by a medicine man, who has his body covered with blood and decorated to represent clouds and rain, many people undergo the operation called "chin-basi," which is the cutting of chest and arms with a piece of flint, and the rubbing in of red ochre. The

[1] Frazer, Vol. III, p. 426. "The Shuswap," J. Teit, London and New York, 1909, pp. 588-90, 601.

people questioned told Dr. Howitt that they were pleased with the rain, and that there is a connection between scars and rainfall. Even little children crowd round the operator, and after they have received the marks, run away expanding their chests and arms while calling for the rain to fall on them.[1]

Among many instances of magical markings assisting in ceremonies which increase the rain and food supply are those of the Torres Strait people, who in the Island of Dubungai entice the turtle to the shore. The men who officiate are painted with a red line from the tip of the nose to the forehead, also down the spine to the small of the back, in order to resemble the mud that streams behind the dugong when he is browsing on the bottom of the estuary.[2] A model of a turtle is painted in the same way, and when the first live turtle for the season is captured, he is carried to the men of the Surbal clan who smear him over with red ochre, afterwards painting themselves with a red mark across the chest, and another across the abdomen to represent the shell of the turtle. The ceremony is concluded by the whirling of bull-roarers round the creature, which is eaten by the turtle clansmen, in order that its spirit may be liberated to go to sea and increase the fecundity of the breeding turtles. Women and children are carefully excluded, and the ceremony is a close approach to something of a religious nature, but after all the emphasis seems to be placed upon food supply, and so the body marking of all the men and the sacred turtle can be regarded as accessory to the magic which is necessary

[1] "Native Tribes of South-East Australia," p. 744.
[2] "Cambridge Expedition," Vol. V, p. 183.

to keep the turtles vigorous. In Mabuiag there are similar turtle cermonies in which the magical marks are lavished chiefly upon a model of the animal, and for the same island there occurs an interesting account of the body marking of a rain-maker whose office is hereditary.[1] A man wishing for rain in order to increase the fertility of his garden goes to the rain-maker, and after stating his needs and paying accordingly, is advised to go at once and get some more thatch on his house before the deluge comes. The rain-maker paints himself black and white, " all along same as clouds, black behind, white he go first," or perhaps he paints his body with black spots to make the clouds come, after which he puts " medicine " on his right hand and waves it towards his body while he chants to the rain. " You no go dance another way, best thing you come taste my body." Of course the rain comes in a deluge and the unfortunate man who asked for it may be imprisoned in his hut for days, after which he has to ask the sorcerer to turn off the magic tap, and in reply to his request for sunshine he is cheered by the words, " To-morrow rain small, next day sun he shine." For the encouragement of the sun the medicine man paints the crown of his head red in imitation of the orb, and after this a broad median line is added in red ochre, which is streaked from the forehead down the middle of the face, and eventually is made into a rhomboidal design which occupies the entire countenance; finally the medicine man covers himself entirely with red.

[1] " Cambridge Expedition," Vol. V, p. 338.

The office of wind-maker is also hereditary, and in order to encourage a breeze, which shall take the ships out for fishing, the medicine man sets up on the shore a number of low bushes when the tide is out. After smearing himself all over with red ochre he waves his arm for the wind to come and stir the low bushes he has set up on the reef. If the payment is considered insufficient the magician resorts to black magic in order to drive the wind away again. A change of colour is necessary, and the red ochre is exchanged for a black covering from head to foot. Then the hands are waved away from the head to drive off the wind.[1]

The most interesting question which arises with a review of these instances of body marking for the production of rain and food supply, is the precise importance which the medicine man himself attaches to the use of his body marks. May we dismiss the marking process as the device of one who, being conscious of his own weakness and deception, seeks some ostentation merely as an aid to imposing on his clients? The reasons for assuming the body paint and changing it according to the nature of the operation may differ with the differing temperaments of the medicine men concerned. Here is one who employs his marking as a means of enhancing his own impressiveness. The painting calls forth in his clients the feeling of self-abasement and a respect for what is magical. The North American rain-maker among the Shuswap seemed to be in earnest over the work, and his marks were without doubt assumed, not as a mere show to impress observers, but as a means of

[1] "Cambridge Expedition," Vol. V, p. 351.

calling forth some recognition from the rain spirit whose aid he sought.

Again the medicine man who advised his client to get some more thatch on his house quickly, actually sent the person away, then assumed the red ochre in order, we think, to attract the attention of some non-human power presiding over the distribution of rainfall; how distinct was this idea of a mysterious power to which paint could appeal, and how far the idea was removed from a conception of a personality it is impossible to say. These instances of body marking in order to control the gifts of nature seem capable of being graded into a series, varying from the most indefinite use of paint to cases which seem to imply a subconscious idea of a non-human power, which might easily be personified. The other instance from Torres Strait does not give much help in determining whether the medicine man has a self consciousness which is uppermost, or whether his main aim is to use paint in order to attract the attention of forces on which he depends. That he conceives of a force merely, is rather unlikely, for everywhere among primitive people there is a tendency to concretion, and it seems more likely that the marks are assumed because the magician feels that he must appeal to the actual personality of the rainfall. For a favourable wind the red ochre was used, and when the payment was unsatisfactory the garb was changed for black. What does this change imply? simply the desire to impress the public? or are we to assume that the medicine man has such close touch with the spiritual forces presiding over the rainfall that he can signal "rain wanted," or "rain go away," simply by changing his covering from red to black. Possibly he conceives of the rain and wind power as a dual personality, one making for good in the way of moderate rain or fair sailing wind, and the other evil making for prolonged downpour and violent gales. The one must be invoked by the signal red, the other is to be called into action by a display of black. There is in no instance evidence of the presence of an admiring crowd, and in one case there is evidence that the rite is carried out secretly, for the man desiring a rainfall is told to go away. A change from a greasy red coat to a greasy black one from head to foot is a troublesome matter for the sake of impressing a person, and in addition there is the smearing of medicine on the hand before waving it towards the body as an invitation to rain or wind. All considered it seems probable that colour used in magical practices is a direct appeal to some power, which with people of lively imagination, and some ability for reasoning by analogy, will easily merge into a conception of a presiding personality or deity. The Dieri appeal to the Murra Murra or rain gods by cicatrization and use of red ochre; an example of body marking which provides a further link in the chain connecting magical and religious practices. Some markings are a vague appeal to something unseen, others are a symbol of a deity, such as scroll of Buddha made on the child's brow during very early infancy, or the sign of the sky god Tira-wa-atius made as an appeal for the good gifts of that god. It may be that the medicine man's practice of assuming red or black for specific purposes is the survival of a one-time concept of two gods, good and evil, symbolized by distinct colours.

For example the Masai have their evil red god who withholds water, and their black deity who loves his people and supplies ample rainfall if suitably invoked.[1]

Marking the Body before Trial by Ordeal, or for a Dangerous Enterprise

The question of body marking as a mute appeal for spiritual aid is also involved in the instances of pigment being used by one who is forced to trial by ordeal, or by a war party. The desire to impress one's foes may be uppermost in the case of an advancing army of Indians or Australians who have used the red war paint very freely. On the contrary, in the case of a man who stands up for trial by ordeal it seems likely that as his means of self-defence are so limited, and his accusers have such a distinct advantage, appeal to a non-human power by some form of body marking is considered essential. In the case of a thief of Burma, who assumes a cabalistic tattoo before making an onslaught on the gold store of the sacred Pagoda,[2] there cannot be desire to impress anyone in particular, for the deed is to be carried out secretly at dead of night, and if any well-defined idea of an appeal is present it is one which seeks to invoke aid from a tutelary power presiding over the robbers' craft.

Some man among the Kurnai has committed a breach of tribal law, an action which is likely to bring down various calamities on his fellows, so he

[1] "The Masai," A. C. Hollis, Oxford, 1909, p. 264.
[2] "The Burman, his Life and Notions," Sir J. G. Scott, p. 143.

must expiate his crime in the manner approved by ancient custom, namely, by standing up practically undefended and allowing the accusers to hurl spears or boomerangs at him.[1] The accused stands out from his people, and it is to be noted that his face is covered with red ochre, stripes of which are continued from the shoulders down the breast where they meet horizontally drawn lines of white and red, which are traced alternately across the abdomen, from the left hip to the right. At a distance of two hundred yards are the aggrieved whose relations have been slain, or perhaps there is the person who makes some charge of incest, etc., against the accused. The one to undergo trial is armed only with a club or a bundle of spears, and near him stands his wife, who will try to ward off the missile weapons with her digging stick. Usually if the man is tried for murder the relations who are hurling clubs and boomerangs paint all over with white as a sign of mourning, but the paint assumed by the defendant seems to be of the nature of a magical protection.

If the Motu people decide to give up a murderer rather than enter upon a blood feud, he retires to his house, where he ornaments and paints himself, after which there is an all night sitting with relatives who consume roast pig.[2] There is here no ordeal, but more correctly an execution, for when day dawns the murderer descends the ladder along with a friend, who turns back when a few rungs from the bottom, leaving his companion to be speared to death by the avenging party from a neighbouring village. The

[1] "Native Tribes of South-East Australia," p. 344.

[2] "Melanesians of British New Guinea," Dr. Seligman, p. 130.

murderer assumes paint which may be considered a magical guard even under these very adverse conditions; but taking into account the feasting, it appears that the paint is assumed before the banquet in order to give distinction to the principal guest whose career is to terminate at daybreak. This suggestion of the paint being socially distinctive is borne out by the custom of the Koita people who allow a homicide to assume a particular tattoo which is a permanent distinction awarded for his prowess.

We have noted the accused man of the Kurnai seeking to minimize the dangers of the ordeal by a use of magical paint, and in other parts of the world, for instance in Africa (Uganda), North America (Point Barrow),[1] Burma, and Northern India, there are similar cases of a man who, feeling that he must embark on a perilous enterprise, seeks magical protection in some form of body marking. The Eskimo who is embarking on a whaling expedition marks his face with a broad streak of blacklead, and the Kadiaks will paint their faces before undertaking the crossing of a wide arm of the sea, or indulging in the dangerous pursuit of the sea otter.

Sir Harry Johnston gives a parallel case for Uganda, where among the Bantu Kavirondo a husband, before setting out to fight, or before starting on any dangerous enterprise, will make a few incisions, not on himself, but on his wife's body.[2] There is in this instance a well-formed idea of the malice of unseen powers, and the idea that these can be guarded against by cicatrization (which, strange to

[1] A.B.E., 1887-8, p. 139.

[2] "Uganda Protectorate," Sir H. Johnston, 1902, p. 728.

say, is practised on the wife of the individual requiring protection). In what way the cicatrization works is a mystery, unless it be by sympathetic magic through wife to husband, the primary source being some ill-defined magical power which is willing to protect if suitably invoked. Certainly there are many examples to show that primitive man can be influenced, even when far distant, by the actions of his friends and relations at home. There is the strange custom of the couvade to prevent injury to the new-born child resulting from any action of the father.[1] In connection with body marking among Kayan women, we noted that the girl must not be tattooed before the male members have returned from their expeditions, and further all the family must rest indoors until the operation is completed.[2]

The idea of the absent one being affected by what occurs at home is very common, and in Laos when an elephant hunter is starting for the chase he warns his wife not to cut her hair or oil her body lest the elephant should break his bonds.[3]

The Dyaks make their wives observe a similar precaution when going pig hunting,[4] and among the Gilyaks children are not allowed to draw when the father is away hunting lest his paths should become as complicated as the drawing.[5] Among Blackfoot Indians no one must use an awl during the absence

[1] Frazer, "Magic Art," Vol. I, p. 119.

[2] "Pagan Tribes of Borneo," Hose and McDougall, Vol. I, p. 262.

[3] E. Aymonier, "Notes sur le Laos," Paris, 1895-7, p. 25.

[4] "Natives of Sarawak," H. Ling Roth, Vol. I, p. 430.

[5] P. Labbé, "Un Bagne Russe l'île de Sakhaline," 1903, p. 268.

of the father lest he should be scratched by eagles,[1] and no male animal may be killed in the house of a Malagasy soldier when he is at war lest the killing of the animal should entail the killing of the man.[2]

With such examples as these before us, it is no stretch of imagination to believe that the men mentioned by Sir H. Johnston mark their wives so that the guardian fetish spirit will communicate good to the husband by sympathetic magic from the wife.

To return to a consideration of body marking made prior to entry upon an enterprise fraught with danger, we cannot do better than refer to the Burman, who is about to make a raid on the sacred Pagoda, and for this reason is marked with a tattoo charm known as the "a-hpee say." The spell, repeated while the tattooing is in progress, is humorous and typical of incantations in general.

"Steal gold from the Pagodas—fine bright gold. Refine it in the fire—repeat the magic words in the house, on the lonely path—before the lucky star at the Pagoda—repeat them a thousand times save one—consecrate the water—draw the circle of the flying galohn. Put it under the left arm, then under the right arm. No harm will befall the safe and invulnerable." [3]

The Burman depends on a vague magic, but the Nagahiya Dôms seek the protection of the Earth Mother when about to commit a felony. Sir H. H. Risley refers to the plotter drawing a circle on the ground and smoothing it over with cow dung on which

[1] "Blackfoot Lodge Tales," G. B. Grinnell, 1893, pp. 237-8.

[2] Dr. Frazer discusses at length the subject of magical telepathy.

[3] Mr. Shway Yoe, "The Burman, his Life and Notions," p. 46.

are drawn five streaks of blood. The left arm has been cut to obtain the blood, and after the streaks have been made in the centre of the sacred circle there is prayer that the night may be dark and the booty ample.[1] These marauders tattoo on the right arm a representation of the five streaks and the curved knife which is used for gashing the left arm. This case is unique so far as our reading goes, for there is not only the tattooing of the sacred symbols for magical protection, but a preliminary ceremony which must be described as a religious rite, inasmuch as it involves appeal to a deity by sacrifice and prayer.

Use of paint during warfare is very common throughout North America and Australia, but as to the exact significance there is little evidence. The Dakotas say that the use of paint was taught to them by the gods,[2] and as will be shown in a succeeding paragraph warriors of Australia and North America go to considerable trouble to get red ochre. In the case of a North American warrior there are ceremonial acts before the digging of the coloured earth, and it is reasonable to assume that such rites point to the existence of some amount of awe.

A little direct evidence of the symbolism of colour was given to Dr. Howitt by men of the Mitchell river, who said that, when about to avenge the death of a tribesman, they painted with pipe clay "because veıy angry at our man being killed, and also to frighten our enemies." "They were painted with red ochre because they had killed our man."[3]

[1] Sir H. H. Risley, "Man," July, 1902.

[2] A.B.E., 1889-90, p. 438.

[3] "Native Tribes of South-East Australia," p. 351.

A medicine man wishing to have kidney fat for magical purposes will retire to the bush, where he lights the "talmam" or magic fire, in front of which he rubs himself with charcoal from head to foot,[1] evidently to put himself in close touch with what is of evil spiritual potence; he makes himself the friend of the powers of darkness. To primitive man the air is filled with spirits of good and evil, chiefly the latter, and what better way of forming an alliance with the evil than by a display of the symbolic colour. Painting with charcoal is followed by dances, incantations, and a display of magical objects. There is calling of the victim's name with a view to making the man walk in his sleep to the magical circle, where foes are ready to extract his fat. Among the Kurnai, a medicine man who wishes to work evil by placing a pebble in an enemy's hand, invariably blackens the stone, and objects which the medicine man pretends to remove from a sick person are covered with red ochre and placed in the magician's bag.[2] A messenger who carries the little carved stick to summon the various divisions of the Kaibara tribe is coloured red, partly no doubt as a magical protection during a lonely journey, and with some reference to maintaining the dignity of the office of messenger.[3]

Before fighting the men of the Gazelle Peninsula mark a stripe on the right breast to give the warrior's arm a surer aim, and the lower part of the face is coloured black, which is supposed to cause the enemy

[1] "Native Tribes of South-East Australia," p. 377.
[2] *Ibid.*, p. 393.
[3] *Ibid.*, p. 679.

to stumble during flight when he hears his pursuer breathing hard.[1]

The Osages, when contemplating the making of an attack on the enemy, will paint their faces afresh.[2] This is the red death paint which is smeared all over the face. On the left cheek, the "peace men" or "chee Zhoo," carry mud, while the aggressors have mud on the right cheek.

Sacredness of Paint and Symbolism of Colour

Any attempt to appreciate the value which primitive man attaches to his body paint may be made, not only by a marshalling of instances which throw light on the conditions under which he uses it, but also by noting whether there are any special efforts to obtain a particular pigment, also whether such efforts are accompanied by ceremonial.

During the month of July or August the Dieri send out an expedition which makes a perilous journey in order to get red ochre.[3] Usually the force consists of from seventy to eighty picked fighting men each of whom is painted across the abdomen with three stripes of red ochre and three stripes of earth tinged with iron ore. Across the arms are two similar stripes of the iron earth. The red ochre is cut from a mine and kneaded into cakes each weighing from seventy to eighty pounds. Encumbered with this load the party has to fight its way back to camp. This ochre is used by the Dieri,

[1] Sinclair, "American Anthropologist," Vol. X, 1908, p. 383.

[2] "American Naturalist," Vol. XVIII, 1884, p. 132.

[3] "Native Tribes of South-East Australia," Dr. Howitt, p. 712.

not only for marking the body during magical ceremonies, but for giving a coat of magical pigment to an inanimate object. There is, among the people just mentioned, a lake whose waters recede during drought until an old stump of a tree becomes visible. This stump is in the charge of a particular family, whose hereditary duty is to cover the wooden stump with grease and red ochre, so that the waters of the lake will not further diminish, and the supply of food fish will not be interfered with.

Among the Cherokee Indians much sacredness attaches to the use of red paint, the colour being symbolic of war, success, and strength acquired by spiritual protection. The word paint in any Indian language is usually understood to mean red paint unless some statement to the contrary is made. Generally the Indian of North America derives his sacred red paint from a soft hæmatite ore found in the hard rocks, from which it can be extricated only after much patient effort. Among the Western tribes, everyone coming to procure paint in this way makes a prayer beside the rock, and in addition to this indication of his awe, he hangs a small sacrifice on a convenient bush or stick, before beginning his digging operations.[1]

M. Dechelette calls attention to the abundance of evidence with respect to use of pigments in neolithic times,[2] and to a great extent in the Magdalenian period, represented by the culture of the caves of Bruniquel, Les Eyzies, and Laugerie Bas, in which considerable quantities of red ochre have been found.

[1] A.B.E., 1897-8, Part I, p. 455.

[2] "Revue Archæologique," 1907, p. 38.

There is also the case of the discovery of a reddened skeleton of the Aurignacian period in Paviland cave near Swansea.[1]

Among the ancient Egyptians red was associated with what was sacred, the word sacred being taken in its broadest application. On the one hand there was a sacrifice of a red bullock to Typhon who was everything that was evil and malignant.[2] In certain festivals the Egyptians reviled anyone who happened to have red hair. In India Ganesa, the lord of mischievous spirits, is symbolized by red stones, and the Cingalese will sacrifice a red cock to a malignant spirit which is causing sickness. Opposed to the conception of the word sacred as expressive of evil influence, there is the idea of the "sacred" being what is holy because of its goodness and purity, as for example the "Book of the Dead," whose most sacred passages are inscribed in scarlet.

The Maoris, too, had a very great regard for the sacred red paint or "Kura" which was used to decorate idols, stages for the dead, sacrifices, chief's houses, and war canoes. The way of rendering anything "taboo" was to make it red, and when a person died his house was thus coloured. As soon as "taboo" was laid on anything the chief erected a post and painted it with "Kura."[3]

It is to be expected that there should be a widespread uniformity of ideas concerning the symbolism of red. Before the historical period Aurignacian man

[1] Sollas, J.A.I., 1913, Vol. XLIII, p. 364.

[2] "The Australian Race," E. M. Curr, Vol. II, p. 17.

[3] Rev. R. Taylor, "New Zealand and its Inhabitants," London, 1870, p. 209.

was using red ochre in connection with burials and cave painting. The sun and blood as life-givers, fertilizers, and requisites of immortality, were fundamental in the civilizations of Egypt, Persia, Assyria, Peru, and Mexico, whose cultures have influenced every part of the world. When in quest for information concerning beliefs in the efficacy of blood letting rites we have but to attend to Australian totemic ceremonies[1] of our own day, or note the little avenging party of the Arunta setting out each smeared with the blood of his fellows to give a symbolic unity.

Black is widely assumed as the representation of evil generally, and of malevolent magic in particular. Black and white are common in mourning ceremonies, the former in Australia, the latter in Melanesia, but a question of extreme interest to the psychologist, as well as to the anthropologist, is the existence of any general laws of universal application with regard to the symbolism of colour. Are there in man emotional states that correspond with the excitation of the retina?

In all psychological inquiry an ample allowance has to be made for deviations from a mean, but probably as a general truth there is a positive correlation between colour and attendant emotion. Apart from the general association of awe and reverence with red as a symbol of life and immortality, and a widespread use of black for the expression of an alliance with the powers of evil in the sense of what is anti-social there does not seem to be any widespread, innate tendency for a particular colour to

[1] "Across Australia," Spencer and Gillen, p. 294.

call forth any specific display of feeling in primitive groups. Conversely there appears to be no universal tendency for man to express a complex mental state, say that of joy or sorrow by resort to a particular colour. White perhaps has some claim to be almost universally regarded as something supernatural, for the instances of the white man being regarded as sacred, also reverence for the white buffalo, owl, and white elephant are but a few of the examples of an association of ideas linking whiteness and purity, an association which is strongly favoured by European people.

Among the Cherokee Indians there is a special association of colours, cardinal points and mental states arising from several common human experiences. The East is definitely associated with red, success, and triumph, the North with blue, defeat, and trouble, the West with black and death, and the South with white, peace, and happiness.[1]

Among the Sioux tribes, as elsewhere, green symbolizes fertility, yellow denotes water, west, and the setting sun, and there is the story of the boy painting himself yellow when going to visit the water spirit with whom he wished to be *en rapport*. The Sioux are people who believe that the use of paint was taught to them by the gods. Blue frequently is an expression of bounty, fertility, and vastness, as, for example, when used by the Pawnee Indians in dedicating the child to the sky god.[2] Naturally enough red, black, and white have some claim to a consistent representation of emotional states; but

[1] American Bureau of Ethnology, 7th report (A.B.E.), p. 342.

[2] A.B.E., 1900-1, pp. 222-33.

taking into account the many environments and the diversified forms of plant and animal life, together with the different ideas associated with such aspects of man's surroundings, it would be surprising if there were the world over a uniform correspondence between colour displayed and emotion excited.

Body Marking in Connection with Death, Mourning, and Execution

Up to the present our inquiry has not included the subject of body marking as a means of expressing those very complex mental states which are associated with death, mourning, and execution. In respect of the last mentioned, the body marking of the executioner gives a very useful clue to primitive beliefs concerning man's spirit, its liberation from the body, and the possibility of its becoming an evil power with which mundane man has to cope.

The examples of body marking as a sign of mourning are so numerous that it will be possible to select only a few of the most important regions for consideration.

In the Chepara tribe the mother of the deceased person has her nose and all her body painted with white stripes of pipe-clay, and in addition to this she has a head-dress of red feathers. After a few months the painting is changed from white to red, a colour which is worn by father, mother, and sisters for a long time; the sister, however, never assumed a coat of white paint, her marking was not commenced until the time for the use of red pigment had arrived.[1]

[1] "Native Tribes of South-East Australia," Dr. Howitt, p. 469.

Among the Kaiabara the sign of mourning is the rubbing of fat and charcoal under the eyes and red ochre over the head and body.

Much could be written concerning the details of body marking in connection with death among the numerous tribes of South Australia, but the massing of instances is in itself of little use without some incident or belief which shows the why and wherefore of the marking, and for the native tribes of South East Australia, Dr. Howitt gives beliefs which render the people's body marking process quite intelligible.

There is a reference to people, who call themselves the Mattari and Kararu, keeping their mourning paint until the spirit footsteps cease to be discovered near the grave of the dead kinsman, and when there is this negative evidence that the spirit has ceased to roam, the white body paint is changed for an application of red ochre, which is soon rubbed off.[1] Food is placed at the grave of the deceased, and a fire is lighted so that the ghost may warm himself. If the food is not touched the people assume that the spirit of their dead relative is not hungry; frequently the great toes of the corpse are tied so that the spirit may not wander. People of the Kaiabara tribe do not mention the name of the dead, and in order to explain who is dead they speak of the father, mother, or brother.[2] The Herbert River tribes break the bones of the corpse to prevent the ghost from wandering. Mr. N. W. Thomas[3] refers to the use of black as a

[1] "Native Tribes of South-East Australia," p. 447.
[2] *Ibid.*, p. 469.
[3] "Natives Tribes of Australia," N. W. Thomas, p. 49.

sign of mourning among the North-Western tribes, and has little doubt that the charcoal is used to deceive the spirit, which will be obliged to leave the relation in peace; an opinion with which Dr. Frazer is in agreement.

Speaking for the Arunta of Central Australia Spencer and Gillen refer to the importance of cicatrization as a sign of mourning. A frequent source of quarrel is the accusation that a man has not mourned sufficiently for his relatives. The cicatrization takes place very shortly after the notice of death is given, and custom decides exactly what each mourner has to do. One young man was observed to cut himself so badly that he could not stand; this youth had fourteen "mourning" scars which he showed with great pride.[1]

Among the Mafulu mountain people of New Guinea black is the sign of mourning, but its use is not confined to the near relatives only; it is common throughout the tribe when a death occurs. The blackening of the face takes place after the funeral and there is ceremonial removal of black paint and mud from the body of the chief.[2]

This ceremonial removal implies that some importance is attached to the body marking, and we shall meet with similar instances of ceremonial removal of the mourning symbols throughout Melanesia.

The death of a person is succeeded (but at what time Dr. Seligman cannot say) by a feast given at the expense of the relatives of the deceased, who

[1] "Across Australia," Messrs. Spencer and Gillen, p. 251.

[2] W. Williamson, "Mafulu Mountain People of New Guinea," p. 260.

supply fish and game,[1] and at this ceremonial banquet the chief mourner is blackened from head to foot. The mourners, other than the widow or widower, blacken the trunk and limbs, but leave the face untouched. The mourning colouring is removed at a special feast held within two years of the interment. Usually the face of the corpse is blackened, and the body is placed outside the hut on a sleeping mat while the grave is prepared. Three or four days after death the widow blackens herself with soot and cocoanut oil. She assumes a neck ornament and bamboo armlets; the brothers of the deceased blacken themselves all over. The widow retains her black paint until it is time to prepare a feast called "rigariga," during which the evidences of mourning are removed at the grave side, by the dead man's sister or mother.[2]

Similar practices prevail in the islands of Torres Strait, but here the process of cicatrization and painting are both used in connection with mourning ceremonies. In Saibai and Dauan a girl whose brother is deceased wears a sign of mourning, which is a cicatrized representation of the brother's nose, on her left shoulder. Strange to say the length of the mark is supposed to be the same length as the nasal organ of the dead relative. This is complimentary to the deceased, and one girl wore a mark twelve centimetres long to show that her brother was a big fine man.[3] Young Miriam adults cicatrized to the extent of having a cut for each relative who had

[1] "Melanesians of British New Guinea," Dr. Seligman, pp. 276-7.

[2] *Ibid.*, p. 585.

[3] "Cambridge Expedition to Torres Strait," Vol: IV, p. 26.

passed over, and there prevailed the custom of allowing the blood from the cicatrix to run on the corpse, possibly to make sure that the ceremonial act of devotion had been noted by the spirit of the deceased. Or the idea may be revival of life in the spirit world. On the cheek of one young woman of Miriam was a peculiar mark like the feathers of a snipe. It was noted that great pride was taken in these mourning scars, possibly because they denoted endurance of physical pain, or because they were the token of compliance with tribal etiquette. The etymology of the word used to denote a cicatrix, made as a symbol of mourning, appears to imply that the original function of this scarification was an expression of grief for relatives; grief probably combined with fear of possible animosity on the part of the liberated spirit. The scar itself is called "Koimai" and the word may be derived from "Koi" meaning great, and "mai" denoting mourning or grief.[1]

The ceremonial painting employed in Mabuiag is thought by Drs. W. H. R. Rivers and A. C. Haddon to be definite and traditional in character. In the death dance of Mabuiag the man who took the part of the ghost covered himself all over with black, and mourners who were not related to the deceased smeared charcoal on the shoulder only, while near relatives used a greyish earth.

At a skull giving ceremony the nearest relative, who is termed "mariget" meaning the ghost hand, is painted black all over;[2] the skull is coloured red and the posts supporting the platform on which the

[1] "Cambridge Expedition to Torres Strait," Vol. IV, p. 29.

[2] *Ibid.*, p. 251.

corpse rests are painted red and black, the colour being applied in alternate stripes. In Mabuiag the "death people," that is the nearest relatives, are painted white with coral mud, and the precaution is taken of carrying out the body feet foremost, so that the ghost will not know his way back to the hut, consequently the relatives will not be troubled by apparitions. Further precautions consist of tying the thumbs and great toes of the corpse, and during the funeral ceremony arrows are shot at the chief mourner who wards them off. Evidently there are several distinct and definite precautions to prevent trouble arising from wandering spirits. In the first place the chief mourner is coloured to propitiate the spirit, who is further prevented from doing harm by tying the hands and feet of the corpse.[1] Similarly in Pulu for the Markai or death dance, men who represent ghosts are painted with charcoal. The Andamanese use olive mud as a sign of mourning, and to propitiate the deceased no doubt, for the spirits of the dead are credited with great power.[2] Relatives seek some of this spiritual force by disinterring the bones, washing them and wearing the skull and other portions as amulets.

Allied with these markings of relatives who wish to propitiate the spirit of the deceased, we have the cases of executioners who mark themselves as a self-inflicted punishment, which is intended to act as a substitute for any revenge the ghost of the person executed might be inclined to take.

[1] "Cambridge Expedition to Torres Strait," Vol. V, p. 252. British Museum Ethnographical Guide, Fig. 66, p. 79.

[2] J.A.I., 1882, p. 333, etc.

The West African executioner who has publicly carried out the death sentence observes several taboos, which include fasting and lying in a hammock for three days without setting foot to the ground. In addition, he has to make incisions on his breast, arms, and other parts of the body. Into these cuts he rubs black pigment, and the ineffaceable scars are artistically arranged so as to give the appearance of a tightly fitting garment. It is believed that the ghost of the victim would cause the executioner to die if he did not draw blood from his own body.[1]

A parallel instance is to be found with the Brazilian Indians, and amongst these people, though it is regrettable that more details are not given, stones and pieces of potsherd are flung at the guards by the man who is about to be executed. The people cry to the thrower telling him to avenge his death before his decease. The marks made, in spite of the guards' attempt to defend themselves, are permanent evidence that all concerned with the execution gave satisfaction to the victim, and as the original says: "What more could any reasonable ghost require."[2]

A few pages back, the question of body marking being the outcome of fear of the spirits of deceased was discussed, and it is notable that the nearest relative, who might reasonably be supposed to exhibit the most marked grief, received the heaviest coat of red ochre, pipe clay, charcoal, or whatever happened to be in fashion. Now from the Finsch Harbour

[1] "Tylor Essays," essay by J. G. Frazer, p. 106. "The Lower Niger and its Tribes," Major A. G. Leonard, London, 1906, p. 180.

[2] J. Lery, "Historia navigationis in Brasiliam quae et America dicitur," 1586, pp. 185, 192.

people of New Guinea, there is an example which serves well to illustrate the fear of deceased relations, and the use of body marks as a protection against malignant ghosts.

The Finsch Harbour people employ the convenient custom of accepting payment for a murdered relative instead of entering into a prolonged blood feud with the people of the murderer. There is, however, the fear that the spirit of the murdered man will be dissatisfied with this. The ghost may show his displeasure by causing the teeth of his relatives to fall out, or by robbing them of their pigs. So when people are accepting a payment for a murdered kinsman, they take care to be marked with chalk on the forehead by the relatives of the murderer. These marks on the face are, of course, a symbol that some steps have been taken to avenge the death by extracting a payment from the murderer or his relatives, and when the ghost is about to turn in fury they are able to show him the facial marks.[1]

Very widespread is the idea of a murderer being pursued by the soul of his victim and some form of purification is thought to be necessary. At the return of the avenging expedition sent out by the Arunta of Central Australia, an old woman meets the party some distance from camp and tests all the shields by rapping each with a spear. The man whose shield does not give forth the true sound is said to be haunted by the soul of the victim, which may have assumed the form of a small bird or other innocent looking creature. The entire party is coloured black

[1] Anthropological Essays to Sir E. B. Tylor, p. 106. "Unter den Papuas," B. Hagen, Wiesbaden, 1899, p. 254.

as a sign of mourning, and the man who is the special object of the ghost's attention must not show his right arm when he is asleep, or paralysis will result. A very useful protection is to tie about the person a portion of some nocturnal animal whose prowling will disturb the avenging ghost.[1] The Naga warriors returning from a head-hunting expedition are taboo, and must not so much as be looked upon by women until cleansed from the blood guilt,[2] and among the Koita people of New Guinea, the murderer must seek seclusion in the forest, for he is "aina," that is something set aside as full of virtue, and he may not be approached with impunity; later he returns to his village and is allowed to assume a particular tattoo.[3]

Considered in the light of such examples as these, which illustrate the fear of restless ghosts, it is evident that body marking has a widely distributed and logical use in securing immunity from malevolent spirits. From the Mtyopi people of South Africa there comes the instance of men of that tribe making a cicatrix under each eye after they have committed a murder.[4] This is a purification ceremony, and, according to Dr. Turner's account, it is very common among the Bantu races. "The marks are supposed to prevent the spirit of the deceased from troubling the man who killed him."

The idea of malevolent human ghosts is, of course, capable of extension to the inclusion of malevolent ghosts of animals which have been killed in hunting.

[1] "Across Australia," Spencer and Gillen, p. 298.

[2] "Naga Tribes of Manipur," T. C. Hodson, p. 175.

[3] "The Melanesians of New Guinea," Dr. Seligman, p. 130.

[4] "Notes of South African Coloured Mine Labourers," Dr. G. A. Turner, pp. 73-4.

Of such instances there is no need to treat fully as they have already been given in some details in the section on body marking with animal forms. The Baganda who have killed a leopard propitiate his ghost by marking themselves with spots and acting like leopards, and the Thompson Indians who have killed a bear will paint with stripes of black and red while singing the bear song, for omission to do this will cause such offence to the bear spirits that no more bears will be killed.[1]

Fear, the deep-rooted fear of some personal injury is the emotion which calls forth all these precautions, and of this dread of the consequences of violence, and liberation of the spirit from the body, there is evidence in the shape of a special three-necked jug from Uganda. The relic is displayed in the British Museum Ethnographical collection, and according to the guide book, the cup was used by a slave who was about to be killed at the funeral of his master. Although only a slave, he had a spirit which might be troublesome later, so the spirit or soul was killed by a magic draught, after which the body could be maltreated without fear that the liberated spiritual part would return to take revenge.[2] Body marking, therefore, becomes fully explicable when considered in conjunction with a series of beliefs respecting malevolent spirits. Mourning scars and pigments are a protection whose employment is a further example of the logical thought processes of primitive man.

[1] "The Baganda," Rev. J. Roscoe, 1911, p. 447. Journal of North Pacific Expedition. James Teit, "Thompson Indians," p. 347 of J.N.P.E., April, 1900.

[2] British Museum Guide to Ethnographical Collections, p. 34.

SUMMARY OF CHAPTERS I AND II

The whole question of body marking in connection with magico-religious practices was approached by a preliminary consideration of the extent to which ceremonies of a positive and negative kind were observed in connection with the marking process. In other words we sought to find to what extent man had connected "taboo," and definite, active, precautionary measures with the custom of imprinting designs on the skin. For inasmuch as such signs of veneration for the process can be discovered, we are entitled to conclude that body marking, for those who take the precautions, is no trivial venture, but one which is in some way capable of affecting adversely the one tattooed, and the operator.

The reasons why puncturing the skin should be regarded with some degree of awe are not far to seek, for in the first place, there is the drawing of blood, which to the savage world over is full of significance as a rejuvenating and immortalizing factor. There is in addition the opening of numerous inlets for evil to enter, and perhaps most important of all the marking is connected with some crisis, some stepping over the threshold of a new phase of social intercourse, some advance from boyhood to manhood, from girlhood to womanhood. Marking during initiation is most important in showing the relation of painting and tattooing to one of their original cultural factors, namely fertility rites.

Among the Kayan we found time and food "taboos" observed by patient and operator, while on the positive side there were sacrificial rites, and statements respecting the house in which the tattooing was to be done. There was a prohibition against operating when members of the family were away from home. Turning to Melanesia it was noted that the tattooing of Koita women was performed in a certain ceremonial order determined by the relative development of the several parts of the body and their functions. The Roro people, too, appear to have much ceremonial connected with the completion of the tattoo, at which time special ornaments are assumed and a very restricted life, involving several taboos, is commenced. In Fiji, too, there is evidence of important ceremonial. Naga girls are under certain disabilities during the time of tattooing, and these include restricted diet and prohibition from visiting another village. In some cases when the operation has been performed away from the native village the girls must not return home until the tattooing is completed. Evidently among the Naga women tattooing is regarded with superstitious fear, which results in the adoption of precautions. When dealing with one or two restrictions in African tribes there were noted those among the Mtyopi, whose marks are made in secret, in default of which a fine is exacted from the father of the girl. There is then among most tribes a seclusion to be observed, which in past time found its most extreme rigour among the inhabitants of New Ireland and Fiji who confined their girls in cages and prohibited the touching of the ground for long periods before the operation was commenced. Dobrizhoffer's evidence respecting tattooing of Abipoine women of Paraguay was found to be congruous in all points with this evidence from the Old World.

The Moko operation performed on a Maori Chief supplied another good instance of taboo in connection with body marking. The restrictions imposed referred to handling of food in a special way, and the ceremonial transfer of the sacredness or "taboo" from chief to god.

This taboo on the chief is probably because of his launching out from one status to another which is higher and nearer to the divine condition.

Following the cases of precautionary observances whose details are definite, there followed a mention of recent anthropological work by M. Henri Junod, Dr. Rivers, Mr. Sinclair, and Drs. Hose and McDougall, all of whom have denoted clearly that the body marking operation, when practised on a woman, and in case of Borneo on men, is one which is regarded with some amount of awe. Primitive man believes that tattooing is not a matter to be lightly dealt with, but there is strong evidence of declining ceremonial.

Among the Ba Thonga marking of women offers something more than a study of declining ritual, for there is still strict seclusion during the operation, special diet and the sacrifice of a fowl at the conclusion. In conversation with M. Junod, the point of body marking having a magico-religious significance was emphasized by him. Sinclair speaks of the increasing difficulty of study in North America on account of reticence on the part of the Indians, but he is hopeful that much may yet be done to elucidate the problems of the significance of tattoo.[1]

[1] A.B.E., 17th report, p. 399.

In addition to the existence of precautions during the marking operation, Chapter I brought forward instances of tattooing having a divine origin, or in some way being definitely connected with a spiritual ancestor. Thus we find the Andamanese telling E. H. Man that their divinity taught them the use of paint for the body, and the North American Indian has a great regard for his sacred red paint, which he takes great trouble to obtain because its use was divinely originated. From Samoa and Fiji inquirers have obtained legends connecting tattooing with divinities. The extent to which marking customs are continued, the elaboration of design on covered parts of the body, and the reticence of the people questioned, likewise the execution of designs by priests and specialists, all seem to point to a deeper meaning than that of decoration. Of course reticence may result from a great variety of causes, including ignorance and lack of understanding of the question, but in the case of Dr. Rivers' [1] inquiry concerning the marking of Toda women, there was certainly an indication that the subject was of grave importance.

Leaving questions of taboo, divine origin, and ceremonial, inquiry passed along to a survey of many expressions of belief in the efficacy of tattoo as a passport in the spirit world. The marks were thought to give some amount of standing, and right of existence, while in case of the Ekoi some commercial advantage was expected from cicatrices made on the arm and shoulder. Kayan women who are suitably tattooed think they will pick up pearls in the bed of the sacred river. The Naga women think they will

[1] "Todas," W. H. R. Rivers, 1906, p. 313.

be recognized by husbands in the spirit world; Hindu and Fijian women contemplate with dread an attempt to enter the next world without their body marks. Ainu women tell their daughters that if they are not tattooed here, the work will be done by a demon at one sitting. The North American Indian mounted on his ghost steed must show his marks to the woman who bars the way to the many lodges, and so on, in a very wide geographical distribution, were noted ideas concerning the practical utility of tattoo and other marks beyond the grave. The whole series illustrates man's readiness to argue from this world to the next by a process of analogy, and corporal marking has been explained as a congruous element of his philosophy.

Is there any evidence of the body being stamped to show that the individual is allied with a supernatural being? From many observers there comes a positive answer. For North America Swanton and Sinclair are able to show body painting according to the direction of a guardian spirit, and Mr. Sinclair has recently given information concerning adoption of the cross, and other religous symbols, by pilgrims to sacred shrines. For India, Dr. Thurston shows the use of branding with the "Chank" and "Chakra," together with a great variety of facial and body markings assumed by the sacred Brahmins. In farther India (Burma chiefly) there is the marking of a scroll representing Buddha in the meditative attitude on the brow of each child. In reference to the Pawnee dedication ceremony there is a most elaborate account of the use of blue and red pigment for helping to assimilate the child to the personality of the sky god. In conclusion of this section the tattooing of the

Omaha girl was mentioned, as an instance which exemplified the importance of ceremonial, which in this particular case has reference to the life-giving power of the sun, treated as a deity whose symbol is painted upon the worshipper. The whole process is accompanied by singing, which bears reference to the sun's ascent to the zenith and the descent of spiritual power upon the one receiving the tattooed symbol. There is a distinct deification of day and night, and a concrete representation of these cosmic forces by a tattooed sun and star. In Aztec religious ceremonies too, corporal marking had a dedicatory and initiatory significance.

The subject of marking tne body with animal or plant designs may be classed along with the section on marking as an expression of moral and religious sentiments. These arise from primitive man's contemplation of the spiritual aspect of animal life, an aspect which he identifies with the spirit parts of his own progenitors, and so body marking with totemic emblems is part of a form of ancestor worship. In North America marking is usually carried out according to the directions of a dream vision, and designs representing the individual totem of the wearer act as guardian spirits. Examples of body marking with an animal design, in Africa, were found to be rare, the two most recent examples being from Nigeria, where a conventionalized lizard design was employed to attract women; but there is little evidence of totemic marking being employed.[1] For India there are examples of the adoption of a design such as the scorpion, but little significance beyond a charm against

[1] J.A.I., 1911, pp. 162-71.

the bite of the creature is claimed, and for Burma, the employment of the animal form in body marks is almost entirely æsthetic and amuletic. Islanders of Torres Strait employ both marks of plants and animals, which are engraved on the body by cicatrization, the designs including the representation of the centipede, snake, turtle, cassowary and cocoanut palm. There is little room for doubt that many of these marks have a totemic significance, which is, however, very rapidly on the decline. Aboriginal tribes of Australia freely employ totemic marks, which are highly conventionalized representations of some animal, plant, heavenly body, or even an inanimate object.[1] The marking is evidently carried out partly by way of compliment to the spiritual parts of ancestors residing in the totemic animals, and to a great extent with a view to gaining for the wearer all the qualities of the totemic animal; for example, stealth, speed, and cunning, which might prove useful in the struggle for existence. Finally in connection with totemic markings, there has for the past few years been an application of anthropological principles to the study of life in ancient Greece, Rome, and Egypt, and there is some evidence to show that the body of a worshipper was marked with a religious symbol.

The commencement of a chapter on body marks, made as an important part of the magico-religious rites of primitive people, opened up an inquiry capable of an almost indefinite extension. When classified briefly, the uses of these marks are extended to such points as alleviation and prevention of sickness and pain, or as a guard against accident and unwelcome

[1] "Cambridge Expedition to Torres Strait," Vol. V.

attentions from evil powers. Examples of the use of body marks for the purposes just named are very widespread, and there is an abundance of instances of painting, tattooing, and cicatrization to ward off the demon of disease. In India the cicatrization is performed by branding, in Timor Laut by incision and burning, in Burma and among the Ainu by tattoo proper, and among the Sakai and others paint is the protective agency.

A charm which is effective in cases of physical sickness is capable of being used with good effect in love sickness. So we find the Torres Strait Islanders (in Mabuiag and elsewhere), also the Sakai, using a form of body paint as a love charm. In Burma the indelible tattoo mark is favoured by amorous maidens. The North American Indian with all his sternness is not too proud to exhibit his feelings by a particular facial paint. And in conclusion it is of interest to note a number of reversions, or perhaps spontaneous adoptions of these practices among criminals of our time; while Cocheris and Sinclair, Lombroso and Lacassagne have a good deal to say of the sailor's tendency to express his sentiments toward the opposite sex by means of tattooing.

Among tattooed designs observed by me in Gallipoli and Malta, the "In Memoriam" figure was common. A sergeant of the R.M.L.I. showed on his forearm the picture of a large gravestone surrounded by yew trees. The inscription "In Memoriam" being supplemented by "In loving Memory of my dear Wife, died May 10th, 1896." A fireman on the *Hunslet* hospital ship exhibited a tattooed representation of a grave and tombstone, over which a sailor stood cap in hand, with lowered head. In order to express sympathy for a shipmate one sailor had tattooed a picture of a steamship over which were the words, *Empress of Ireland.* Sentiments of joy were in one case represented by a tattooed design of a racehorse which had brought to his backer the sum of £30.

At no time more than in the stress of the twentieth century has the problem of perpetual youth exercised the brains of inventive genius. A long time ago primitive woman solved the problem of combating old age, and her method was one of body marking of a magical nature. The Ainus have great faith in tattooing and re-tattooing as a restorative of youth, and from the Pima of North America and the Maori girl of New Zealand there come similar instances of belief in the rejuvenating power of tattooing. Such ideas are probably close to the original concept of red ochre and blood as life-giving tokens.

To the medicine man the magical red ochre is quite indispensable, and one cannot conceive of a ceremony of black or white magic in North America, Australia, or Torres Strait, without the employment of an attractive coat of red or black. What is more interesting than the existence of a wide distribution in use of red ochre are the facts of ritual and pains taken to secure the pigment. The paint is assumed, apparently not merely to impress a spectator, but as a dynamic factor essential to success of a rudimentary kind, there are ideas of a soul which is capable of surviving physical death. Should such a soul decide to be vindictive, the surviving relatives or any who have caused offence become apprehensive of their safety. So we find in West Africa and among the Amazonian Indians, that the executioner voluntarily assumes certain marks, which are evidence for the ghost that there has been a self-inflicted punishment rendering further retribution unnecessary. The Motu people, who decide to accept a blood fine, take care to assume a facial paint mark which explains to the ghost of their deceased relative that his death has not been disregarded, but on the contrary the penalty has been paid. For fighting and trial by ordeal some form of marking is thought necessary. The painting may be an appeal to the powers who are thought to shape the course of the conflict, and in fact, whatever be the crisis, whether child-birth, puberty, sickness, love, marriage, mourning, fighting, revengeful enterprise, or consecration to divine service, the ritual is incomplete unless a magico-religious aid is given in the form of body marking. The body marks in a mute way accomplish that which is expected of prayer and incantation, or most frequently the body marks are combined with spell or prayer to bring pressure to bear on the non-human powers which are thought to sway man's destiny.

CHAPTER III

BODY MARKING FOR SOCIAL AND ANTI-SOCIAL PURPOSES

Psychological processes involved in body marking for social purposes—Tribal marking—Tattooing in social and anti-social groups—Individual marks to denote social status—Tattooing and the social status of women—Markings to gratify the sentiment of pride—Tattooing in secret societies.

PROFESSOR WILLIAM JAMES has emphasized very strongly the importance of social tendencies in the evolution of material and moral culture, and has pointed his remarks on the human being's love of companionship by analysing the feelings of the man condemned to solitary confinement, a punishment thought by Professor James, and most of us perhaps, to be too cruel for any civilized nation to tolerate, and, further, there is the mention of the tumultuous emotions of the human being who comes into touch with civilization after a long sojourn in the wilds.[1]

The subject of body marking on its magico-religious side has been dealt with in Chapters I and II. There now remains the task of showing the manner in which painting, tattooing, and scarifying have assisted in the formation and maintenance of social units.

Grouping may be an evolved and acquired process resulting from utilitarianism and suggestion from

[1] "Principles of Psychology."

original minds. The open question of the existence of a "gregarious instinct" does not necessarily form part of this discussion. For the purpose in view it suffices to show the manner in which body marks have contributed to growth of communal feeling.

Body marking of the family, tribal, clan, and totemic varieties, together with tattooed symbols of witches and secret societies, likewise the practice of smearing members of a dangerous expedition with the same colour, possibly with each other's blood, all show desire for concerted action and mutual help.

It is with this question of group formation and maintenance, also acquisition of social status and its preservation, that the present chapter deals. Marking of children during infancy may indicate a desire to distinguish them from the progeny of hostile neighbours. Andaman islanders commence cicatrizing their children at the age of eight years and complete the marks at puberty. In conversation with a missionary named Howell, who has spent some thirty years on the Congo, between the estuary and Stanley Falls, the point of decline of tribal markings was mentioned, and in viewing photographs of infants of nine or twelve months, he said that twenty years ago the child would have been marked with the tribal cicatrices at that age. Information from Torday and Joyce shows that the marking is frequently carried out during early childhood, but is not complete until puberty in some instances. " Chez les Banbala les incisions sont pratiqués pendant l'enfance, chez les tribus orientales des que l'enfant peut marcher ce sont les femmes qui pratiquant l'operation. Chez les Bangongo si la cicatrization n'est pas complète quand le patient atteint l'âge de la puberté, elle reste inachevée, chez les Bengendi cependant elle peut être continuée." [1]

Apparently in the Congo region of Africa the marking becomes more complex, and instead of being carried out at an initiation ceremony as among the Andamanese, or native Australian tribes of Port Lincoln, it is usually accomplished at the time the child begins to walk, so we seem to recede to a period when the child was identified with the family by permanent markings, as soon as there was a chance of his straying away. The employment of body marks to denote clans, totems, and families illustrates stages in the evolution of group consciousness and a sense of corporate existence. Occasionally, as in the Western Islands of Torres Strait, a man shows two marks, the one indicating connection with the father's group, the other with the mother's,[2] thus illustrating the interesting passage probably from mother right to father right. Lastly there is the individual mark, which shows that with the slow growth of self-consciousness, a man evolves an identity and positive self-emotion which requires some expression. So we find the man of New Georgia adopting the turtle or frigate bird as his emblem, or the North American Indian painting on his body a representation of his Manitu or guardian spirit. Dr. Howitt gives the marks which distinguish the clans of the Kurnai; Spencer and Gillen show totemic paintings on the backs of the Arunta people,

[1] Torday and Joyce, "Documents Ethnographique du Congo Belge," 1910, p. 166.

[2] "Cambridge Expedition to Torres Strait," Vol. V. p. 168.

and Torday and Joyce, for the Congo, show the family markings. Again for North America Swanton has dealt with family marks of the Haida, and Hill Tout mentions the employment of the mark indicating possession of an individual tutelary spirit. Among the Kwakiutl there is for a period the disbanding of the natural families, and the aggregation of members of the same spiritual community, or secret society, in which a particular facial paint, together with dances and other ceremonial items are observed.

Briefly, these forms of body marking mentioned in Chapter III indicate the growth of self-consciousness in the social group, also the attainment of complex sentiments of pride, hatred, and ambition, with acquired tendencies towards rivalry and pugnacity, all of which require some form of activity to express them, and considerable time with culture contact must be allowed for their development.

Tribal Markings

Very probably the designs employed in tribal markings were suggested by the marks observed on each member of a herd of animals such as zebras, or the less distinctive markings of the kangaroo or opossum. The peculiar colourings of the toucan, hornbill, and similar birds would no doubt suggest some form of design, which would make the individuals of a group resemble one another. Mr. Starcke says: "the type of marks must be referred to the animal kingdom, yet we cannot discover any tradition or myth which relates to the custom."[1] Dr. Seligman gives illustrations to show that the Melanesians of British New Guinea borrow a design very finely from the beak of the hornbill,[2] and in speaking of the tribal marks of the Urabunna, Spencer and Gillen supply the type of legend which Starcke thought to be absent.[3]

The Urabunna state that long ago in Waraka there lived two hawks, Wantu Wantu and Irritja, each of whom owned a tree and a nest of children. Wantu Wantu, the larger and stronger, made Irritja catch black fellows as food for his offspring, but Irritja himself was kind-hearted and fed his youngsters on wallabies. Returning to the nest one day Irritja saw the little hawk "Kutta Kutta" and warned him to flee, saying: "Hello, you alone! the old man Wantu Wantu is coming up behind, you had better flee." But Kutta Kutta, who had a very good opinion of himself, said, "Not I, if the old man wants to fight let him come on." The sight of the old man Wantu Wantu damped the courage of Kutta Kutta, so he fled to his brother the bell bird, and to him related the tale of woe. To cut a long story short the bell bird came to the trees where Wantu Wantu and Irritja nested, and severed almost through the bases of the trunks, so that the trees collapsed when the hawks alighted. Irritja cried, "Do not kill me, I do not eat the black fellows," so the bell bird spared him and said, "I think it would

[1] Starcke, "The Primitive Family," pp. 42 and 62. "Evolution of Decorative Art," H. Balfour, 1893, pp. 63 *et seq.*

[2] "Melanesians of British New Guinea."

[3] "Across Australia," Vol. I, p. 24.

be a very good thing if you marked your backs like my feathers," and while this painful proceeding was in progress the bell bird sang. The final word is that the flesh of the hawks Wantu Wantu and Irritja are "taboo" to the Urabunna to this day, because Irritja was kind to them, and Wantu Wantu's flesh would give them pains inside, because he used to be their enemy.

Previously when dealing with the origin of body marks the cases of a belief in divine origins were discussed. Such origins are said to have occurred among the Fijians, Andamanese, Ainu, and North American Indians, but the designs referred to are not the tribal markings now under discussion. There is for the Sakai a legend of the origin of tribal marks given by Skeat and Blagden in "Pagan Races of the Malay Peninsula." It appears that the Senoi had decided to leave the main stem of the Sakai in order to found a new home and establish themselves as a separate unit. Discussion soon resulted in the selection of a paint pattern for the breast, but there was greater difficulty in deciding what facial mark should be assumed. At this stage the wife of a magician intruded into the solemn debate, and was rewarded for her curiosity by a flat-handed blow on the face, which left five digit marks, and so the perplexed council formed a decision that woman should bear five tribal marks on the cheek and the men three.[1]

Are there among the accounts of tribal markings any present-day accounts or ancient legends, which reveal that these marks have, or had at one time, an

[1] "Pagan Races of the Malay Peninsula," p. 281.

important social significance? In 1895 a French trader pushed his way up the Congo into the Wangala and Balobo districts and came to a halt among the Mongo tribe near the River Bussera. Trading and collecting were going well when suddenly the whole business was stopped by the Mongo Chief and a palaver was arranged. The only demand was that the trader should become one of the tribe, to which he gave assent, and asked how the initiation was to be accomplished. The outcome of the palaver was that the trader was refused all commerce and collecting until he had become one of the tribe by receiving the scars,[1] an operation to which he gave assent. The marking was carried out by a medicine man, and the trader took little notice of the affair, hoping to grow a beard over the marks when he returned a wealthy man. Unfortunately blood poisoning set in, and the young man died at the home of a London surgeon, whose aid he had sought for the removal of the scars in which colouring matter had been placed.

There was no doubt as to the Mongo idea of what was implied in the word "tribesman," and the tattooing of Englishmen who have been among savages shows the regard of primitive man for this body marking process, as an outward emblem of the bond of sympathy which exists between the individuals of the group.

In the year 1816 John Rutherford fell captive to the Maoris and was tattooed with Moko designs on the face and the body from hips to knees. Rutherford appears to have made himself quite at home after the painful proceedings were over, for he married two

[1] Frobenius, "Childhood of Man," English translation, p. 30.

Maori girls of high rank, and when tired of his domestic responsibilities contrived to escape, and in 1828 was exhibiting himself in London.[1] A similar experience fell to the lot of James Caddell, who was the only man saved from a vessel named the *Sydney Cove*. He owed his escape from cannibalistic practices to the fact that he had touched the mat of a great chief, an act which would render him full of virtue. Caddell also did well, and report says that he became a noble, led fighting escapades, and assumed the warrior's Moko designs.

M. Bossu gives an interesting account of the details of his adoption by the Arkansas who tattooed a mark of a roebuck on his thigh. At the completion of the design they all danced and shouted for joy at the event of welcoming into their society one whom they admired. The pipe of peace was smoked and M. Bossu was told that all the allies of the Arkansas would welcome him as a brother when he showed the tattooed design, which was one of the insignia of a warrior or chief.[2]

The identifying of a newly-born child with the tribe is sometimes considered necessary, and on the fifth day after birth the child of the deer clan of the Omahas is painted with red spots on its back to imitate a fawn. On the arms and chest are red stripes to resemble the markings of the totemic animal. All the head men of the deer clan are required to be present at the ceremony, and their unity with the child

[1] "Moko" by Major-General Robley, ch. VI, p. 98.

[2] Bancroft, "Native Races of Pacific States," Vol. I, p. 388. M. Bossu, "Travels through Louisiana," 1750 (London, 1771), Vol. I, p. 107.

and one another is expressed by painting red spots on the chest of each member.[1]

Incidents such as the foregoing illustrate the importance of marking, without which those who have been so long accustomed to it would feel that there was a lack of expression of the sympathy that should exist among tribesmen. The devolution of this use of tribal marking must have been very slow in its passage to the merely ornamental function which it is now fulfilling in so many cases. Primitive, deeply-rooted emotions would die slowly.

Anything like a detailed survey of tribal marks in any one continent—America, Africa, or Australia—would be impracticable. And as the aim of this book is not a detailed account of technique, perhaps it will be well to confine our attention to a few instances of tribal marking, noting where possible the mixture of markings as indicative of a slow though definite mutation of ideas. Any ceremonial which implies a magico-religious feeling in connection with the marking is important, also distinctions between marking at child-birth or soon after, and a performance of the operation at initiation deserve attention. Such distinctions and tendencies are valuable only so far as they reflect the mental processes which underlie them; and in the case of a borrowing and mixture of designs until they are no longer a clue to the tribal relations of the wearer, one may note the gradually ascending self-consciousness and evolution of feelings of self-elation, as opposed to the more rudimentary and early reliance on mutual aid.

[1] Dr. Frazer, "Totemism and Exogamy," Vol. I, p. 31. A.B.E., 3rd report, p. 245.

The existence of ceremonial in connection with the infliction of tribal marks seems to imply that there is some fear beyond that which prompts the marking as a social process. There is in such instances of allied ceremonial, namely, among the Andamanese,[1] and certain Australian tribes as, for example, the Yerkla and the Yuin, a fear of something non-human in its operation, and perhaps careful research among the people who still associate ceremonial with tribal marking would reveal a legend relating to commands of ancestors of the tribe. Marking at child-birth, or soon after weaning, shows a tendency to revert to the form of marking which was likely to exist under the regime of mother right, the marking probably being carried out by the parent in response to the play of a tender parental emotion, which led to an idea of protecting the infant by allying it with the family group. The evidence afforded by tombs, monuments and mummified remains shows clearly that body marking of various kinds was employed in Egypt at a very early date.[2] Egyptian women stained the nails of their fingers and toes a yellowish red with the juice of the henna plant, and painted their faces with a sort of rouge. The eyelids and eyebrows were painted with a preparation of antimony named " Kohl," and under the eyes were thick lines of paint to make them appear large and full. Both men and women sometimes decorated

[1] E. H. Man, " Andamanese." Quatrefages, " Les Pygmes." " Pagan Tribes of Borneo," Hose and McDougall.

[2] See collection of palettes in University College Museum and elsewhere. " Primitive Art in Egypt," Jean Capart, 1905, pp. 29-33.

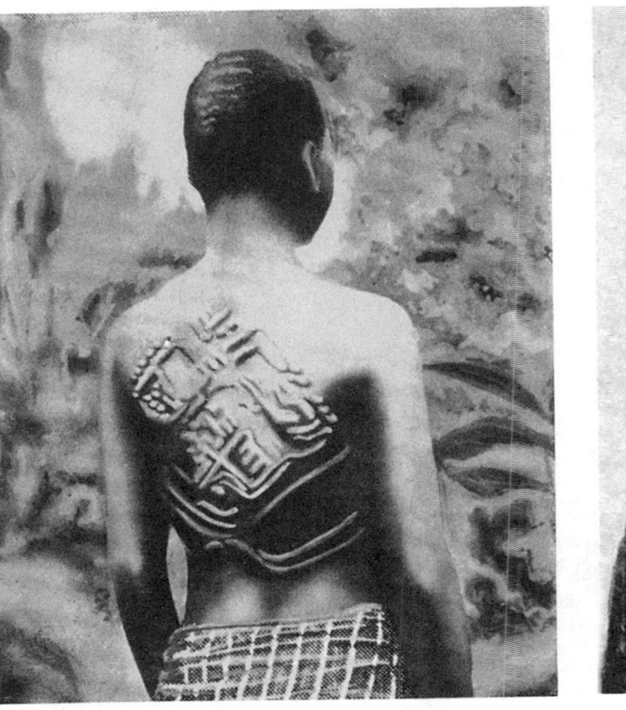

MANYEMA WOMAN, BELGIAN CONGO.

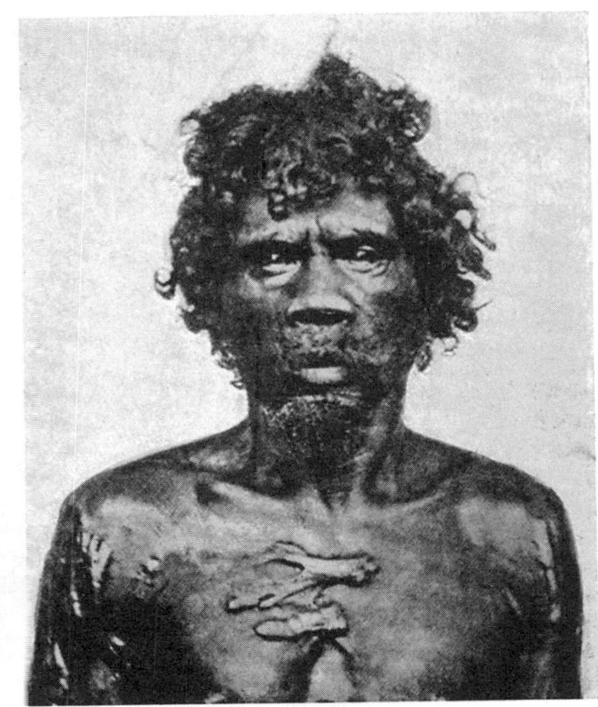

NATIVE AUSTRALIAN.

SIMPLE AND COMPLEX SCARIFICATION.

their bodies with tattoo markings which originally may have had a religious or tribal import.[1] The whole question of tattoo in Egypt is reviewed in the final chapter relating to the antiquity of body marking (pp. 325, 334).

The Congo region provides the best examples of cicatrization carried to a fine art, and on the backs of Ma Neyma women the cicatrized designs extend from the small of the back to the neck and laterally to the middle of the sides. The markings consist of a series of rhomboidal figures, the one within the other, and within each rhomboid is a symmetrical meandering curve, the whole outline being made by numerous, distinct, circular keloids. Cicatrization is widespread among the Bantu peoples, and is also especially noticeable in the North-East Central region among the Akikuyu, Masai, and Naivasha. In addition to the process of cicatrization people of the Kasai watershed paint with the red dust of the tukula wood, and the Bena Lubua of the Kasai district, Congo Free State, carve little wooden figures showing cicatrization marks, including circles, curves, and triangles.[2]

The marks sometimes tend to be of a very simple nature consisting only of from three to five rows of dots across the forehead, as among the Shilluk people.[3] Widespread in the Uganda Protectorate is the custom of cicatrizing by means of caustic juice, and the speciality of the treatment in this region lies

[1] E. A. Wallis Budge, Guide to Egyptian Galleries, British Museum, p. 82.

[2] British Museum, Guide to the Ethnographical Collections.

[3] "Shilluk People," Westermann, p. 24 of the introduction. "Uganda Protectorate," Sir H. H. Johnston, 1902, p. 556.

in the fact that the scars are so tiny and close together as to have the effect of tattooing.

In addition to the fact that tattooing proper would not show to advantage under the dark skin of the negro, there is to be considered the natural tendency of negroes' flesh to form in keloids, even after the simple operation of vaccination. Healing is said to be aided rather than retarded by rubbing in pigments. Usually scars are made more prominent and indelible by the rubbing in of charcoal, woodash, and gunpowder. "Formerly," says Werner,[1] "the various scars always indicated the tribe to which a person belonged, and children were marked with the mother's pattern; now the tribal marks are no longer strictly retained." Dr. Frazer[2] discourses on the common practice of having marks incised or tattooed on the body. He notes that for Africa there is usually no reason to regard such marks as imitations of totems, for the design is the same for each member of the tribe, whereas in totemic clans there would be a differentiation of markings for totemic groups. Another very simple form of marking is that employed by some Bushmen who tattoo straight lines on the arms, shoulders, and cheeks, and equally simple are the body markings of Hottentots, who, like the Bushmen, tattoo their cheeks, smear their bodies with grease, and paint their faces. J. Dowd[3] remarks that tribal marking probably originated at a time when mother right and descent were universal, and the process would be exceptionally useful at some

[1] "Native Races of British Afiica," A. Werner, p. 40.

[2] Dr. Frazer, "Totemism and Exogamy," Vol. IV, p. 197.

[3] "The Negro Races" by J. Dowd, 1907, pp. 42, 57, 327.

remote time when children were identified as group members, rather than individuals, each of whom possessed a personal name. All of the same blood on the mother's side would be designated by a common tattoo.[1] In the Banana Zone a great variety of style exists and there are skin patterns to designate families.

Among the Dahomans body marks scarcely exist, but in Nigeria they are exceedingly common and varied as the recent researches of Major Tremearne show.[2] The Somali and Galla people of the "Horn of Africa" cicatrize geometrical designs of very neat construction, usually on the upper arm, face, or abdomen. The marks are of a very simple kind including rectangles, rhomboids, and other figures, stated by Dr. Paulitschke to be tribal and family markings, and no mention of a deeper significance is made. Paulitschke thinks many scars may be of therapeutic origin.[3]

By far the most elaborate accounts of body marks are to be gleaned from the publications of the Museum for the Belgian Congo,[4] also from the researches of Dr. Turner, who has examined many hundreds of coloured mine labourers in Johannesburg, and so has had the opportunity of viewing numerous specimens side by side, and studying them in a comparative way. The Bushongo are above all other people of the Congo region addicted to the use

[1] "Das Mutterrecht," J. J. Bachofen, 1861, p. 335.

[2] J.A.I., 1911, pp. 162-71.

[3] "Somal Galla und Harari," Dr. Von Philipp Paulitschke, p. 86. "Die Geistige Cultur der Danakil, etc," Berlin, 1896, Vol. I, p. 96.

[4] "Documents Ethnographique du Congo Belge," Messrs. Torday and Joyce, 1910, p. 154.

of red pigment made from the tukula wood. This is applied to the husband and children, by the wife, before a social function such as a dance. Cicatrization is practised for tribal markings, which are given to both sexes, and the mark is usually carried on the temple. The mark of the Ba Mbala is composed of three groups each consisting of three cicatrized marks, and among the Ba Ngongo the badge is three concentric circles on each temple. Whether or no

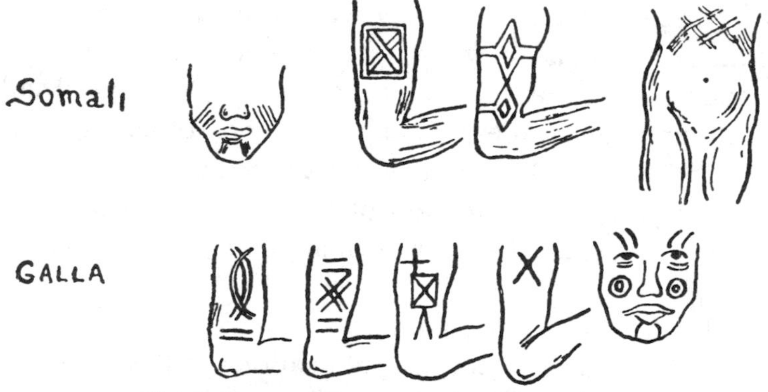

Simple Forms of Geometric, Scarified Design.

there is any mystic significance in the use of three is not stated. The Ba Ngendi marking is made up of two lines cut from the corner of each eye to the middle of each ear. In addition to the tribal marks of the Ba Mbala there are among these people cicatrized designs of a solely ornamental nature traced on the shoulders of the men, or on the abdomens of the women.

Some points of interest arise in connection with the time at which the marking takes place, and naturally we should expect one of the most ancient methods to be the marking of the child, by the mother, during infancy, the designs being those of the mother herself. Among the Ba Mbala the incisions are made about the time that the child can walk, a time at which it might have strayed away and become a unit of another social group. Marking of Ba Ngongo children is carried out at intervals between infancy and puberty, but if the operation is not complete by that date "elle reste inachevée," among the Ba Ngendi, however, the process is sometimes carried to completion after puberty is passed. The Ba Kango display designs not unlike those of the Bushongo, namely, a series of parallel cicatrices on the lower part of the abdomen. Some men carry the marks on one side of the abdomen only. Lozenge-shaped marks near the external corner of the eye and concentric circles on the temples are also common, and in addition to these devices it is usual for women to cicatrize the neck freely, and in consequence of the sexual varieties of marking and the complication of ornamental scars with tribal, there is an ever increasing difficulty in distinguishing the one mark from the other, so here the process of evolution from tribal marks to an expression of the æsthetic sense, by the marking of ornamental cicatrices, is observed in a very interesting stage. Dr. Turner remarks that tribal scars are rapidly changing or disappearing especially in the case of natives who are being brought into closer contact with Europeans. The Makuka cicatrize some deep cuts right across the forehead, at the corners of the mouth and on the chin, and deep folds are formed just as if one pinched the the skin of these parts between the thumb and finger. On the abdomen of the Makuka are large lozenge shaped figures each containing a smaller lozenge, the entire design having the appearance of wire netting. The M'Xosa employ faint patterns on the abdomen and these bear a striking contrast to the heavy nodules with which the Mtyopi mark themselves. The Yao mark is a half moon with the convexity upward, placed between the eyes. Among the Amemba the tribal sign is a vertical mark down the centre of the forehead, made by blistering with cashew and rubbing in a black pigment.[1]

Recent researches by A. C. Hollis[2] show that the Masai and Nandi still employ markings, which are both tattoo proper and cicatrized designs scratched with thorns. Among maidens and warriors the process is optional, and the information given seems to point to the decline of tribal marks in favour of ornamental scars. Such a transition, of course, indicates a very important change in mental activity, for whereas the underlying social tendency, coupled with the emotion of fear, and a sense of ownership, will account for the tribal scars, there is a much more complicated mental process behind ornamental marking, which involves some degree of introspection, self-consciousness, and rivalry.

About the age of ten or twelve, girls of the Bargesu begin to make on body and forehead markings which are signs of clan membership. The wounds were made with an iron needle attached to a ring worn by the girl. Wood ashes are rubbed into the wounds which are spaced according to the fashions

[1] Dr. Turner, "Anthropological Notes of South African Coloured Mine Labourers," p. 73.

[2] Hollis, "The Masai," p. 341; "The Nandi," p. 30.

of the clan to which the girl belonged. A girl who had not keloids on the forehead and breast would not be accepted in marriage, neither would she be allowed to join adult women.[1]

Australia is a good field of research for the student of tribal marking, and at present expert opinion is not agreed as to what marks are tribal, which are merely ornamental, and to what extent the process of cicatrization is carried out at initiation, with or without ceremonial.[2]

Any reference to body marking among mythical ancestors can be regarded as an indication of considerable antiquity, and the Kurnai have a story of a mythical ancestor Buryil Bornu, who was deceived in some way by a woman. The story goes on to say that on returning he became very much enraged and began to paint himself in preparation for fighting with the man whose wife had played this trick. Dr Howitt remarks that although it is generally held that raised scars do not indicate the tribe, and are merely ornamental, there are some instances which show that examples of this cicatrization are undertaken to distinguish tribesmen.[3] Further, among the Kurnai a man has his private mark to distinguish him as the owner of an opossum skin rug. In the Yerkla tribe the cicatrices are made by the medicine man at initiation, and a legend relates how these scars came to be made in the first instance.

Not only are there well authenticated instances of body marks of a tribal significance, but also cicatrices

[1] "The Bargesu," J. Roscoe, Cambridge, 1924, p. 27.
[2] Dr. Howitt, "Native Tribes of South-East Australia," p. 712.
[3] *Ibid.*, p. 744.

which are significant of sub-class names. In the Budera sub-class of the Kurnai each member has three cicatrices from breast to breast and three on each shoulder. People of the Kura sub-class distinguish themselves by one horizontal mark between the breasts and three vertically on the side of the biceps of each arm. In the Budu sub-class there are three horizontal marks between the breasts, above these two V-shaped incisions, and on the biceps five horizontal lines. The possibility of an ancient and magico-religious rite having existed is pointed out by the fact that the members of a group do not mark one another indiscriminately, but such marking is executed by the medicine man. The marks doubtless assisted in preserving observance of the laws of totemism and exogamy.

For the Yuin it may be said that the scars are not made until after the initiation ceremonies, and at this point Dr. Howitt gives the example of a Yuin man who had cicatrices vertically round the upper arm in order to make the boomerangs glance off, an instance which is paralleled by one in Saibai, where at initiation, cicatrices were made to cause arrows to glance off the youth when fighting,[1] and yet another parallel from Burma where tattooing proper can preserve from spear thrusts and gun-shot wounds. So convinced is the Burman of the efficacy of his tattooed designs that he will invite a European to discharge his revolver at him.[2]

Reverting to the question of tribal marks in Australia, in the neighbourhood of Moreton Bay

[1] "Cambridge Expedition to Torres Strait," Vol. V, p. 215.
[2] Sir G. Scott, "The Burman, his Life and Notions," ch. V.

scars are cut below the nipples when the boy is initiated. When the youth is a little older a second row of scars is made below the first, while an old man holds the boy's ears to keep away the pain. Messrs. Fison and Howitt [1] are doubtful as to the meaning, tribal or otherwise, of any Australian cicatrization, a doubt which is also mentioned by Mr. E. M. Curr.[2] The opinions of these observers are supported by the most recent accounts of Australian aborigines, and no doubt as time goes on, it will be increasingly difficult to say that any mark has a special significance, so rapidly is the practice declining in many places, or perhaps more correctly the practice continues, but the former significance is disappearing.

Messrs. Spencer and Gillen are unable to say with confidence that the marks are tribal,[3] and Mr. W. E. Roth is equally undecided,[4] but an older observer and explorer, namely, E. J. Eyre, whose account was published in 1845, is of the opinion that many scars are beyond doubt a tribal distinction.[5]

The writings of this explorer speak of the great varieties of form, number, and arrangement, of the scars employed by different tribes, so that a stranger meeting with another anywhere in the woods may at once tell from the manner in which he is tattooed, the

[1] "Kamilaroi and Kurnai," p. 66.

[2] "Australian Race," Vol. II, pp. 468, 475.

[3] Spencer and Gillen, "Native Tribes of Central Australia," pp. 41, 43.

[4] W. E. Roth, "Ethnological Studies among the Aborigines of New South Wales and Queensland."

[5] Eyre, Journals of the Expedition of Discovery into Central Australia, London, 1845, Vol. II, p. 333.

country and tribe to which he belongs, if not very remote. Continuing we have the words "each tribe has a distinctive mode of making incisions."

If we look to-day at the process of transition, from tribal to ornamental marking, which is taking place in Africa, there seems to be a strong probability that Australian marking experienced a similar change, but unfortunately there does not seem to have been any accurately reported observation of the process of devolution. Schurmann[1] says that the marks are now purely ornamental; but it is difficult to see that they were always so, and in all likelihood there were powerful motives leading to the making of the incisions at initiation ceremonies. Schurmann also gives an account of the conferring of tribal marks in the neighbourhood of Port Lincoln. The youth who had been initiated was covered with coagulated blood from the veins of the assembled company, and while kneeling on all fours he received, on the covering of blood, small marks to indicate the position of the cicatrices which were to be made by the medicine man, who used a sharp stone implement. The incisions named "Manka" are held in such veneration that it would be deemed a great profanation to allude to them in the presence of women, and all points considered there is a very strong probability, that in the neighbourhood of Port Lincoln at any rate, tribal marking was a very sacred and important part of the initiation ceremony.

For Borneo it may be stated that keloids are

[1] C. W. Schurmann, "Aboriginal Tribes of Port Lincoln," 1879, pp. 228-31.

unknown. Tattooing among men is widespread, but the designs can no longer be trusted to give a clue to the tribe, so great has been the borrowing, chiefly from the Kayans. A point of great interest is, that "among travelling tribes it is usual to submit to the pattern of the host,"[1] and if this holds good for Borneo, one wonders whether research would reveal any such custom in Australia and Africa. Certainly such a convention would very rapidly lead to a great confusion of marks, which were once quite distinctive.

It would be reasonable to turn to the tribal markings of the Andamanese for some clue to the original ideas regarding the value of tribal marks. Mr. Man recognizes no special ceremonial in connection with the cicatrization, which he alleges is carried out for ornament, and as a test of endurance.[2] But there is some importance in the statement, that very seldom is a child of either sex allowed to remain untattooed after the age of eight years, a custom which may take us back to very remote times when the children had to receive means of identification before their wandering began. For no doubt after hostilities there would be an exchange of captives. Certainly this cicatrization, carried out with a piece of quartz, is not for the purpose of distinguishing ranks of society, for the Chief's children are marked in the same manner as the commoners, neither does any status or profit attach to the office of body marker.

The account of M. de Quatrefages concerning these tribal markings is of exceptional interest by reason of the mention of connected taboo and

[1] "Pagan Tribes of Borneo," Vol. I, p. 244.
[2] J.A.I., 1882, p. 331.

ceremonial. In the Southern Andaman Islands both sexes scarify their entire bodies in a very simple way, by little horizontal and vertical incisions in alternating series. Women usually operate, and it is revelant to state these points: (1) the first three incisions must be made low on the back; (2) these primary cuts can be inflicted by a man only, although a woman may go forward with the subsequent marking; (3) the three first incisions are made with an arrow used for hunting wild pigs; and the remainder of the marks are inscribed with a piece of glass or quartz; (4) while the wounds are open the patient must abstain from the flesh of the pig. Assuming that these statements are quiet correct, the tribal marking of the Andamanese involved both ceremonial and taboo, two circumstances which usually denote some degree of awe and fear of powers against which the rites are a protection, or by whose permission the rite is exercised.

Not only would tribal markings be useful in establishing the unity of the social group, but the ownership of property in the form of wives could be made more certain.[1] At the present day the Naga women are tattooed, and females from the North are much sought after by Southern men because, however fierce the feuds, a tattooed woman goes unscathed. Women belonging to the Californian tribes, among whom warfare was incessant,[2] were tattooed so that each tribe could recover its own women when negotiations for peace were commenced, and ransoms had been paid. Dialects were so similar, and differences of appearance so inconsider-

[1] "Naga Tribes of Manipur," Hodson, pp. 30, 31.
[2] S. Powers, "Tribes of California," pp. 20, 96, 148, 242.

able, that some mark of ownership was necessary, and beyond such a sign there were no marks ornamental or otherwise. Very early in child life the sense of ownership is present, and the result is frequently some degree of rivalry or stimulation of natural self-assertion. Among these Californian and Naga warriors there is the same sense of ownership at work; hence women, in common with other property, have to receive means of identification. With this reservation, that whereas women receive a mark of the community, material objects such as skins and weapons are stamped with the crest of the individual owner. The Haida, too, have their family names and crests, and each member receives on the body a representation of the bear, wolf, eagle, or some family of fishes. A chief who exacts allegiance from several others, tattooes each of the emblems of his subjects on his own body, so he assimilates various virtues, and at the same time gives expression to his feelings, which involve no small amount of pride, sense of ownership, and sentiment of sympathy.[1]

Opinions respecting tribal markings among the Sakai are at present in such a plastic state that no one cares to say definitely what are tribal and what are ornamental markings. A perusal of information supplied by Messrs. Skeat and Blagden leaves the impression that the Sakai, Semang, and Jakun have entered upon a complication of marks so great, that unless the problem is very quickly elucidated, one never will know of any special meaning being attached to a particular design. Reviewing the summary of

[1] Mr. Swanton, American Bureau of Ethnology, 1888-9, p. 402. This work, p. 268.

accounts supplied, there appears to be a Sakai tribal mark consisting of lines on the cheek, and fifteen women were observed to bear these identical markings. The men paint fern fronds on the chest; but as three marks are used as a pain cure for children it is possible that the fern frond designs are more amuletic than tribal. The wife of a Sakai chief had four distinct scarifications on the left cheek, and faint marks on the right; these she said were Sakai tribal marks, for she was a person of the Sakai tribe.[1] These instances, considered with the legend concerning the origin of tribal marks, given a few pages previously, are perhaps sufficient to suggest that at one time the Sakai had a tribal sign differing for the sexes, but that progress of ornamental marking, and contact with the Semangs, has tended to confuse the several tribal, amuletic, and ornamental marks.

Modern Tattooing of a Social or Anti-Social Group

Interesting cases of present-day employment of tattooing to express social solidarity are common enough among soldiers, and for schoolboys M. Lombroso gives examples. Military men not infrequently mark themselves with something which shows allegiance to their profession, for example, the date of a battle, cross-guns, a flag, a cannon, or a pyramid of bullets. Naval men prefer a ship or an anchor, and sometimes the marking does not merely connect the wearer with some particular army, but further identifies him with a certain corps. Thus a

[1] Skeat and Blagden, "Pagan Races of the Malay Peninsula," pp. 30, 31, 35, 41.

cavalryman tattooed a horse on himself. Musicians have marked the body with a representation of a violin or drum, and other people wishing to identify themselves with a particular trade have marked on the body two crossed knives to denote the butcher, or a barrel to designate the cooper. The criminal allies himself with his nefarious business in a way which cannot be mistaken, and there is a considerable expression of sentiments of lust, hatred, and revenge, by the tattooing of mottoes and maledictory epithets on the body. One criminal had on his chest two poiniards, and near them the words "je jure de me venger" (I swear to avenge myself). This threat the old Piedmontese sailor had carried into effect by robbing and killing.[1] A Venetian had on his chest the inscription "malheur à moi! Quel sera ma fin?" (misfortune to me, whatever will be my end?). Again, another criminal sentiment of despair was, "Né sous une mauvaise étoile" (born under an evil star). While in prison another desperado tattooed on his chest a poiniard, above which were the words "mort aux bourgeois" (death to the citizens). In 1878 M. Lombroso examined a criminal of Naples who had tattooed across his chest the words "je ne suis qu'un pauvre malheureux" (I am only a poor unfortunate). Malassen had on his chest a guillotine tattooed in red and black, and near by in red letters were the words, "j'ai mal commencé, je finirai mal" (I commenced badly and I shall finish badly). Other lugubrious mottoes were: "La vie n'est qu' une illusion," "mort

[1] "L'Homme Criminel," Lombroso, Vol. I, pp. 289, 292. "Le Criminel," Dr. Emile Laurent, Paris, 1908, p. 109. "Les Tatouages," A. Lacassagne, Paris, 1881.

aux officers français," "la liberté ou la morte," "morte aux gendarmes," "la gendarmerie sera mon tombeau"; and so forth in infinite variety to give expression to the intensely strong passions that were raging within. One criminal, who was about thirty-four years of age (most of which time had been spent in jail), had not on his body an untattooed space as great as a crown piece (la surface d'un écu qui ne fut tatouée). He bore the words "martyr de la liberté," which were quite surrounded by a tattooed serpent eleven centimetres long, and on his nose was a cross which he had tried to erase with acetic acid. One criminal, who had made a speciality of maiming horses, had allied himself with his crime by tattooing the head of a horse, and to express his sympathy with the brigand Mottino, he had tattooed a portrait of that person. There is also the example of a man who had spent a lifetime in forgery tattooing himself with the implements of his craft. A soldier, who was tattooed in the same way as each member of his regiment, said to M. Lombroso, "Voyez vous monsieur, nous sommes comme les moutons, que l'un de nous fasse une chose, tous aussitôt l'imitent, au risque même de se faire du mal." He expressed very clearly the soldier's sentiment that the regimental unity was preserved only by members marking in a similar way; a practice superseded by wearing of uniforms or clan tartans. It appears that the emotions working to produce such a uniform marking are not greatly different from those which prompt the body marking of primitive man, who wishes to be allied with his tribe or clan, except that these markings of criminals are strongly anti-social in function.

Twenty pupils who were leaving the college of Castellamonte tattooed themselves with a device having a connection with their college, "ignorant que le tatouage fut un usage des barbares et des galeriens." The observations of M. Lombroso find confirmation in the researches of A. T. Sinclair,[1] who has carried on a prolonged investigation of the subject of tattooing by civilized peoples of the present day. The majority of Scandinavian deep water sailors are tattooed and ninety per cent. of the men serving in the U.S.A. navy bear some tattooed device, while among Cape Cod fishermen only about ten per cent. are without tattoo marks. In France the designs of a crossed cleaver and knife were borne by many butchers, the barrel by a cooper, and the saw and hammer by a carpenter, and these practices, which also hold some ground in Germany, A. T. Sinclair regards as a survival of old guild customs. With this view Lacassagne is at variance after a careful comparison of tattooed designs with emblems of cities, mottoes of companies, and heraldic devices.[2]

Marking to Denote the Social Status of an Individual[3]

Leaving the subject of marking for the purpose of expressing those emotions which lead to a preservation of group stability, we turn to a very wide field

[1] A. T. Sinclair, "American Anthropologist," 1908, Vol. X, p. 361.

[2] "Les Tatouages," A. Lacassagne, Paris, 1881, p. 115.

[3] "The Social and Political Systems of Central Polynesia," R. W. Williamson, 1924. Gives many instances and references for tattooing in relation to social status.

of inquiry among examples of body marking, carried out for the purpose of giving some distinction to a particular individual, who is respected on account of age, social status, or prowess in fighting and hunting.

There can be little doubt that public opinion regarding the treatment of old people has varied considerably from place to place and time to time. Probably on account of infirmity, and limitation of means of sustenance, old people have been abandoned or killed among hunting tribes. On the contrary there are many examples of body marking to show that age is with some a cause for deferential treatment and all works on Australian native tribes emphasize the important social standing of the old men. Dr. Nassau, speaking for West Africa, refers to a widespread respect for the aged, to whom the young must not approach within several yards, or again among the Masai it is customary for young boys to salute the old men, who return the compliment by spitting at the youths,[1] this being a usual Masai salutation, and saying, "Ngai give you long life." In Australia old men have many privileges of eating and marrying which are not accorded to young boys,[2] for the uninitiated must search for the best food which is given to the old men, and for some time after initiation a youth may have no more than a temporary attachment to some young woman who is married to an old man.

Speaking for Tahiti, Charles Darwin[3] said that many

[1] "The Masai," Hollis, p. 316.
[2] "Across Australia," Spencer and Gillen, p. 316.
[3] "A Voyage Round the World," Darwin, p. 430.

of the elder people had their feet covered with small figures so placed as to resemble a sock, an indelible marking which prevents a man from assuming the manners of a young dandy. General remarks on the New Zealand shore natives visited in 1769 show that at that period it was usual for both sexes to stain themselves in the same manner. A black stain was used by the woman for colouring the lips, but the men generally carried the custom to greater lengths and had patches on many parts of the body. A man added a quantity every year of his life so that some of the elders were almost covered with the stain.[1]

Women of the Californian tribes tattoo with three blue lines extending perpendicularly from the centres and corners of the lower lips to the chin, and among some tribes of this region similar lines are added to the arms and backs of the hands.[2] As the women grow older the lines are developed in width and depth of colour in order to indicate increasing social importance.

Ainu women tattoo moustaches, which are commenced during childhood, and enlarged each year until the women marry.[3] The circular marks on the arms are increased in number year by year, and are believed by Commander St. John to be definitely indicative of age.[4] In the Admiralty Islands the old women are distinguished by a coat of black paint,

[1] Journal of Rt. Hon. Sir Joseph Banks, 1769, p. 233.

[2] "Native Races of the Pacific States," Bancroft, 1875, Vol. I, p. 332.

[3] Commander St. John, R.N., J.A.I., 1872, p. 249.

[4] "Living Races of Mankind," Hutchinson, Gregory and Lydekker, Vol. I, p. 34.

and in New Zealand any self-respecting old man would practise depilation, for should his facial Moko be covered with beard, he would receive the opprobrious epithet of "E-weki" (old man).[1] In this instance there was no question of assuming additional marks, but rather the necessity of retaining the exposure of youthful scars was emphasized. Among the Salish tribes the use of red and yellow ochres, white clay, charcoal, and powdered hæmatite is common. In addition to expressing rank and calling there are markings which are distinctive of age.[2] Young women usually paint their cheeks with red, which is not unbecoming when applied thinly, and elderly women usually paint the whole face to the level of the eyes. Cicatrization in Treasury Island, in the Solomon Group, was carried out by placing little piles of touch wood on the skin in circular heaps which were ignited.[3] The marks so obtained were not assumed by young people; only men and women of maturity were observed to wear them.

Already in speaking of tribal marking it has become evident that in some instances, at any rate, such marks have been assumed at initiation. At the time of the initiation ceremonies there is usually another form of body marking which may be regarded as a magical aid to the giving of a particular status to the youths under treatment. Such cases of marking at initiation might have been correctly classified

[1] "Moko," Major-General Robley, p. 29.

[2] "British North America," C. Hill Tout, 1907, p. 73.

[3] "Solomon Islands and their Natives," H. B. Guppy, 1887, p. 137.

with examples of tattooing and painting for magico-religious purposes, but, after all, the social aspect of initiation is the more impressive and fundamental reason for the ceremonial, while magico-religious practices such as body painting, whirling the bull roarer, and putting goodness into the boys from Daramulun, are but magico-religious aids to the completion of what is essentially a social function.

In the Melanesian area of British New Guinea[1] boys are initiated at a ceremony termed "aruaru," which takes place when the candidates are about twelve years of age. The actual ceremony is preceded by a period of seclusion of ten months' duration, during which anklets and belts are made. During the whole of this period each boy is covered from head to foot with red pigment, the assumption of which indicates the survival of a one-time idea of blood as an adjunct in fertility rites. Paint is a magical aid to the launching of the boy into man's estate, the blood colour symbolizing new life and vigour. Among the Sakai, too, there is sprinkling with the juice of a fern before the youth may join the ranks of men and marry.[2] In Tutu, Torres Strait, initiates are covered with soot to which a fresh coat is added each day. Elder men sit on mats belonging to their respective clans, and if a man sat on a mat other than one of his own clan he was painted black. A medicine made from bark is supposed to be a love lubricant, for the youth is

[1] Dr. Seligman, "Melanesians of British New Guinea," p. 260.

[2] "Pagan Races of the Malay Peninsula," Skeat and Blagden, p. 47.

rubbed on the abdomen, on the palm of the hand, and behind the ears, while a little is also placed on the nose, knees, and feet. This "girl medicine" will act in such a way as to make the newly initiated boy successful in attracting females.[1]

The people of Mabuiag proceed somewhat differently, for, prior to initiation, the mother's brother blackens the boy all over with Kubi, a charred husk of the cocoanut, and a red line is painted round the forehead, at the insertion of the scalp hair. Another red line passes down the centre of the nose and meets a broad red band painted across the face at the level of the nostrils. Meanwhile such moral precepts as the following are given:

"When you want to speak some word you speak true, no tell lie, tell lies no good, s'pose you bad boy, you dead quick. You touch nothing belong another man he call you bad boy, s'pose man send you for anything you go quick, you no too much run about," and along such lines the wholesome advice continues. In the Cape York tribes the men who are about to take part in these initiation ceremonies paint their transverse abdominal scars with red and white. Each boy is told the clan into which he must marry, and is anointed with "bush medicine" in the hollow of the femur, the groin, and clavicle, to make him grow quickly. Older boys of the Solomon Islands have to submit themselves to the tattooing operation before they obtain the rights of manhood, and H. B. Guppy was informed that they were kept

[1] "Cambridge Expedition to Torres Strait," Vol. V, pp. 209, 220.

isolated during the process, but after it is complete they are at liberty to marry.[1]

The significance of this use of paint or other form of body marking seems to be illustrated by the case of the Bova tribe, in which initiation ceremonies are somewhat elaborate. Two circles are drawn, and on the outer fringe of the outer circle women are allowed to be present. The boy about to be initiated is covered red from head to foot, a garb which is supposed to render him able to enter safely into the inner circle when the images of gods are seen, the red paint acting as a magical protection in the holy of holies. After the completion of these sacred ceremonies the youth washes off the red paint and gives himself a coat of white.[2]

There is no doubt a good deal of pride assumed by a man who has publicly shown contempt for physical pain, and for the gratification of this pride and the earning of a superior social status, the North American Indian, or the Tamil of Southern India, would swing on the flesh hook for long periods. Tattooing appears in some instances to be quite disconnected from any magical aspect of initiation, but it is just used as a test to find whether the candidate can show stoicism which justifies his inclusion in the ranks of men.[3] With a view to this, together with the hope of receiving flattery from the girls, this painful tattooing process is cheerfully undertaken. The Rt. Hon. Sir Joseph Banks noticed a positive

[1] "Solomon Islands and their Natives," H. B. Guppy, 1887, p. 136.

[2] "Aborigines of New South Wales," Frazer, p. 17.

[3] The process is at once a test and expression of emotional states.

correlation between the extent to which the Maori used amoca, and the density of the population of the area in which the tattooing was practised. The more populous the country the greater the number of well tattooed persons. Sir Joseph Banks was of the opinion that the process was called forth by the tendency toward emulation in bearing pain, for where the population was sparse, the amoca was almost absent; there being a lack of incentive to gain social status by fortitude during a painful operation.[1] For the Society Islands,[2] the same writer says that the markings are shown with great pride both by men and women, but whether as a mark of beauty or as a proof of perseverence in bearing pain he cannot say.[3] Observation carried out in 1769 is extremely useful, but even at that date the reasons for practices do not seem to have been particularly clear, and it should be remembered that scientific ethnological inquiry was undeveloped. In the Society Islands the operation was performed between the ages of fourteen and eighteen years, and Sir Joseph Banks never saw a person of maturity without it. The writer was puzzled to account for the universality of body marking. He feels certain that some superstition was connected with it.

A Shan youth is considered to have reached manhood when he has been tattooed, but until he has shown courage sufficient to endure the pain he has the status of a child.[4] The usual tattoo has the

[1] Journal of the Rt. Hon. Sir Joseph Banks, 1769, p. 233.
[2] Tahiti.
[3] Journal of the Rt. Hon. Sir Joseph Banks, 1769, p. 130.
[4] "The Shans at Home," Mrs. Leslie Milne, 1910, pp. 66, 67, 68.

appearance of breeches[1] from waist to knee, the favourite colours being red and blue. Opium is sometimes given, and the patient is encouraged to be brave by the operator saying, "If you wriggle too much people will think you are only a little boy," and friends sitting round say, "If you spoil the tattoo no girl will admire you," a few remarks which show clearly that for the Shans this operation is the outcome of a feeling of egotism and a desire for the gratification of a sentiment of pride. The sexual instinct is at work, and together with the primary tendency to self-assertion, it accounts for the adoption of some ceremony which enhances the social status, and improves relations with the opposite sex. Mrs. Milne says that no girl will recognize a man of marriageable age until his legs are tattooed, an account which agrees quite well with the independent observations of Shway Yoc,[2] a pseudonym under which Sir G. Scott published his well-known work.

In Polynesia the young chief of eighteen leads the way to the hut specially selected for the tattooing, and following him are a number of youths of from fourteen to eighteen years of age. Female relations hold the young man, and groaning is considered to show a want of courage. When about as much as the palm of one's hand is done, which takes an hour, another patient is admitted. When all the tattooed are healed, a great dance is arranged in order that the tattoo marks may be displayed, and the youths may have an opportunity of receiving congratulations

[1] The "breeches" tattoo has a wide distribution, viz., Shan States, Borneo, Samoa, Tahiti, Easter Island, New Zealand.

[2] "The Burman, his Life and Notions," ch. V, pp. 39-47.

from the fair sex. The observer of these practices says that they are an indispensable sign of manhood, and the practice is rarely discontinued, in spite of the fact that the marking is almost covered with the clothes that are now fashionable.[1]

At one time tattooing was done in Yucatan and Nicaragua by lacerating with stone hatchets and rubbing the wounds with powdered coal or black earth. The favourite devices were stripes, serpents, and birds, the making of which was a slow and painful process, demanding much fortitude.[2]

There has from the earliest recorded period been a custom among peoples of various levels of culture to divide the community into chiefs, freeman, and slaves, and among various devices used to express the social distinctions separating these groups tattooing has been very prominent.

Restrictions as to the reservation of a particular tattoo to denote a certain social status are not now so rigidly enforced as was at one time usual with the Kayan. Formerly the wives and daughters tattooed the thighs only, while all others were permitted to decorate only the ankles and calves. It is nevertheless possible even at the present day to distinguish between the markings of those of high and low rank. A woman of low class is tattooed free hand, that is, without any previous stamping of an outline design on the skin, and very naturally the work is not so symmetrical, neither are the figures or lines so numerous. The flexor surface of the

[1] "Melanesians and Polynesians," G. Brown, 1910.

[2] Bancroft, "Native Races of the Pacific States of North America," Vol. II, p. 733.

forearm of a chief's daughter is usually tattooed with such signs as full moons, the head of the hornbill, the bows of a boat, and spirals; while the supinator surface reveals transverse zigzag patterns known as rattan leaves; the design terminating in a bundle of tuber roots.[1]

A Maori by the name of Tupai Kupa gave M. Frobenius an explanation of the various Moko curves, each flourish of which had a particular name and significance.[2] The chief gave a narration of the incidents which had led to the assumption of each particular work, and sketched the patterns for each of the noble families.[3] D'Urville has professed to see in the Maori Moko a complete analogy to European heraldry, with this difference, that whereas a coat of arms attests the merit of ancestors, the Maori design advertises the merits of the person decorated. One Maori chief, on examining the seal of a British officer, asked if the coat of arms thereon was the " Moko " of the officer's family. It is also significant of the status-giving function of Moko, that slaves were excluded from the reception of designs, and for designating a woman of high rank the tattoo was carried from the heel, right up the calf of the leg, to a point where it became hidden by the short skirt.[4]

For Polynesia Ratzel has some evidence respecting tattooing as an indication of social status.[5] In the Society Islands, the Marquesas, and Carolines, common people are tattooed on the loins only, while

[1] " Pagan Tribes of Borneo," Vol. I, p. 255.
[2] " Childhood of Man," L. Frobenius, p. 36.
[3] " Moko " by Robley, p. 17.
[4] *Ibid.*, pp. 22, 38.
[5] Ratzel, " History of Mankind," Vol. I, p. 196.

"Erri" or "Ariki," the nobility, are distinguished by large circular markings all over the body. In the Gilbert Islands a poor man who is tattooed enjoys more influence in the general council than a rich man whose surface is blank. The people of Rotuma indicate social or caste distinctions by tattooing in different ways, but strangely enough, the chief is but slightly decorated, while persons of lower rank show decoration all over the person. By way of contrast the people of the Marshall Islands reserve tattooing for their chiefs only, and in Mortlock Island differences of rank are shown by decoration of the legs.

Among Guinea negroes it is a common custom for free women to have one, two, or three narrow lines from the wrist up the back of each arm and down the back.[1] The Tsalisens of Formosa[2] use tattooing for the decoration of both sexes, but among the men, only the chief and the males of his family are allowed to use this means of ornament. A suggestion of totemism is found among the Red Karens of Burma, and in this clan each member bears the crest of his nobility tattooed on his back in the design of a rising sun.[3]

"Cher les Thraces on considerait le tatouage comme une marque honorifique. C'était ainsi qu'on distinguait les nobles du vulgaire. Pour d'autre nations il fut au contraire une preuve de servitude."[4] Although tattooing may be a badge of slavery according to the words of Cocheris above quoted, it appears

[1] "Living Races of Mankind," Hutchinson, Gregory and Lydekker, p. 368.

[2] "Formosa, Past and Present," Davidson, 1903, p. 565.

[3] "Things Indian," W. Crooke, p. 461.

[4] "Les Parure Primitives," Cocheris, p. 38.

from Herodotus that it was in one instance a sign of escape from slavery. A slave who escaped to the Temple of Hercules in Egypt and was tattooed there could not be retaken by his master; the device tattooed was scarcely a sign of freedom, but rather of bondage to the Temple instead of to a private owner.[1]

Before Japan had any records of her own, Chinese travellers, writing early in the Christian era, note that the men of Japan all tattoo their faces[2] and ornament their bodies with designs. Differences of rank are indicated by the position and size of the patterns. Then came the reversion of feeling, and from the dawn of history to the Middle Ages this form of marking was confined to lower classes.

Cocheris states that the inhabitants of the Marquesas Islands are not less remarkable for their decoration than the New Zealanders.[3] They are by gifts of nature worthy to act as models to the sculptor, and to add to natural charms they have the entire body covered with coloured incisions. The designs indicate not only the tribe of the individual but also castes and official functions. " Il-y-a des signes pour les guerriers, les nobles, les mercenaires, les artisans, et les veufs."

The records of A. von Humboldt show that South American Indians of the Orinoco express poverty and destitution by saying, " the man is so wretched that he cannot paint his half body,"[4] and

[1] Herodotus, Vol. II, p.113.
[2] Things Japanese," B. H. Chamberlain, p. 399.
[3] " Les Parure Primitives," Cocheris, p. 44.
[4] " Native Races of the Pacific States," Vol. I, pp. 48, 72.

for North America Bancroft gives instances of body marking as a sign of rank. In tattooing, the colour is applied by drawing a thread under the skin or pricking it with a needle. Different tribes, and different ranks of the same tribe, have each a different form of tattooing. The plebeian female of certain bands is permitted to adorn her chin with but one vertical line in the centre, and one parallel to it on either side. The more fortunate nobles mark two vertical lines from each corner of the mouth. Among the Kadiaks the " more the female chin is tattooed the greater her respectability." [1]

In Yucatan face-colouring and the tattooing of hands was a privilege accorded to the brave, but most of the examples given refer to markings which show social distinction by accident of birth. The Mayas tattooed as an honorific sign.[2] Joyce summarizes the evidence of Sahagun and Landa respecting tattoo in Mexico. The more the Aztec men tattooed themselves, the greater the respect they commanded. The decoration was usually applied at marriage, the design being first painted, then pricked in. Women also covered the body with tattoo from the waist upward with the exception of the breasts. Probably the custom was of long standing since ornaments simulating tattoo are often seen on the faces of monumental figures.[3]

[1] " Native Races of the Pacific States," Bancroft, Vol. II, p. 741. For distribution of practice of chin tattoo of women see Buckland. J.A.I., Vol. XVII, 1888, p. 319.

[2] " Manuel d'Archæologie Americaine," H. Beuchat, p. 454.

[3] " Mexican Archæology," T. A. Joyce, London, 1912, Fig. 11, p. 295, also " Historia de la Cosas de la Nueva España," Bernardino de Sahagun, and D. G. Brinton in " Rig Veda Americanus," Library of Aboriginal American Literature, Vol. VIII, Philadelphia, 1890.

Tattooing and the Social Status of Women

A further study of the employment of marks to indicate social status very naturally falls into three divisions: (*a*) Tattooing of women to indicate womanhood, completion of marriage contract, number of children (and in one case the sharing of hunting honours awarded to the husband). From North America, among the Omahas, there is the practice of tattooing a maid in honour of a chief's exploits. (*b*) The tattooing of men to show prowess in head-hunting, killing of animals, membership of a secret society. (*c*) Finally, in a third division of miscellaneous instances, there are the practices of tattooing criminals to preserve social order, the recording of mythology by skin marking, also body marking for communication and pecuniary reward.

The numerous and widespread examples of tattooing girls at puberty, which have been to some extent dwelt upon in previous pages, are intended to illustrate a tendency to associate with body marking both ceremonial and taboo, positive and negative rites, which usually denote the presence of the sacred.

In addition to being the signs of womanhood and a marriageable age, the marks probably form part of the mysticism which is necessary for launching the maiden forth into the higher dignities attaching to the office of wife and mother. The ceremonial and taboos in favour with Melanesians, Nagas, Kayans and Ba Thonga during the tattooing of women having been mentioned, there remains a list of people who tattoo their women at puberty. The function may be devoid of ceremonial, or there may be traces of former rites.

Dr. Thurston says that it is usual to tattoo Toda women before puberty, but that in some instances the operation is neglected until after this period.[1] Generally, however, it is accomplished before the birth of the first child. Dots and circles are marked on the chest, arms, back, and legs, and there is a statement that the women so marked must have borne one or more children. Dr. Rivers[2] remarks that the facts concerning tattooing of Toda women are not understood. Among the Atagals of Formosa[3] both sexes tattoo as a sign of puberty, and females on entering womanhood add a rather complex design in pale blue leading from the mouth to the ear, measuring nearly an inch in width. The Yam and Tutu girls of Torres Strait[4] have the entire body blackened at puberty, and the use of this colour seems to suggest, not so much a giving of social status at womanhood, as the survival of a superstitious regard for fertility rites.

In Paraguay, for girls at puberty, there is a blue marking which is increased at marriage.[5] With the aid of a thorn dipped in blue or violet pigment a line a centimetre wide is made from the roots of the hair, down the nose to the top lip. At the time of marriage this band is prolonged to the chin point. The Haida and all tribes of the North Pacific coast are addicted to the practice of tattooing girls at puberty. The

[1] "Ethnographical Notes in Southern India," p. 382.

[2] "The Todas," W. H. R. Rivers, 1906, pp. 313, 576.

[3] "Formosa, Past and Present," J. W. Davidson, 1903, p. 565.

[4] "Cambridge Expedition to Torres Strait," Vol. IV, p. 29.

[5] M. Dobrizhoffer, "Abipoines of Paraquay," London, 1822, Vol. II, p. 19.

Salish usually tattoo women only; the facial marks are very simple, consisting of parallel lines, spots, crosses, angles, and squares.[1] There are generally three diverging lines from the corners of the mouth, and two parallel lines from the centre of the lower lip to the chin. Mr. Hill Tout says that these designs are added after the puberty rites in order to mark the new status. The Rev. David Cranz,[2] a missionary in Greenland for thirty years, says that the Eskimo mother performs the tattooing operation during the childhood of her daughter for fear she might not get a husband. Turning to more modern accounts of the Eskimo, there is a reference to the tattooing of the tribes of Behring Strait, especially among those people inhabiting the Siberian Coast and the St. Lawrence Island. On the Tundra to the south of the Yukon, only a few women tattoo, and the simple design usually consists of three, five, or six lines radiating from the under-lip to the chin, while in some instances lines are marked on the back of the wrist and forearm. In former years the women of the Hudson Bay Eskimo were fancifully tattooed with curved lines and rows of dots on the neck, arms and legs, up to mid-thigh.[3] The practice is declining rapidly as a result of the Shamans saying that it brings ill-luck. At the present day, among the Hudson Bay Eskimo, there is just the tattooing of a few dots on the face at puberty, the operation being performed by an old woman.

Any inquiry as to the reason for one sex preferring

[1] Hill Tout, "British North America," p. 74.

[2] David Cranz, "History of Greenland," London, 1767, Vol. I, p. 138.

[3] A.B.E., 1896-7, Part I, p. 50; 1889-90, p. 207.

the other to be tattooed is difficult to get, and most inquirers fail to receive any answer beyond the statement given in New Ireland that no woman likes an untattooed man, and vice versa.[1] Certainly it is anticipated that lack of tattoo marks will be cause for shame; the individual will feel self-abased, and to a desire to avoid such emotions, the act must be attributed. Attempts to push inquiries further met with some little success in the case of investigations in Fiji, by Sir Basil Thomson,[2] who says that shortly before puberty every Fijian girl was tattooed. The operation was not carried out merely for the sake of ornament, because the decorations were limited to a broad horizontal band in parts, covered by the " liku." The operation is still often carried out by three old women, two of whom hold the patient, while a third uses the fleam. The patient lies on mats outside the door of the hut, and the horizontal band tattooed consists of an intercrossing of parallel lines and lozenges. The instrument used is a toothed comb, which has been dipped in oil and charcoal contained in a cocoanut shell. The operation must be performed when all men are absent in the fields, and a ceremonial feast is given by the girl's parents. In some instances there is in addition to the tattooing of a horizontal band round the middle, the marking of barbed lines and dots on the fingers of young girls, so that the ornamental marks may be displayed to advantage when handing food to chiefs. G. Brown states that

[1] " Melanesians and Polynesians," G. Brown, 1910.

[2] " The Fijians, a Study of Decay of Custom," Basil Thomson, 1908, p. 217, and A. B. Brewster, " The Hill Tribes of Fiji," 1922, p. 185, etc.

tattooing of the buttocks has undoubtedly some hidden sexual significance. It is said to have been installed by the god Ndengei, and it is believed that in the last journey of the Shades an untattooed woman will be subject to various indignities. So there is secrecy during the operation, a ceremonial feast, a divine patron, and a belief in the advantage of tattoo marks after death. Fear of ridicule, and an anticipation of shame are the motives leading to tattooing, and should a girl refuse to receive the usual decoration her peculiarity would be whispered abroad, with the result that there would be great difficulty in securing a husband. In an attempt to get at the origin of the sexual superstition, this inquirer attempted to obtain on the Ra Coast some ancient chants sung in honour of the tattooing operation, but either the people had forgotten the songs, or they considered them unfit for repetition. Eventually a young man rendered an extremely lascivious ode in praise of tattooing, but in it there were no religious motives mentioned. Vaturemba, a chief in the Tholo hills, chuckled wickedly when questioned, and declared that physically there was the greatest difference between mating with a tattooed or an untattooed woman. The idea of marriage with an untattooed woman filled him with disgust, and he intimated that tattooing was considered as a stimulus to the sexual passion in the woman herself.[1]

In the Solomon Islands a girl is not sought in marriage until her charms have been enhanced by tattooing. This painful and tedious process is accom-

[1] "Living Races of Mankind," Hutchinson, Gregory and Lydekker, Vol. I, p. 37.

plished by a sorceress called "tindălo," or ghost, a name which appears to indicate that the operation is in some way connected with superstition, and a vague sense of awe. The operation is carried out to the accompaniment of musical instruments, and vocalists render a chorus from about sunset until sunrise, when the tattooing commences. Usually the patient suffers without a murmur, and the next day she has the joyful thought that she has entered the ranks of womanhood and is eligible for marriage. A husband who can pay well for his bride is secured, and when the marriage is solemnized the guests of the parents must include all those who helped to defray the cost of tattooing.[1]

Sometimes the body marking is performed after marriage or at child-birth, and among the Pima of North America,[2] also with the Niam-Niams of Africa there are these customs. Among the Pima both bride and bridegroom tattoo immediately after the marriage. In Formosa bride and bridegroom are tattooed by a priestess.[3] In Mabuiag the significance of marking the bride appears to be rather different, as it is more of the nature of a temporary ornament than an indelible mark, assumed also by the husband to express a bond of union. The Mabuiag bride blackens her skin all over before adding a red or white line along each side of the nose, then extends this marking over the eyebrow to the ear. The Benabendi husband shows affection for his wife by having her tattooed, and the practice is causing much competition

[1] "Childhood of Man," L. Frobenius, p. 36 (for parallel instances).

[2] A.B.E., 1904-5, pp. 161-2.

[3] "Among Head-Hunters of Formosa," J. B. Montgomery McGovern, 1922, p. 160.

and price-cutting among the operators.[1] For the Ainus the Rev. Batchelor, in "Ainus and their Folk-lore," says the mother impresses upon the daughter the necessity of being tattooed, but Mr. Landor says that sometimes the husband tattooes his wife shortly after marriage.[2] After child-birth the Fijian woman marks with a semicircular patch, which is tattooed at each corner of the mouth as an indication of matronly reserve; sometimes the patches are joined by lines following the curves of the lips.[3] Chukchee women mark their daughters of ten years or even younger by drawing a soot-coloured thread under the skin. Childless women tattoo on both cheeks three equidistant lines running all round the chin as a charm against continued sterility.[4] The Mtyopi men and women mark with a linear cheek decoration, which in the case of females denotes an abortive birth, also that the fœtus was a male.[5] Probably there is in this a survival of some ancient propitiatory rite, thought necessary when the natural course of events in pregnancy and child-birth was not followed. Toda women, at the time of child-birth, are obliged to undergo a ceremonial isolation with accompanying rites, which include marking of keloids on the wrist. During the fifth month of pregnancy the woman goes to live alone in a hut whose distance from the village is determined by the sacredness of the settlement. The

[1] L. Frobenius, "Childhood of Man," p. 63.

[2] "Hairy Ainu," S. Landor, p. 254.

[3] "The Fijians, a Study of Decay of Custom," Basil Thomson, 1908, p. 217.

[4] "Jesup Expedition to North Pacific," Vol. VII, p. 254.

[5] "Anthropological Notes on South African Coloured Mine Labourers," G. A. Turner, p. 73.

journey to the hut is made on the day of new moon, and when the woman has taken holy water, made by pouring it on the back of a calf, she holds a little bundle of threads in the fire until they are all aglow, then burns herself on the wrists.[1] In all, four marks are made, two on each hand, one at the base of the thumb, and another on the styloid process of the radius. Visiting relatives stand at a distance and ask whether the hand burning performance is accomplished. There seems in this and the isolation to be the use of body marking as part of a purification ceremony.

Miscellaneous Marks to Gratify Pride

Self-assertion, emulation, and pugnacity are all very evident among the men of a society where there is considerable competition for the honours of the chase, and the favours of the opposite sex. These emotions culminate in the formation of a complex sentiment of pride, which seeks permanently to record any social distinction obtained. And the record is made at times on the body of a child.[2]

The Motu murderer, who is about to be delivered to his enemies, assumes a coat of paint and spends his last night in revelry, while among the Koita a homicide is entitled to wear decorations which vary somewhat with the sex of his victim. For a man successfully done to death the homicide is allowed to wear a longitudinal line down the back, on each

[1] "Todas," W. H. R. Rivers, p. 313.
[2] "In Primitive New Guinea," J. H. Holmes, 1924, p. 86.

side of and about two inches from the middle line, also a design on the deltoid region of each upper arm, and a V-shaped marking on the chest and shoulders. The homicide is "aina," that is virtuous, set aside as dangerous when in contact with others, and for a time he must live alone in the forest. After seclusion there is a feast in his honour, and at this time an account of the exploit is given; it seems that this great credit is due to the secrecy with which the venture has been carried out.[1] At a dance formerly performed at a cannibal feast, where the enemies taken were cut up and eaten in order to get their virtues, youths painted their faces white, which was relieved by the addition of a dark line down the centre of the forehead, nose, and chin. Such marks are made probably as ornaments for the special occasion, temporary signs of satisfaction at the honour of dining off a victim, and so they differ considerably from the Koita tattoo which is a permanent badge to show individual merit.

A Sarawak Kayan who has taken the head of an enemy has the back of the hands and fingers covered with tattoo designs. If he has had only a share in the slaughter he will have a finger, or more generally a thumb tattooed. Theoretically, the Dyak who has committed a successful murderous attack on an enemy tattooes the backs of his hands, but in practice the custom is not merely confined to the brave, and observers Hose and McDougall frequently had occasion to note that a man with tattooed hands was a wastrel

[1] "Melanesians of British New Guinea," p. 130. D. Jenness and A. Ballantyne, "The Northern D'Entrecasteaux," 1920, p. 55.

and of no account with his own people.[1] Pryer notes that among the Dusuns, the men who took heads generally had a tattoo mark for each one taken; the marks made on the arm were looked upon as signs of bravery, though, as a rule, the heads were obtained in a most cowardly manner by the murder of a woman or child.[2] The recently published book "Papua," by the Lieutenant-Governor, Mr. Murray,[3] shows that many murderers are tried at Port Moresby, and no small number of these are people who have sought favours with the opposite sex by taking a head. A girl does not like a man who has done no deed of this kind, and, as in the case of the Dusuns and Kayans, it is considered a meritorious act to take the head of a defenceless person. Possession of the head of a woman or child rightly indicates great prowess, for it means that the head-hunter was within or very near to the inner defences of the hostile camp.

Dr. Haddon confirms these reports by stating that the Kayan design for head taking is a rosette at the back of the hand, and on more than one occasion Dr. Haddon was asked when he was going to have his hands tattooed; it seemed strange that one so wonderful in other ways should not have this simple sign of valour. The mark is made to show a woman that the murderer has courage to protect her, and a further stimulus to the act is the belief that in the next world those beheaded will become the slaves of the murderer. The demand for a human head at

[1] "Pagan Tribes of Borneo," Vol. I, pp. 247, 273. Also "British North Borneo," Owen Rutter, 1922, p. 335.

[2] J.A.I., Vol. XVI, p. 233.

[3] "Papua," J. P. Murray, London, 1912, p. 197.

some Kayan and Kenyah ceremonies is so great that the resident governor finds it convenient to keep one or two museum specimens for loan on these exciting occasions in order to prevent bloodshed.[1]

Concerning the tribes of the lower Mississippi,[2] there are body marks which are assumed only by warriors who are noted because of some famous enemy they have killed. The decoration commemorative of the fact is the design composed of a very great number of parallel red and blue lines on the abdomen. Figures of suns and serpents are imprinted on the bodies of warriors, as well as on chiefs and honoured men. Youths tattoo on the nose, but not elsewhere until they have performed some valorous act. When they have killed an enemy and brought back his scalp they have a right to have themselves tattooed, also to ornament themselves with figures suitable for the occasion. Those who have distinguished themselves have a war club on the right shoulder, and beneath this is the hieroglyphic sign of the conquered nation. Among the Poncas a father sometimes records his honours on the body of his daughter.[3] Captain F. R. Barton reports a similar practice in New Guinea, the recipient being the daughter of a successful voyager.[4] The designs tattooed are cosmic symbols, and frequently the mark of honour has reference to thunder and war. Among the Omaha the tattoo is not connected with war, but with achievements relating

[1] "Head-Hunters, Black, White, and Brown," Dr. A. C. Haddon, 1901, pp. 306-95.

[2] A.B.E. Bulletin, 1911, p. 56-7.

[3] A.B.E., 1905-6, 27th report, p. 219.

[4] J.A.I., 1918, p. 22, "Tattooing in South-East New Guinea."

to hunting and the maintenance of peace with other tribes. The Osages tattoo sacred pipe designs on the chest of the keeper of the sacred pipes, by means of which visions are obtained, and if the keeper has cut off heads in battle, the skulls of enemies are also represented by tattoo. These marks are to some extent honorific, but there was an explanation to the effect that tattooing the skull of a slain enemy on the body of the victor drew to the wearer all the strength and unexpended years of the foe, so that the tattooed man had his life lengthened by appropriating to himself the unexpired days of his enemy.

The tattooing of the Omaha girl with the cosmic symbols, sun and star, as a sign of her father's valour, is carried out with great ceremonial, which includes the erection of a scaffold and the assumption of a position facing the rising sun.[1] Two heralds stand at the door of the lodge and call the names of those who are to sing during the tattooing. These singers must be men who have received public war honours in the form of a round spot, representing the sun, in the middle of the forehead.[2]

The designs given in tattoo to a Ponca girl as honorific marks for her father's deeds are a star, a sun, and four small crosses. The whole design represents day and night as generative forces whose power is to be conferred upon the maiden. The marks have then a double function, for whereas the operation is to commemorate the honours of the parent, the designs are a plea for the perpetuation of all life, and human life in particular. At meetings

[1] A.B.E., 1905-6, p. 503

[2] *Ibid.*, p. 507.

of the Ho-hewachi, or society of honoured men, only those who have received war honours can beat the drum. Before a man could sing his song he had to relate his war honours, saying what they were, and for what deeds they had been publicly awarded. As a proof of the truth of what was being said the woman who had received his honorific marks came forward and danced. The credential entitling to the admittance of a man to the "Ho-hewachi" (or society of braves) was the right to tattoo on a maid certain cosmic symbols. M. Bossu states that in his time (1756) there were tattoo marks as a sign of valour among the Osages,[1] and a man who assumed a mark to which he was not entitled had to submit to having it flayed out, a practice indicating that the honours were highly esteemed; neither was there any sign of the deterioration in importance which may be observed in Borneo to-day.

Some years ago, before the Chukchee were as peaceful as they are to-day, a man who had killed a Russian or other enemy tattooed a dot on the back of his right wrist. For each similar performance a dot was added until these marks sometimes formed a line from the wrist to the elbow.[2] M. Lombroso notes among soldiers a tendency to commemorate an achievement by tattooing the date of a battle in which they had taken part, a very interesting adoption of an old-time custom.[3]

Very similar are the motives of self-assertion,

[1] M. Bossu, "The Osages," 1756, London, 1771, Vol. I, p. 164.

[2] "The Chukchee," "Jesup Expedition to North Pacific," Vol. VII, p. 254.

[3] Lombroso, 1895, "L'Homme Criminel," Vol. I, p. 268.

pride, pugnacity, and love of approbation which call for markings to distinguish the man who has shown skill in the chase.

The islanders of Torres Strait are distinguished by a large complicated oval scar only slightly raised and of neat construction. This design, which represents a turtle, occupies the right shoulder, and is occasionally repeated on the left.[1] It is probable that a young man was not allowed to bear a cicatrix until he had killed his first turtle or dugong. In modern times, among the maritime Chukchee, a man who has succeeded in killing his first whale, or polar bear, has a simple mark tattooed near every joint of his limbs.[2] Near Plover Bay the man whose ancestors had been great whale killers imprinted marks on a cover he owned; the design being representative of the flukes of the whale.[3] An earlier report states that among the Point Barrow Eskimo those men who have been captains of whaling umiaks,[4] and have taken whales, have somewhere on their persons marks to indicate these whaling exploits, while in particular cases the marks form an exact tally of the number of animals killed. For instance, "Anoru" had a broad band across each cheek from the corners of the mouth, made up of many indistinct lines, which were said to indicate many whales. Amaiyuna had the "flukes" of seven whales in a line across his chest, and another man had two small marks

[1] "Cambridge Expedition to Torres Strait," 1908, Vol. IV, p. 23.

[2] "Jesup Expedition to North Pacific," Vol. VII, p. 254.

[3] A.B.E., 1896-7, Part I, p. 322.

[4] *Ibid.*, 1887-8, p. 139.

on the forearm. Niaksara, the wife of Anoru, just mentioned for his whaling exploits, also had a little mark tattooed at each corner of her mouth, and these she said were "whale marks," indicating that she was the wife of a successful whale man—an interesting case of transferred honour not entirely unlike the instances of the North American warriors having war honours recorded by tattooing cosmic symbols on their daughters.

Marking of the Body on Admission to a Secret Society Illustrates the Anti-social Use of Tattooing

Few primitive people are unable to boast of the possession of a secret society into which the new members are initiated, often with abominable rites. And although in isolated instances such societies may punish evil-doers, they are in the main anti-social tyrannical organizations. West Africa is a hot bed of such institutions, and others are to be found in New Guinea and Melanesia generally, the "Duk Duk" being one of the most powerful. As membership of such a society is a title of respect, those who have been initiated sometimes adopt a particular body or facial mark which, on account of the power of the society, will not fail to induce in the tribesmen some degree of servility. Along with primitive secret societies can be considered any institutions which exist for purposes of brigandage, or the committal of political crimes.[1]

At the initiation of a man into the Donga thieving

[1] "Primitive Secret Societies," H. Webster, New York, 1908.

caste there is ceremonial bathing, also anointing, and cicatrizing of the tongue by burning. Shortly after the branding ceremony the patient is allowed a place in the general company, and he is obliged to partake of a ceremonial feast.[1] When a Badaga, who has been excommunicated from the caste, is received once more into the fellowship of the thieves his tongue is burned with sandal wood.

With the Kwakiutl all persons who have the same supernatural protector are grouped together in a secret society, during whose times of activity the natural families are disorganized, and there is a regrouping around spiritual guardians, including a cannibal spirit, a ghost, a grizzly bear, and a fool spirit. The ritual consists of a pretence to visit the abode of the spirit guardian, and there is a long pantomime display representing the adventures. During this ceremony facial paint is used by each member, who assumes designs which are supposed to be a portrayal of the particular patron spirit, and by these the members are allied one to another and to their spirit guardian.[2]

Three cuts on the breast of a Koranna man of Central South Africa indicated a kind of freemasonry, for he was a member of a secret society whose privilege it was to move over a large tract of country with safety, because of the scars which denoted membership of so powerful an organization. The man said : " I can go through all the valleys inhabited by Korannas and Griquas, and wherever I go, when

[1] Dr. Thurston, " Ethnographical Notes in Southern India," p. 402.

[2] " Totemism and Exogamy," Frazer, Vol. III, pp. 514, 517.

I open my coat and show them three cuts I am sure to be well received." [1] Among the Egba of North-West Central Africa, membership of the secret society is indicated by cuts on the cheek, the marks being of gridiron shape placed on each side of the face, and with regard to the number of the incisions,[2] it is noted that they are invariably arranged in threes or multiples of three. Newland states that too much importance has been attached to these secret society marks during legal inquiries.[3]

Initiation into the secret society of the Ojibwa Indians is accomplished in several successive stages, each of which is denoted by the assumption of a particular colour of paint.[4] The man who wishes to become a member of the ghost society first paints one red stripe across the face from near the ears to the tip of the nose, and a similar band is added across the eyes, temples, and the root of the nose. The upper half of the face is painted green and the lower half red, while green is also used for the forehead and the left side of the face. Finally four spots of vermilion are made with the tips of the fingers upon the forehead and the green surface of the left cheek. After this ceremonial painting the novice is a fully fledged member of the Ojibwa ghost society.

There is now considerable tattooing among the lower classes of the West Indies. The " Nañigo," a

[1] Dr. Holub, J.A.I., Vol. X, August, 1880, p. 7.

[2] " Living Races of Mankind " by Hutchinson, Gregory and Lydekker, p. 368.

[3] " Sierra Leone, its People, Products, and Secret Societies," H. O. Newland, 1916, p. 177.

[4] A.B.E., 1888-9, p. 627.

cut-throat secret society of Cuba,[1] had each member marked on the biceps of the arms, and for modern reversions to the primitive practice of body marking to show membership of such a society, the pages of M. Lombroso's report may be consulted.[2]

Many Cammoristes of Naples bear a tattoo mark which represents a grating, behind which is a prisoner, and above this the initials Q.F.Q.P. (*quando Finiranno queste pene*). Another man, in addition to the design of a grating and prisoner, had the motto " Courage galeriens, pour voler et piller, nous devons tout mettre à sang et à feu." Another Cammoriste had tattooed on himself two keys united by chains. Yet another member of the secret society of anarchists had the tattooed design of a serpent, and on the arm a mysterious alphabet, a kind of secret code used for correspondence among the Cammoristes. In Barière, also in the South of Spain, there is a secret society whose members are known to one another by tattooed epigrams, such as " c'est à due," " Y and L," words which they exchange in a low voice when they meet. One man informed M. Lombroso that in this particular band there were ranks of office, the importance of which was denoted by the extent of the tattooing. " Plus nous sommes tatoué, plus il a d'autorité sur ses compagnons." " Au contraire celui qui n'est pas bien tatoué ne jouit d'aucune influence—il n'a pas l'estime de la compagnie." [3]

By some operation of a law of contrast, tattooing instead of being an honorific mark has been given to

[1] A. T. Sinclair, " American Anthropologist," Vol. XI, 1909, p. 362.

[2] " L'Homme Criminel," Vol. I, p. 273.

[3] Lombroso, pp. 285, 286, 289.

produce in the recipient a feeling of shame, a somewhat complex mental state, involving a conception of oneself in relation to others, but essentially built up on the primary emotion of negative self-feeling.

During the days of unqualified native rule in Burma,[1] an offender was often led about mounted on an ass, with the name of his crime tattooed in blue on his forehead. Under the authority of Burmese kings incorrigible offenders were tattooed on the cheek with a circle, or perhaps they were marked across the chest with the title of the offence.

Cocheris states[2] that there has been a practice of tattooing criminals in France, England, and Russia. In Japan those who were convicted of having robbed to the extent of a hundred francs were marked with a cross, and for each additional crime a similar tattoo mark was added, so that when brought for trial it was known to what extent a prisoner had been convicted in the past. Mr. B. H. Chamberlain[3] outlines the uses of tattooing as an honorific mark in the early days of Japanese national life, but adds that, "from the dawn of history to the Middle Ages the marking was confined to criminals." W. W. Rockhill reports meeting a Chinese criminal wearing the cangue,[4] and tattooed on the left temple with an account of his crime.[5] With the dawn of Western civilization tattooing fell into very great disrepute, and was prohibited by law; nevertheless

[1] "Things Indian," Wm. Crooke, p. 463.
[2] "Les Parure Primitives," Cocheris, p. 39.
[3] "Things Japanese," B. H. Chamberlain, p. 399.
[4] A heavy wooden yoke.
[5] "Diary of a Journey through Mongolia and Tibet," Washington, 1894, p. 58.

it flourished among bravadoes, who tattooed on the chest some scene of blood and thunder to give them a terrifying aspect when fighting. In conclusion of the paragraph on tattooing as a means of preserving order by appealing to the instinct of self-abasement, here is a reference to an incident which occurred at the Old Bailey early in April, 1913. Three men who had previously been deported returned, succeeded in evading the authorities who supervise alien immigration, and were subsequently tried for theft. The judge passed sentence and added: "I hope before the prisoners get out that there will be an act passed so that men shall be marked when ordered to be deported, not in a way to damage their appearance, but in some part of the body where it can be known at once." [1]

Historical stories including tales of national heroes, also mythology, have power to appeal to man's emotions, which are excited time after time as the narrative is read and re-read, for during each perusal there is an act of reproductive imagination, which conjures up images of scenes and people as the narrative proceeds. Thus, in course of time, permanent sentiments are engendered toward some particular story or song. Such sentiments have at times found expression in tattooing, and M. Cocheris[2] states that some Japanese designs bear special reference to stories of history, Japanese legends, and classical mythology. Mr. Risley,[3] dealing with the

[1] See also "Natives of Sarawak," Ling Roth, 1896, Vol. II, p. 92. Example of Coward's tattoo.

[2] "Les Parures Primitives," Cocheris, p. 53.

[3] "Man," July, 1902.

tattooing of a piece of Dôm mythology, gives some interesting details. King Harris Chandra was so generous that he gave all he had to the poor and sold himself to a Dôm at Benares, who employed him to watch his cremation ground at night. While thus engaged his wife, who had also been sold, came to cremate the body of her son, but as she had no fees, and the darkness prevented Harris Chandra from recognizing her, she was turned away. Presently the sun arose, the woman returned and was recognized, while Vishnu appeared and restored the son to life.

This little narrative appeals to the Dôms so much that they show their appreciation of it by tattooing the whole of the scene on their bodies in two pictures. The first scene shows Harris Chandra standing guarding the pyre, while near him is the Ganges, represented by a wavy line, and some trees indicated by dots. Scene two shows a large rising sun, the Ganges, trees, and in addition, standing between two heaps of logs, are Harris Chandra and his wife hand in hand. The technique is as crude as can be, but the case is very interesting as an illustration of the use of tattooing to give expression to sentiments, which are formed by the play of imagination in following a story appealing to the innate emotion of tenderness.

In New Zealand there prevailed at one time a horrible practice of taking a slave's head and tattooing it for sale, almost a unique example of the use of "Moko" as a means of profit.[1] The Takelma of South-West Oregon tattoo their girls on the left arm with a series of short parallel marks, which are used for

[1] "Moko," Robley, p. 24. Frontispiece, this work, tattoo on forehead may be post mortem.

the purpose of measuring off strings of shell money.[1] M. Cocheris[2] mentions the tattooing of the mother and her infant when the birth has taken place in a Paris hospital, so that there is the chance of tracing the parent in case of infanticide or desertion. The same author gives instances of a man tattooing his last will and testament on his chest, which is a practice similar to the marking of sailors who wish that the body, if washed ashore, shall be buried with suitable honours. A strange case of utilitarian scarification is reported by A. Werner.[3] It appears that the Makua of British Central Africa make a series of cuts above the eyes deep enough to form little pouches in which snuff is kept.

An appropriate closure to the section dealing with magico-religious aspects of body marking should, after summarizing observations, endeavour to explain the practices of tattooing in the light of psychological and sociological considerations. Comparison of primitive man's views and practices in the body marking art with other activities shows a satisfactory congruity of thought and purpose.

The Levy Bruhl[4] and other writers would deny the logic of primitive man, but in the data relating to magico-religious beliefs we have shown that in approaching a supreme being or supra-human force, likewise in appeasing ghosts or placating demons of disease and pain, corporal markings are part of a

[1] J.A.I., April, 1907, p. 264.

[2] "Les Parure Primitives" by M. Cocheris, p. 61.

[3] "Natives of British Central Africa," London, 1906, p. 39.

[4] "Les Fonctions Mentales dans les Sociétés Inférieurs," Paris, 1910.

system of ideas in general congruous. Burial of red ochre with the deceased, reddening of skeletons, and similar practices in prehistoric times may rightly be regarded as the earliest attempts to secure continuity of existence and rejuvenation by blood symbols. Long before the dawn of history, possibly in the period preceding the first wide dispersal of man, a strong magico-religious system of ideas had centred around the use of pigments as an aid to solving the problem of continued existence after death.

With the march of time concepts became more clearly defined, though in general, action of a magico-religious nature resulted from impelling ideas which scarcely advanced beyond the subconscious. Originators of new ideas have been few, but to these are due the world's advance in social, religious, and political doctrine. Probably there is a "psychic unity," not in the sense of a factor responsible for numerous similar inventions widely disparate in time and area, but in the sense of a unity of emotion which accounts for rapid adoption of an idea that solves some difficulty such as acquisition of immortality, passage through the crisis of puberty, or securing immunity from pain and sickness.

SUMMARY OF CHAPTERS I, II, AND III

Is it possible to explain man's ready adoption of body marking practices with their attendant beliefs and ritual by postulating a common emotional basis? Probably a consensus of opinion favours the monogenetic theory of man's origin, and correlated with evolution of a nervous system and its muscular co-ordination there would be an undifferentiated emotional basis. There is no universal acceptance of the meaning of the term "instinct," and psychologists are not in agreement respecting the primary emotions and the manner in which these have contributed to the formation of complex sentiments, with their appropriate social expression in the form of institutions and ideas.

Prehistoric archæology makes clear that man, during prehistoric ages, was attempting to give concrete expression to his emotions by certain methods of burial, use of pigments, and mural paintings. Material evidence and inference suggest a common basis of emotion and thought which later became modified, and specialized in well-known areas of characterization, from which migratory waves travelled extensively, hence practices, among people who are ethnologically and geographically disparate, are facts suggestive of the likelihood of dispersal, as opposed to the theory of repeated independent evolution.[1] Associations of body marking with various aspects of

[1] Sollas, "Ancient Hunters," second edition, p. 234. Elliot Smith, "Evolution of the Dragon," "Migration of Early Culture," etc.

human culture and endeavour have been detailed in Chapters I, II, and III, and there remains only the task of a brief presentation of summarized facts with some comment on social and psychological dynamic factors.

Ideas Concerning Deity, Heaven, and a Spirit Life Apart from the Body.—Aztecs painted and cicatrized in connection with their worship. The North American Indian, so it was thought, would be searched for his tattoo marks by the spirit guarding the way to the many lodges, and death paint showing the clan marks is needed to ensure recognition. The Ekoi in a spirit world would barter keloids for food. Men of the Egyptian Middle Empire assumed tattoo marks associating themselves with the goddess Neith. There are many Dravidian women who believe that they will be ill-treated by Parameshwar if found in the spirit world without tatto marks. Branded marks dedicate girls to temple service. Painted stripes indicate adherence to Vishnu or Siva. The Ainu woman is threatened with forcible tattooing in the spirit world if she neglects it here. Tattoo marks ensure recognition of Naga women by their husbands in heaven. Only Kayan women who are tattooed will be able to pick up pearls in the bed of the sacred river. Fijian women who are untattooed will be dragged through thorns. Such are a few of the instances detailed in previous pages to show a relationship between body marking and survival after death.

References to a divine origin of body marking were given for North America, and instances of gods teaching the use of paint were quoted. The Ponca invite the sun to judge of the chastity of a maid receiving tattooed war symbols of her father. The Pawnees dedicate their babies to the sky god with much painting and colour symbolism. The Andaman Islanders were taught the use of paint by a goddess. In like manner were the Ainus taught to tattoo their women, and in Fiji and Samoa there are legends of divine origin of tattooing. In the Solomons tattooing is in the hands of a " tindālo " or ghost. Priests or priestesses tattoo, the former in Samoa, the latter in Formosa. The tattooing of a Maori chief was a sacred rite carried out by priests who observed sacrifice and taboo.

Totemism,[1] has a religious as well as a social aspect, and body marking with totemic devices may be looked upon as a form of ancestor worship which identifies the individual with his group, and its spiritual precursors who have assumed animal form. There is totemic body marking in North America (tattoo), Australia (by painting), Torres Strait (by cicatrizing). Body marking certainly has a definite connection with totemism, and the geographical distributions may be compared by consideration of the accompanying map. Wundt marks the function of painting and tattooing in connection with totemism.[2]

Puberty, Marriage, and Fertility of Women are intimately connected with tattooing by puncture in North America, South America, India, New Guinea,

[1] For distribution see map. Frazer's " Totemism and Exogamy," Vol. IV, and this work, p. 25.

[2] " Elements of Folk Psychology," translation, E. L. Schaub, London, 1916.

Fiji, New Zealand, and the whole Pacific. In Africa cicatrization is essential for the marriageability of girls in most tribes, and in some instances important ritual and taboo survive, of which the following is typical: " The girls are cut on the back and loins in such a manner as to leave raised scars. They then receive the 'Boondoo' names, and after recovery from the painful operation are released from Boondoo with great ceremony and gesticulation by some who personate Boondoo devils with hideous masks."[1] Chin tattooing of women has a wide distribution in India, Japan, Egypt, Arabia, New Guinea, New Zealand, Alaska, California, Greenland. Marquesan women like those of Eastern Bedouin Arabs tattoo their lips with a gridiron pattern in a tint like blue-black writing ink.[2]

Tribal and Clan Distinctions are clearly indicated by body marking according to the three main methods. The American continents illustrate the use of puncture tattoo and painting for this purpose. Cicatrization subserves the same functions in Africa and Australia. Moko was tribal as well as personal and heraldic.

Social Status and Heraldry have been denoted by body marking in all parts of the world. The best examples are to be gleaned from North America, including the Aztecs, the Abipoines of Paraguay, Easter Island, Marquesas, Tahiti, New Zealand, Borneo and Samoa. Tattoo by puncture is the form

[1] Griffith, " Sierra Leone," J.A.I., February, 1887, p. 309.

[2] F. W. Christian, " Eastern Pacific Islands," 1910, p. 197. For map of chin tattoo see A. W. Buckland, J.A.I., Vol. XVII, 1888.

of marking most frequently and definitely associated with social position and lineage. A statement relating to Kayan tattooing is one which well describes the social importance of the practice in all parts of the world. Nowadays class restrictions as regards tattoo are not so closely observed, but it is always possible to distinguish between the designs of a chief's daughter, an ordinary free woman, and a slave by the number of lines composing the figures of the designs, the fewer these lines the lower the rank of the woman. Moreover, the designs of the lower class women are not nearly so complex, and they are generally tattooed freehand.[1]

Head-Hunting shows a clear line of coincidence with tattooing by puncture. The associated customs have the strongest union along the coast of Eastern Asia from Formosa through the Philippines and Borneo to New Guinea. In this region the records of homicides are kept by tattooed stars or other devices. Passing northward the practice has affected the Chukchee and Eskimo, who record their prowess by tattooed lines and dots. In the latter case skill relates to whaling, not to capture of human heads. Certain North American Indians confer their war honours on a daughter by tattooed symbols, and themselves assume the tattoo marks of a conquered foe as insignia of prowess and social status.

Mourning Ceremonies have been and are still accompanied in most parts of the world, among uncivilized and semi-civilized people, by gashing and painting. There is no doubt that these practices

[1] "Pagan Tribes of Borneo," Vol. I, p. 255.

result from fear of ghosts and a desire to propitiate possible malignant spirits.

The Medicine Man is ubiquitous in primitive society, and wherever his operations are in progress we find him with appropriate painted garbs for dealing with wind, rain, comets, eclipses, revenge on an enemy, diagnosing cause of death, detecting crime, visiting the spirit world, or grappling with the demon of disease.

As a General Amuletic and Prophylactic practice tattooing by puncture has a wide distribution for avoiding the evil eye, curing rheumatism and defective eyesight, attracting women, making weapons glance off; and among belligerent and criminal classes puncturing designs expresses crude emotions and sentiments.

Captain James Cook remarked: " The universality of tattooing is a curious subject for speculation." I do not think that any investigator would claim that tattooing by puncture is a simple and obvious practice which might reasonably be expected to occur spontaneously in a large number of widely separated areas. The elaborate beliefs, taboos, and ritual associated with this craft lend support to a belief that we must look for a centre of origin, and lines of migration, together with creative causes and dynamic social and psychological forces which shall adequately account for facts of wide dispersal and long survival.

There can be no doubt concerning some fundamental activities of the human mind from long before the dawn of the historical period. Such activities have, I think, centred around problems of nutrition, fecundity, and that elusive something which distinguishes a corpse from a thinking, willing, self-directing being. The intimate and widespread connection of body marking with fundamental thought processes of individuals and societies has been discussed in preceding pages. The relationship of body marking to a supernatural being; to totemism (which has a nutritional aspect); with puberty; marriageability and fecundity of women; also with tribal and clan distinctions, social status and heraldry; likewise with head-hunting, ghosts, medicine men and their magic, all constitute the social and psychological factors of our problem.

There was no doubt a definite reason for the invention of each form of body marking. Scarifying was originally therapeutic with subsequent borrowing of ideas from painting and tattooing. That painting first symbolized life, fertility and preservation after death, is clear from archæological evidence discussed in Chapter VI. The numerous examples of marked female figurines from prehistoric sites in Egypt suggest the association of body marking with a fertility cult which persists all over the world to-day in the marking of women at puberty. Initiatory rites for boys and girls are always accompanied by painting or tattooing, perhaps both. And what are these puberty rites but the insignia of arrival at a state of manhood or womanhood with consequent possibilities of reproduction? Palæolithic man of Europe employed red ochre as a blood symbol typifying life and regeneration. From these basic ideas of marking to assist fertility and continued existence, other beliefs and practices have originated by conscious creation and transfer, while migration has everywhere been assisted by Polynesian wanderings and pearl fishery. These wanderers may be "Divine" originators to which native legends and myths refer. Long after the original import of marking has been forgotten, the practice is accepted with conviction without logically adequate grounds for such acceptance. Continuing our hypothetical reconstruction of the dynamic force of body marking in a developing social system we may say that totemic marking is closely allied with fertility cults of animals which provide a food supply; with a vague idea of continued existence after life in this world; and the use of red ochre to assist the process was followed by more concrete ideas of heaven and a deity. At each stage painting and tattooing played their part in giving the concrete and tangible proofs of ability to enter heaven, or alliance with a superhuman being. In this connection there developed the practice of painting and scarifying to appease ghosts of the deceased.

The medicine man and his marking give a number of definite subsidiary ideas arising from the basic concepts of fertility and survival after death. Thus we have paint to assist in rain-making, preparing love charms, and exorcising demons of disease.

In areas of Assam, inhabited by Naga tribes, also among the Kayan of Borneo, are seen an association of beliefs in connection with tattooing which give a clear idea of the unity of original concepts. Successful head-hunting, possibly a form of blood-sacrifice, is necessary for fertility of the land and marriageability. Tattooing distinguishes the successful head-hunter and marriageable woman, while in both areas women are said to be recognized and privileged in heaven because of their marking. On the social side in many parts of the world there are family, clan, tribal, secret society, and personal markings with special designs and elaborations for persons of high rank. In cases where tattooing is completed at puberty, the operation is commenced at a much earlier age, and there is in Africa at any rate definite evidence to show that tribal marking was formerly carried out during the first few months of infancy. In Polynesia chiefs are held to be of divine origin, and the tattooing is elaborate in technique, ceremonial, and precaution. All this evidence respecting the social importance of tattooing and painting gives the impression that corporal marking is the visible sign of the history of human society from the family onward in growing complexity.

Here one idea will survive, and there another, or perhaps two or three ideas exist in unison with definite rites, taboos, and explanations. All of these points have been elaborated in the preceding chapters which show clearly how, in appealing to fundamental concepts and thought processes, likewise by ministering to social requirements, the migration of body marking customs has been rendered possible.

The question of dispersal from a centre, in which a few fundamental ideas were developed and elaborated from crude palæolithic and neolithic concepts allied with painting and tattooing, forms the subject of Chapter VI.

CHAPTER IV

TECHNIQUE OF BODY MARKING

Artistic taste—Development of symmetry and proportion—The naturalistic school of tattooing—Growth of æsthetic sense.

THE present chapter is a consideration of the technique of body marking apart from cognate anthropological problems. One realizes that the specialized nature of puncture tattooing, combined with the occurrence of identical beliefs, ritual, and restrictions of a peculiar kind in connection with the art, at widely separated points, are sufficient guarantee of the spread of the custom, as opposed to the one-time idea of evolution along similar lines from disparate origins. There should perhaps be the admission that hypotheses relating to migration of culture do not find support from the technique of tattooing in widely separated regions, though the borrowing of patterns locally is beyond question, and may be seen to-day in the transfer of designs from South-East to Western New Guinea. "Tattooing is not a custom of Western New Guinea," says W. N. Beaver. "But now and again one sees men, who have spent years in other parts of New Guinea, come back to their own parts with a series of tattoo marks." [1] This is corroborated by Holmes.[2] The

[1] "Unexplored New Guinea," 1922, p. 169.

[2] J. H. Holmes, "In Primitive New Guinea," 1924, p. 84.

frigate bird pattern and its derivative, the chevron, are widespread in the Pacific, but the ultimate products evolved from these are numerous and distinctive.

Apart from chin tattooing of women, the technique of this art does not help considerably in mapping lines of distribution over widely separated countries, for patterns have developed very distinctively in many areas. A technologist might urge the cause of independent evolution by stressing disparity of style and *modus operandi*. But the dependence of style on biotic factors such as plant and animal life, and the consequent development of such distinctive schools as the Moko of New Zealand, Samoan tattoo, Japanese, Burmese, Haida, and Bornean styles, leading to great disparity of motive and design, should not be disregarded. So far as migration is concerned, the main point is the presence of the craft itself, and its alliance with concepts and practices of a kind not likely to arise repeatedly by independent processes of thought.

An investigator should not, however, overlook the comparative side of the tattooer's art, but the personal equation is a troublesome factor. I have always seen in Marquesan circular designs, as shown by Von Langsdorf,[1] a resemblance to involutes and other forms of Moko. Christian appears to be impressed with the differences.[2] Petrie and Myers do not agree with regard to resemblances between modern Egyptian tattoo marks and those of North Africa.[3] The scroll work on thighs of Kayan women

[1] "Voyages and Travels," London, 1813. This work, p. 61.
[2] "Eastern Pacific Islands," p. 93.
[3] J.A.I., 1903, p. 84.

is an incipient Moko with incomplete spirals and curves. It is interesting to note in this connection that the Polynesians passed along the cost of Borneo from whence they voyaged to Oahu in the Sandwich Islands about 450 A.D. St. Johnston states that there is a resemblance between Motu designs given in Haddon's "Evolution of Art," and letters inscribed on an ancient stone column of Asoka in Northern India.[1] The "breeches tattoo" for women has been noted in New Zealand, Easter Island, Marquesas, and Tonga, while in Samoa the men have such a design still tattooed though covered by the "liku."[2] The chevron, possibly derived by bisecting the frigate bird design, has a wide vogue in the Pacific, being employed to the exclusion of every other mark, in tattooing covering the entire body of a Gilbert Islander, figured by Joest.[3] Long marks on the phalanges of women in Samoa and the Liu Kiu Islands (north of Formosa) are idential in form, and in the latter case are extended to denote increase in age.[4] There are many undeniable sun designs in modern Egyptian tattooing; painted cosmic symbols occur in Australia including sun designs for the sun totem men; tattooed and painted cosmic symbols including suns are found in North America; but one

[1] Percy S. Smith, "Memoirs of Polynesian Society," Vol. IV. "Life of Whare Wananga," 1915, and "Hawaiki," 1921, p. 283. Also "Islanders of the Pacific," T. R. St. Johnston, 1921, p. 83.

[2] Marquardt, "Tatowirung in Samoa," 1899. Beechey, "Narrative of Voyage in the Pacific," 1827. Tasman's description of Tonga, 1642, see "Savage Island," B. Thomson, p. 91.

[3] Joest, "Die Tatowirung," 1887, etc.

[4] "Cruise of Marchesa," F. H. H. Guillemard, 1889, p. 29. Capt. Basil Hall, "Voyage of Alceste and Lyra," and Beechey's "Narrative of Voyage in Pacific," 1827.

could not trace out a migrating line of tattooed suns without pressing into service many vague circular marks of unknown identity. The Bena Luba and Baluba have a form of cicatrization quite different from that of other African peoples. The parallel lines round the mouth correspond to chin tattooing of women in several parts of the world.[1] The involute has a curious and presumably fortuitous resemblance to common Moko patterns.

The evidence collated in these pages leaves the impression of an origin of tattoo in prehistoric times from painting; the association of these practices with magical beliefs, ceremonials, and taboos, also a development in cultural centres and spread from thence over the whole world. But the evidence is unequivocal respecting evolution of designs and instruments along peculiar lines in isolated centres. Belief and ritual have persisted with little alteration, technique has been influenced by local conditions including plant and animal life, geometric forms in everyday use, and the innate aptitude for artistic success. Proficiency depends on co-ordination of hand and eye, appreciation of form, colour, spatial relationships, patient perseverance, and numerous physical and psychological factors which could be unravelled only by a lengthy discussion and analysis.

Probably the consideration of body marking in its æsthetic aspects is of less interest to the ethnologist than to the student of comparative art. A study of æsthetic values is carried out with some facility as the observer is concerned with externals only, and there is no question of extracting information respecting

[1] See "Moko" by Robley, and "Man," Torday, January, 1913.

hidden significance, taboo, ceremonial, and other points.

For the space of a chapter the present inquiry is concerned with purely technological problems; but these cannot, of course, be wholly divorced from psychological considerations relating to sensory perceptivity and its possible racial variations. According to experiments among Todas,[1] Veddas,[2] and islanders of Torres Strait [3] norms of sensory perceptivity are much the same for several primitive races and civilized man. But such work within the realm of experimental psychology has not advanced sufficiently to warrant a dogmatic statement respecting questions of æsthetic sense in various branches of the human family.

A step preliminary to the inquiry into use of body marking as an ornament should be the arrangement of examples in three classes: (1) The crudest of all in which there are no underlying principles to guide a community, but each individual is instructed to make a few marks which are sanctioned by custom. Form and colour are unstudied, and the single aim is to make the individual conform to the practices of his social group. (2) There is a stage which one may term the "geometrical" which reaches its acme of excellence in the "Moko" of New Zealand, though it has some very fair exponents in the Congo region. (3) There is a phase where man recognizes underlying principles of form, colour and perspective. What is more, there is the giving of motion to animal

[1] Rivers, "The Todas," 1906.
[2] Seligman, "Veddas of Ceylon," 1906.
[3] "Cambridge Expedition to Torres Strait," 1898.

forms which are displayed with the most minute accuracy.

Following upon this there is for the anthropologist considerable interest in a review of the factors, social and psychological, which combine to form a permanent artistic style and what is still more complex, there arises the debatable question of man's power to transmit to offspring self-acquired skill. In a word, suppose a Japanese artist spends a lifetime in artistic work and so develops a neuro-muscular basis which guarantees excellence, can this be transmitted to his offspring? Must the child rely solely on his own individual education? What part does heredity play? and to what extent is environment responsible for artistic productions? Such problems are, however, outside the scope of this chapter which deals with quality, convention, subject, motive, motion, and other items with regard to which divergent styles of any artistic product may be compared.

Primitive Artistic Taste

Feathers, shells, and nowadays brilliantly coloured prints are highly prized as ornament, but when feathers are scarce a few spots of paint will suffice to gratify the desire for self-assertion. A native of the Port Moresby district will apply a few spots of paint to his nose, chin, and cheek-bones, when going ashore with his white master to visit a strange village, his desire being to impress the strangers he is visiting, and to direct some amount of admiration toward himself.[1] For any social event, such as a dance, there is a crude ornamentation adopted in response to a desire to stand well in the estimation of those present, and the absence of all ceremony, also the free choice of colour, and the method of its application seem to indicate that the colour is assumed for no reason other than that of gratifying a self-regarding sentiment. Favourite colours among the Mafulu people are red, greyish yellow, and black, and the staining of the face is usually of a very simple character. One side may be yellow, the other grey, to which spots of red are added.[2]

Body marking of all kinds is common among the Indians of South America, and for Guiana there is evidence of very crude ornamental painting.[3] The Savannah Indians favour red paint, the Forest Indians carmine, while the use of white and yellow clay mixed with natural oils and resins is widespread. The colouring is applied either in masses or patterns, and the adoption of a pattern may be looked upon as a step forward in the evolution of the art of body marking. A man who wants to dress really well will give his feet and ankles a coat of red, the trunk will be coloured blue-black, or perhaps adorned with intricate patterns of black and red, and over the place from which the eyebrows have been removed he will paint red arcs. Ackawoi women are extremely fond of brilliant face paint, and a blue-black band is usually painted round the edge of the mouth, also from the corners of the mouth to the ears.

[1] Seligman, "Melanesians of British New Guinea."

[2] Williamson, "Mafulu Mountain People of New Guinea," pp. 41, 42, 220.

[3] "Among the Indians of Guiana," Sir E. I. M. Thurn, p. 196.

Fuegians, like Andamanese, have a colour code which expresses emotional states in detailed accuracy.

Although the art of tattooing proper made great advance in North America especially among the Haida, the Dené, and others, painting never lost ground as a means of ornament, or as an expression of emotions connected with magico-religious observances. With regard to the Kwakiutl, Professor Boas says,[1] the people paint the face and especially the eyebrows with small sticks, after first applying a coat of greased red ochre. A black fungus yields a dark pigment, which, mixed with gum, makes a cosmetic protection against sunburn. If none of the fungus is available, ochre or charcoal is used instead. Warriors smear their faces with tallow, over which they rub coal made of soft red cedar, then they polish until the paint begins to shine. Finally they wet the tip of the little finger and use it to imprint designs by scratching lines on the background of black paint. Painting the faces of the dead with clan totem marks is likewise practised among the Osages.

The Andamanese have for a long period been isolated in their small islands, and so one might turn to them in the expectation of finding a well preserved sample of ancient types of body marking; for when contact with other peoples is denied, there is no infusion of new ideas, and ancient customs are likely to be accurately preserved. Mr. Dobson speaks of a young man, evidently the dandy of the tribe, strutting about in full dress obviously very proud of himself on account of his attractive personal appearance. His full dress consisted of a coat of fresh

[1] "Jesup Expedition," Vol. V, Part II, p. 451.

olive-coloured paint on one side of the body and red on the other. Half his face was red, the other half olive, and the red paint on his body terminated in a festooned border along the chest and abdomen. Arms and legs were adorned in a similar way by a festooned border passing down the outer side of the legs, like the stripe down military trousers.[1] Mr. A. R. Brown believes that painting, though tending now to mere formality, has a real psychological function in keeping alive ideas and sentiments that will on occasion play an important part in influencing conduct.[2]

Here is still another example of this crude marking, which implies an adoption of some individual standard, there being at the time no evolved principles of art which must be followed by all members. For men of Yam and Tutu (Torres Strait) there is face painting which is quite unconventional, and limited only by the resources and ingenuity of the individual. The observers saw young men and girls with the two sides of the face painted in different colours, and symmetry in lines and dots was rarely observed. The people were always very proud of their decorations, and behaved in a serious manner though the effect was generally ludicrous to Europeans.[3]

These instances of crude markings as ornament in North and South America, Andaman Islands, Torres Strait and Melanesia, are grouped to illustrate the initial stage in the evolution of ornamental markings. Yet simple as this stage is, it involves a very important step in the advance of psychic development.

[1] "Andaman Islands," 1874, G. E. Dobson, p. 465.
[2] "Andaman Islanders," A. R. Brown, 1922, p. 275.
[3] "Cambridge Expedition to Torres Strait," Vol. IV, p. 29.

Individuality has asserted itself, and there is a free play of the emotions of self-assertion and emulation, which are closely connected with the sex instinct and the sentiment of love. Man has arrived at a stage when he is capable of adopting consciously or unconsciously a means of adding to sexual charms. Not only does such crude marking imply a considerable advance of thought, but it also involves and illustrates the very first step in the evolution of geometrical designs which are at first quite unsymmetrical. The North American Indians of the Kwakiutl tribe trace patterns on their face paint with the forefinger; some Indians of Guiana apply the colour in masses, while others, who had probably observed animal markings, make some attempt at plastering the clay in more or less definite patterns. The Andaman Islander has some idea of completing the chest and abdominal designs by means of a festooned border, and an elementary notion of symmetry is apparent in the adoption of similar designs taking the form of side stripes for the legs. In many instances a curious want of balance is noticeable, and among Paumotuan figures are some in which half only of the body is tattooed.[1] Boggiani[2] shows a Paraguan Indian with two distinct patterns, one for each half of the face. The tattooed designs are elaborate and well executed but there is no balance. Moko, on the other hand, is a classic example of perfectly balanced curves and spirals.

[1] "Abbildungen zur Geschichte der Schrift," Heinrich Wuttke, Leipzig, 1873, Plate X.

[2] Boggiani Guido, "Viaggi d'un Artista nell America Meridionale," Rome, 1895, Fig. 78, p. 165.

An interesting reversal to unbalanced ornament occurred in the reigns of Charles I and Queen Anne. Many people decorated themselves with irregularly

Tattoo adopted by Women of the Tobas Tribe, West Central South America.

distributed patches in the form of owls, rings, crescents, crowns, and even a coach and horses.[1] Webb, Planché, and other writers on facial markings in England have extracted their information from Bulwer's "Artificial Changeling," published 1650.

[1] W. M. Webb, "Heritage of Dress," London, 1907, p. 279. Planché, "Encyclopædia of Costume," 1876, Vol. I, p. 388.

Development of Symmetry and Proportion

The second stage in the evolution of bodily decoration may be regarded as a development of the process of making symmetrical scratches on a coat of paint. Probably some accidental insertion of earth or other matter into a cut suggested the rubbing in of red ochre, or other substance such as charcoal, or gunpowder. The unsymmetrical stage of the ornamental process involves a relatively small degree of skill, for as the instances show, the colouring is applied in a most irregular way without any regard to a standard combination of colours. The spots and lines are usually applied without any idea of a symmetrical distribution. To make the wearer conspicuous is the sole end in view, and the modern buffoon resorts to the same technique. With the advance to a definite conception of geometrical forms, and the placing of these so as to give a proper balance, we are touching upon a process which involves no small amount of skill. In the first place there must be a preconceived plan, and what is more difficult than the planning of each part in relation to the whole, there is required a fine co-ordination of hand and eye, also a delicate muscular movement. These requirements cause the art of body marking to pass from each and every individual into the hands of specialists, who are usually of high social status and are well remunerated.

Within this section of body marking with geometrical designs, perhaps it is possible to arrange several examples in a gradually ascending series, taking as the criteria the regularity of the figures, the symmetry with which they are arranged, the extent of the surface covered, and the minuteness of detail.

It would be difficult to conceive of geometrical figures more simple than the tribal and ornamental marks of the Galla, whose designs are chiefly the rectangle, rhombus, parallel lines, crosses, concentric circles, and intersecting arcs, all of which must be classed among the elements of geometric designing.[1] The designs, though so simple, show a fairly advanced idea of symmetry, and in this respect they are to be contrasted with the marks of the Urabunna of Australia, whose tribal design is very simple and unsymmetrical. The design (if this term is permissible) consists of a number of cuts down each side of the spine, these being placed in a most irregular manner.

The marks of Ainu women are important because of the way in which they illustrate how ideas may be in advance of the powers of execution. The artist evidently had in mind a fairly complex pattern, produced by the winding of a narrow strip of bandage. The technical skill was so slight that the marks became confused when the worker forgot just where the overlapping of the bandage should be shown.[2]

To the Bushongo, too, one may turn for a fairly simple form of geometrical ornament, consisting of lozenge-shaped marks, the outlines of which are composed of numerous circular cicatrices.

The operator has made some attempt at a rhomboidal figure, which here and there is quite successfully executed. In other places the result is scarcely a

[1] See this work, p. 184.

[2] Savage Landor, "The Hairy Ainu," 1893, p. 253.

successful one, there being very little more than a confusion of circular keloids.

Other designs adopted by the Bushongo may be selected from a great quantity of material to illustrate

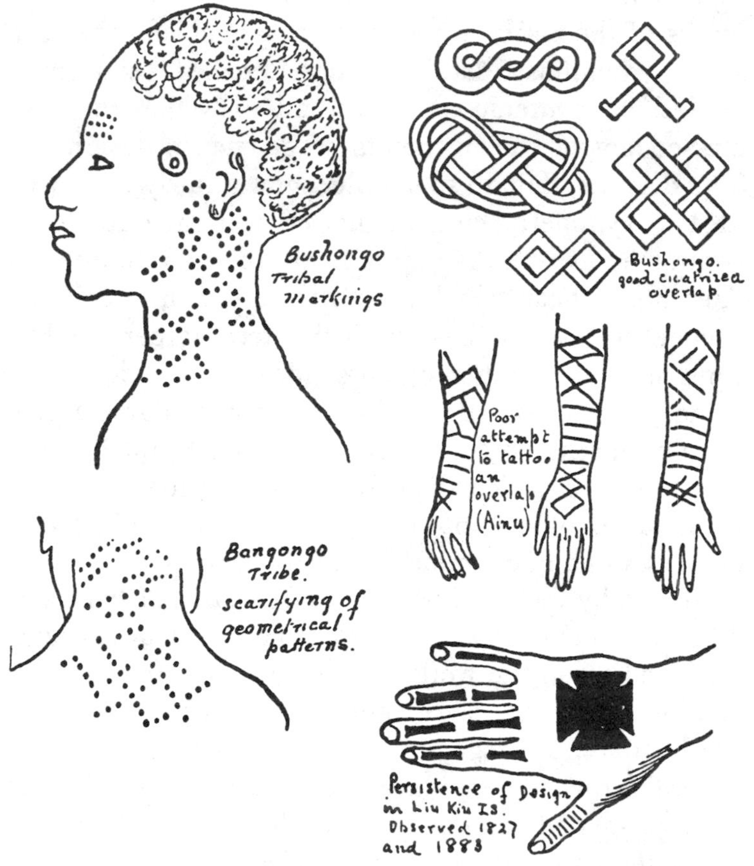

Simple Geometric Designs.

a very definite step in the evolution of geometrical marking, namely, the ability to represent with accuracy the overlapping and intertwining of geometrical figures, which, though simple in themselves, are not easy to combine artistically, with due observance of accuracy in representing the crossing and overlapping.

The Mekeo, Motu and Koita people of British New Guinea have a well-conceived idea of a variety of geometrical patterns, including the zigzag, triangle, and undulating marks of some regularity. The illustration given shows the breast and abdomen of a marriageable girl decorated with designs, which are arranged with perfect symmetry, although there is nothing elaborate in any particular mark. An enlargement of the V-shaped neck design, or "gado," assumed at marriage, shows how certain parts of the skin are left untattooed with very good effect in producing the formation of small triangles within the large triangular design.[1] A large part of the body is covered, and in no instance is there any irregularity in the placing of the patterns, for those of the left half of the body are in each instance balanced by precisely similar markings on the right. The tattoo assumed as an honorific mark by the Koita homicide is simple but effective, and it illustrated the worker's ability to depart from a geometrical figure, based on a combination of straight lines, in order to attack the more difficult task of representing well-balanced arcs, which, placed end on end, produce a regular undulating curve.

The Melanesians have copied their triangular designs from the beak of the hornbill, and not only are the derivatives applied to the body, but also to posts in club-houses as Dr. Seligman's sketches show.[2]

[1] Is the cross an addition due to Christian influence?

[2] "Melanesians of British New Guinea," Seligman, pp. 211, 237-8, 631.

Dr. Seligman speaks of the derivation of designs from the markings of the beak of the hornbill and the shape of dogs' teeth. Careful inquiry certainly shows that a considerable part of the ornamental and symbolic marking of the body is the outcome of careful observation of natural marks on the feathers of birds or the fur and hair of animals.[1]

In the case of these Melanesian markings on the body, also in ornamenting portions of club-houses and chiefs' dwellings, it is difficult to say whether the design was copied from the animal on to the wood of club-houses, and from there on to the human body. If technique is any guide, the designs were for some time practised on wood until some degree of proficiency was attained, then there arose the idea of transferring the markings to the body for purposes of personal ornament.[2]

Turning to the geometrical markings employed on hands, feet, and thighs by the Long Wai, and other Bornean people, it becomes evident that we have entered a field of research in which the skill in representing geometric patterns is on a plane much higher than any yet considered. The designs advance beyond a symmetrical arrangement of straight-lined figures, and on wrists and thighs there is a very considerable amount of scroll work of excellent quality, coming almost into effective competition with the best work the Maori can produce. The general effect of the scroll work is quite good, but when details are

[1] J.A.I., Vol. XLVIII, 1918, p. 22. "Tattooing in South-East New Guinea," Capt. F. R. Barton.

[2] "Evolution of Decorative Art." H. Balfour, "Conscious and Unconscious Variation in Copying." See "Melanesians of British New Guinea," Seligman, pp. 211, 237, 631.

considered there is not the precision and accuracy of the work found in Maori " Moko " designs, which are bolder, less involved, and more complete. One thinks of " Moko " of New Zealand as the Bornean attempts taken over and completed by a master hand.[1]

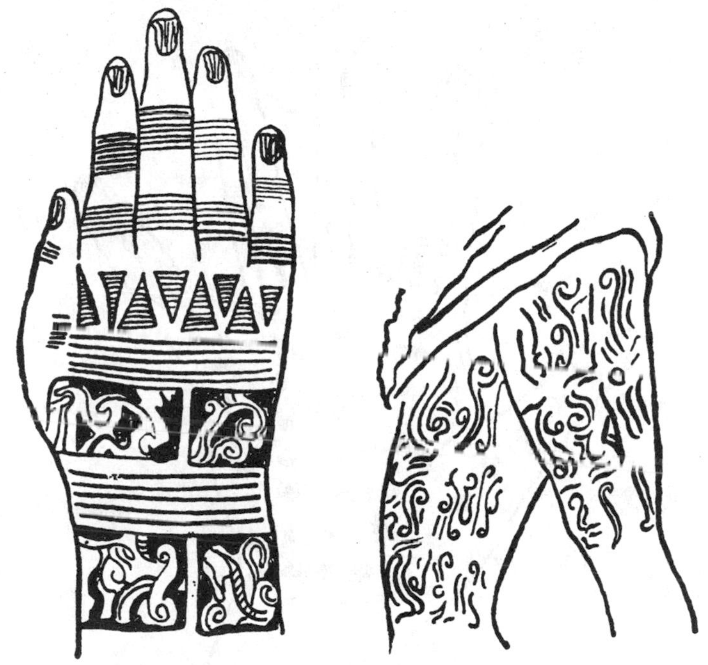

Tattoo Marks of Long Wai Women, Borneo.

The Kayan tattooing of hands is effective to an extraordinary degree, especially when one considers the simplicity of the units composing the designs. For usually there is nothing more elaborate than straight parallel lines, triangles, and some amount of scroll work.

The Maltese cross design (page 256) is notable for

[1] " Pagan Tribes of Borneo," Hose and McDougall, Vol. I, pp. 270 *et seq*. " Moko," Robley.

its exactness of outline, and still more remarkable for its persistence as an ornamental mark for women of the Liu Kiu Islands. In the "Cruise of the Marchesa," M. Guillemard mentions visiting the Liu Kiu Islands in 1883, and noting that the cross

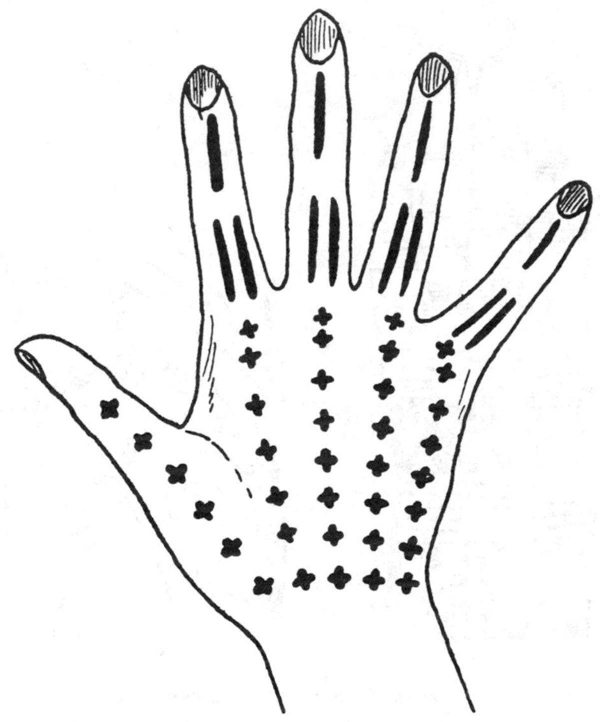

Hand Tattooing of Samoan Women.

was a favourite design, also that the marks on the phalanges varied in extent with the age of the individual.[1] The entire hand tattoo is not completed until marriage. M. Guillemard states that the design he noticed in 1883 is exactly described in Beechey's "Narrative of a Voyage in the Pacific" (1827).[2]

[1] Compare with tattooed phalanges of Samoan women.
[2] "Cruise of Marchesa," Guillemard, p. 39.

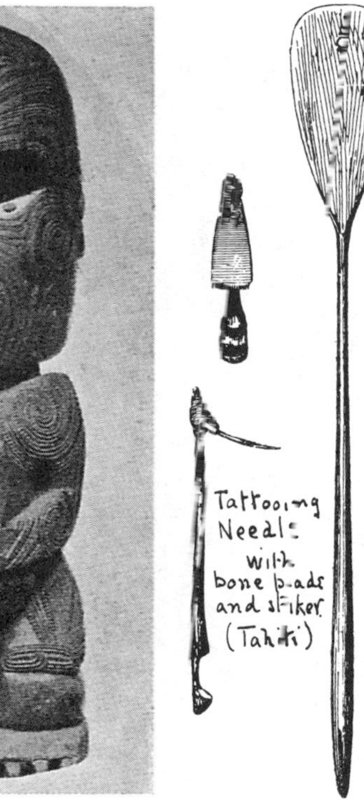

WOODEN FIGURE FROM A MAORI CHIEF'S HOUSE; THE USUAL TATTOO OF A MAN, NEW ZEALAND.

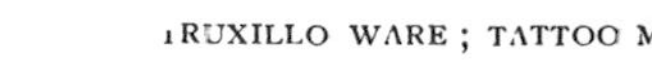

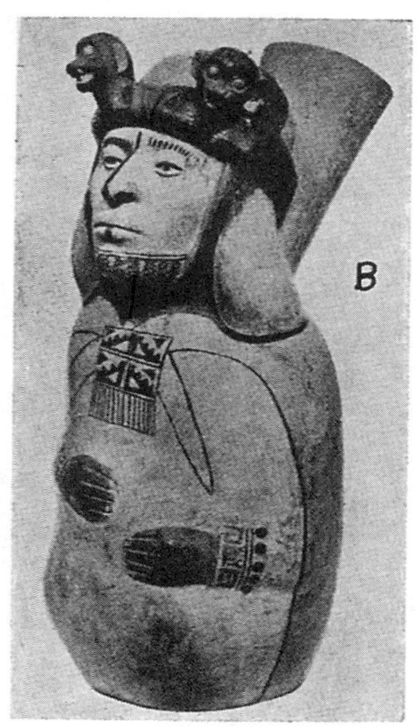

TRUXILLO WARE; TATTOO MARKS ON FACE.

(A and B show use of tattoo for decoration.)

In approaching a short consideration of Maori Moko designs, we have to deal with the greatest proficiency in marking with geometrical figures, which were employed both by warriors who tattooed the entire face, and women who adopted lip and chin designs only. The most striking features in connection with Maori Moko are the perfect symmetry of individual marks, the balance of designs on right and left cheeks, and upper and lower lips, finally the minute accuracy of detail; for nowhere is there any trace of confusion, and it is evident that a master mind was at work thinking out, not only the size and intricacies of each mark, but in addition a clear conception of the finished product, and the relation of each part to the whole design.[1]

With the Maoris, as also is the case among the Motu and Koita peoples of New Guinea, there is employment of body tattoo marks similar to those on objects of use and ornament. The Melanesians of British New Guinea were found to adopt the design from the beak of the hornbill, both for body marking and ornamenting posts of club-houses. Likewise with the Maoris, the spiral (which is the basis of all their ornament) is employed, not only in Moko, but extensively in ornamenting the posts of houses, prows of canoes, and the funnel from which a chief is fed during the tattooing operation.

The technique of the New Guinea markings suggests considerable practice before the designs were transferred to the body, but with reference to Maori markings, those on materials such as wood are almost, if not quite, as perfect as those on the individual.

[1] See Frontispiece.

One very interesting point in connection with Maori art, Moko and otherwise, is the fact that the spiral, whose underlying geometric principles and construction are very elaborate, should have been selected as a basis on which to build up complex ornament. To the artist's credit be it said that no more difficult geometrical figure could have been selected, especially when one takes into account the fact that no preliminary geometrical construction was employed. The artist simply traced the designs freehand with black, then went over these with a small adze which had been dipped in red ochre. In addition to the employment of the spiral, the Maori artist used the parabolic curve, the involute of a circle, and the ionic involute. The geometrical construction of these figures is exceedingly complicated, and difficult to realize even with the use of a good set of mathematical instruments. So great must have been the skill of the artist, whose delicate co-ordination of hand and eye enabled him successfully to complete these designs freehand, that "Moko" at its best must be regarded as the acme of excellence in the geometrical stage of the evolution of the fine art of body marking. Major-General Robley says of the ornamentation of New Zealand women: "I have seen the arms and body so covered with powerful blue marks, that the women looked as if they had on them a tight-fitting figured chintz dress." No doubt the degree of beauty in ornament depended on the amount which the artist was likely to receive, and such a supposition is guaranteed by the lines:[1]

[1] Robley, "Moko," p. 43.

> " He who pays well, let him
> Be beautifully ornamented,
> But he who forgets the operator,
> Let him be done carelessly,
> Be the lines far apart."

Again by Ratzel's verse referring to the tattooer's art in Polynesia, the connection between skill and payment are illustrated.

> " Every line be duly drawn
> On the man whose rich and great
> Shape your figures fair and straight,
> On the man who cannot pay
> Make them crooked, coarse and splay."[1]

C. Hose and W. McDougall [2] mention the interruption of the tattooing process in order that the operator may begin bargaining, or receive an instalment of the payment, and evidently there is good reason for thinking that not every pattern must be taken as an exposition of the degree of skill attained. The quality of the artist's work varies with the amount of remuneration given, and in addition to this difficulty in assessing values, there is that of deliberate conventionalizing of animal forms, as in Haida designs, which leave the critic in doubt respecting the artist's appreciation of animal outline.[3] Social and religious conventions may be repressive to naturalism and free development of observational power.

[1] " History of Mankind," 1896, Vol. I, p. 196.

[2] " Pagan Tribes of Borneo," Hose and McDougall, Vol. I, p. 252.

[3] This work, p. 268.

Samoan Tattooing

The art of Samoa is to be considered hardly inferior to that of New Zealand, and researches of M. Carl Marquardt show that tattooing is still extensively practised. The excellent illustrations given in "Die Tatowirung in Samoa" [1] justify the linking of the Samoan with the Maori tattooing as final units of an ascending evolutionary series of geometrical patterns. The Samoan art has not received the consideration which it deserves, because of the extreme reticence of those who practise it, and the fact that the most elaborate markings are covered by the loin cloth.

For the most part there is a symmetrical arrangement of lines, dots and crosses on the backs of the hands[2] to form zigzags and rhomboids, and at the back of each knee, where the operation is extremely painful, there is a finely-pointed star. The oblong, lozenge, triangle, and V-shaped marks are exceedingly well employed, sometimes in combination, as when the oblong is placed inside the rhomboid. The inner frontal aspect of the thighs shows a remarkable series of lines of frigate bird pattern which gradually converge as they approach the groin, and one mark peculiar to the Samoan designs is a kind of highly ornamental fish-hook carrying numerous barbs. Another mark is similar to our sign for denoting the Cardinal points, and so original

[1] "Die Tatowirung in Samoa," Carl Marquardt, p. 15.

[2] This work, p. 260.

is the tattooing in Samoa that it may almost be considered in a technological sense as an independent school of the body marking art.

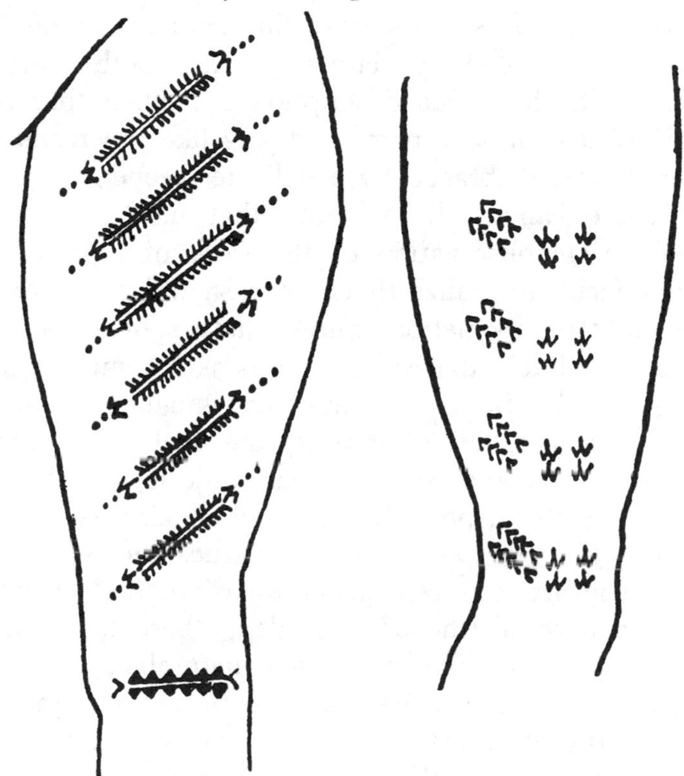

Thigh Tattooing of Samoan Women.

For an account of the general effect of covering the human body with neatly executed designs, well correlated, and selected with a view to enhancing the naturally graceful curves of the figure, it would be difficult to find one more apt than given by Darwin.

Describing a native of Tahiti,[1] the author says that the ornamental markings follow the curvature of

[1] "A Voyage round the World," Darwin, p. 430.

the body so gracefully that they have a very elegant effect. One common pattern, which varies in detail with different individuals, is very like the crown of a palm tree; it springs from the central line of the back and gracefully curves round both sides.[1] Darwin concludes his description by saying that the body of a man so ornamented was like the trunk of a noble tree embraced by a delicate creeper.

There can be little doubt that most ornament results from observation of the work of nature, for it is difficult to realize that a man should conceive of a variety of geometric figures, quite spontaneously. It is more likely that such designs as he employs are suggested by forms of leaves, markings on plants, fruits, animals, birds, insects, the scales of fishes, spiral shells, and many other objects, exhibiting symmetrically disposed patterns of regular geometric form. If such postulation be true, the stage of geometric art is a representation of nature's handiwork, and those who operate along these lines must be regarded as pupils of the naturalistic school, whose masters are to be found in Burma and Japan. To North America reference may be made for examples of crude efforts in the portrayal of animal form. Haida animals[2] are too conventional and anthropomorphic to reveal a correct idea of skill, but in the cicatrized animal designs from Torres Strait[3] there is obvious appreciation of natural anmal outline. Christian speaks appreciatively of tattooed

[1] "Evolution of Decorative Art," H. Balfour, p. 26. "Adaptation of design to space available."

[2] This work, p. 268.

[3] "Cambridge Expedition to Torres Strait," 1898, Vol. V, Plates IX, X.

animal forms in Anua, an island of the Paumotus. "The design is very beautiful and consists of faithfully rendered representations of sea urchins, quaint zoophytes, just like plates out of a naturalist's album."[1]

The Naturalistic School of Tattooing

In making an attempt to illustrate the development which has taken place in the naturalistic school, we might take the tattooed animal designs of the Haida as representative of that stage in which the portrait is quite easily recognized, although the outline is in some instances highly conventionalized, and there is absolutely no attempt at giving motion to the figures. The "bear" is too highly conventionalized to give a clue to his identity, but how far this is the result of inability to draw correctly, and to what extent it results from intentional deviation from a true likeness, it is difficult to say. The human attributes of the face are no doubt given, not because of inability faithfully to show a likeness of a bear, but by deliberate intention of the artist, who desired above all to indicate his alliance with the bear spirit, which like other animal spirits was anthropomorphically conceived. The frog is fairly easy to recognize; but again in the squid there is the human countenance which gives such a ludicrous result.

The efforts of the totemic islanders of Torres Strait display a considerable amount of skill in

[1] "Eastern Pacific Islands," F. W. Christian, 1910, p. 199.

giving in their cicatrized body marks, a correct outline of animal form.[1] In the case of two dogs facing one another, there is a moderately successful attempt at realism in showing this casual meeting of two animals, each of which appears to be watching with some caution the movements of the other.

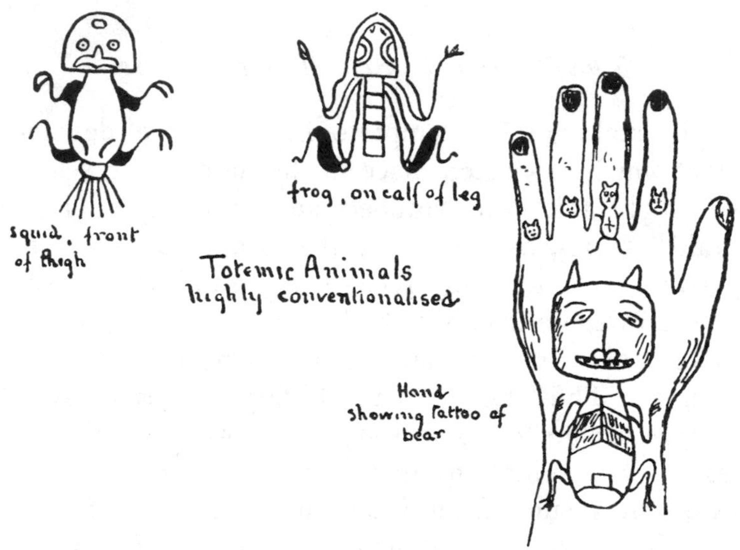

Tattoo Marks of the Haida Tribe, Queen Charlotte Islands, N.W. Canada.

The cassowary is fairly true in outline to the original it represents, but details will not bear close scrutiny; a remark which also applies to the representations of a turtle and a stinging ray, so well known in most Pacific waters. (See also p. 97.)

The designs of animals so far considered have been confined to cicatrized marks in Torres Strait

[1] "Cambridge Expedition to Torres Strait," Vol. V, Plates V, IX, X. Of these designs some are applied to the human body. Others appear only on drums and pipes.

(where the pattern is touched with red ochre on festive occasions), and tattoo by puncture among the Haida. Tamil markings are also of a simple nature, consisting of more or less realistic representations of animals, plants, and human beings in tattooed

Totemic Designs used by Islanders of Torres Strait.

puncture filled in with red or blue; some designs exhibit a combination of two colours. The tattooed designs of Burma and Japan, with their delicate variegated backgrounds of colour, are too complicated to represent in outline tracings, and for clear ideas concerning the products of the tattooers' art in India, Burma, and Japan, it is well to resort to descriptive passages from those who have made personal investigation. The coloured plates given in Joest's "Die Tatowirung" are very instructive with regard to Japanese colour designs and style.

A Tamil man engaged at the Madras Museum said: "While I was in Colombo I made the acquaintance of a Cingalese, a professional tattooer, who had an album of patterns; I was attracted by their beauty and submitted to the operation." A good deal of the tattooed marking of Southern India is the result of visits to Burma, and Tamil men sometimes return covered with the most elaborate devices. Dr. Thurston examined a hundred and thirty men who were stripped for anthropometrical measurement, and in each instance he found on the chest, upper arm, forearm, wrist, backs of hands, and shoulders devices in blue, with occasional employment of red. Among the devices mentioned are a steamboat, cross and anchor, a sailing boat, royal arms, crown and flags, crossed swords, bugles, Queen Alexandra, a dancing girl, heart and cross, shepherdess, a Burmese lady, the word "mercy," some flowers in a pot, the elephant, scorpion, finally a lizard, and bracelets.[1] No claim is made for symbolism attaching to any particular design, but the sentiments connected therewith are apparent.

Final Stage in Artistic Evolution of Tattooing

The tattooing of Burmese and Japanese artists must be considered as the final stage in the evolution of ornamental markings, and a decision respecting

[1] "Ethnographical Notes in South India," p. 378.

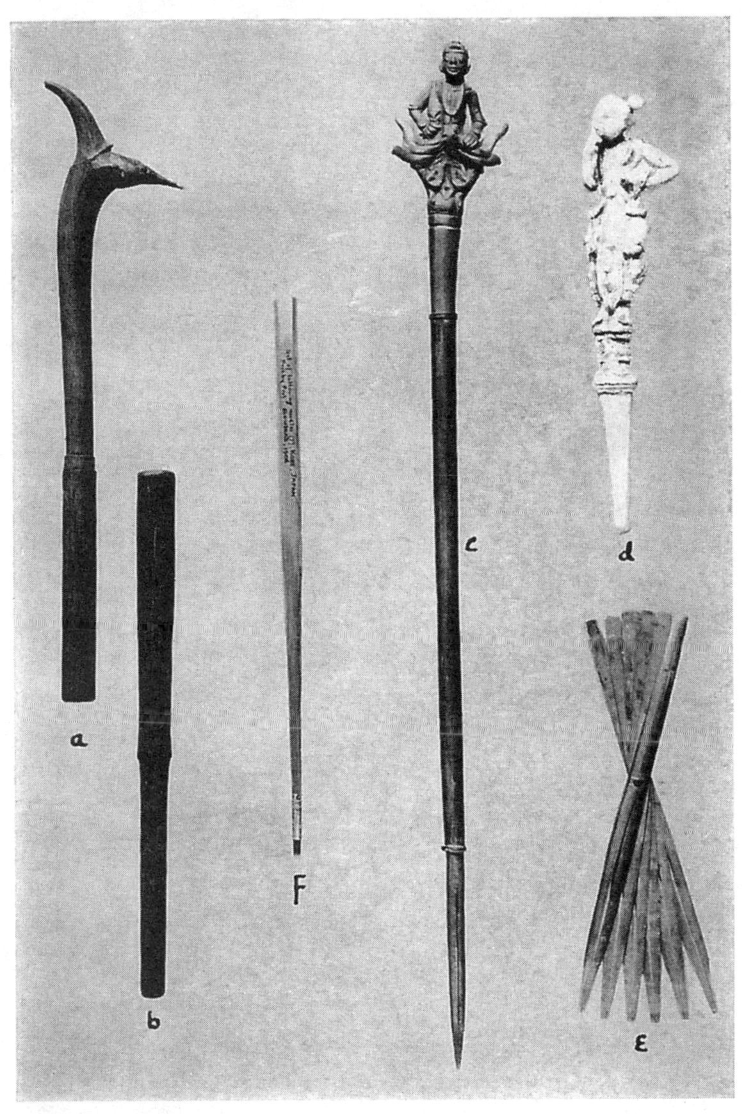

(a) TATTOOING INSTRUMENT, SARAWAK, BORNEO. (b) TATOOING STRIKER. SARAWAK, BORNEO.
(c) COMPLETE TATTOOING INSTRUMENT, BURMA. (d) LEAD WEIGHT FOR THE SAME. (e) TATTOOING NEEDLE, OPENED OUT TO SHOW COMPOUND STRUCTURE.
(f) TATTOOING NEEDLES, MOUNTED, JAPAN.

(From specimens in Pitt Rivers Museum.)

the superiority of one of these schools of art is extremely difficult to make. Perhaps the honours should be accorded to the Japanese artist, not because of the superior accuracy of detail, or faithfulness of outline in marking his animal figures, but because of the absolutely life-like pose, or more correctly, "motion" of the figures, which include the tree blown by the wind, the fish swimming lazily with an occasional lash of his tail, or a fin movement, and the graceful swoop of a bird on the wing.

The Burmese artist works with a pricker two feet long weighted at the top with the brass figure of Buddha, and having its point split into four fine needles which are capable of holding colouring matter. The operator holds the instrument in his right hand, while the left is used as a rest and guide. The designs are shown in an album before opium is administered, then the patient selects his patterns and indicates the parts of the body on which he would like these to be tattooed. A skilful artist will tattoo fifteen figures in a little over half an hour, and the markings are usually faithful portrayals of tigers, cats, monkeys, elephants, rats, baboons, and compound animals. Usually each representation is surrounded by rough oval tracery composed of letters of the alphabet, which form a curious and effective framework, having in some instances a cabalistic meaning.

In Japan also figures are outlined with a brush of camel's hair, and the designs are pricked in with an instrument which terminates so as to accommodate varying numbers of fine needles selected according to the length and nature of the curved outline which has to be followed. The pigments used are black Indian ink, which looks blue under the skin, vermilion, madder, and yellow. The work is done with such rapidity that an elaborate design of a dragon covering the entire front of the forearm will be completed in a couple of hours, and during such an operation it is unusual for blood to be drawn, so great is the skill of the artist in avoiding a puncture of the dermis or true vascular skin. An elaborate snake design ten inches in length I saw completed by a tattooer in Waterloo Road. Three colours were used, and the process occupied about eighty minutes. Whatever may be said of the beauties of Moko, the artists certainly never attained anything approaching the delicate precision of a Japanese worker, and the cheek of a Maori would frequently be streaming with blood, while some punctures, or grooves, would be so deep as to perforate the cheek in such a manner that the smoke from the warrior's pipe issued therefrom.

An interesting description of the tattooer's workshop in Yokohama, accompanied by an illustration,[1] shows that though the process of tattooing is entirely ornamental it may have in Japan some lingering magical significance,[2] for as Cocheris shows, "Sa maison est remplie d'imagies fantastiques, dragons vomissant des flammes, poissons ailés, oiseaux fabuleux, monstres humaines, qui s'en disputent les murailles." If there is no lingering connection

[1] "Les Parures Primitive" by Cocheris, p. 53.

[2] Tattooing in Japan is now forbidden by Government. French Authority also proscribes the tattooing practice in Marquesan Islands.

between tattooing and magic, no association of the body marking art with ideas of what is uncanny and abnormal, why the fabulous monsters, winged fishes, and demons, as ornaments, both in the form of solid objects in the workshop, and as patterns on the patient's body?

As an instance of the artistic product of the Burmese tattooer there is the classic example of a tattooed man from Burma,[1] around whom no small amount of romance gathered. Whether the detention and tattooing operation was forcible or not is extremely difficult to decide; probably Sinclair is correct in stating that the man went to Burma in order to receive his ornament for exhibition in Europe and America. Such a point is scarcely relevant, but the factor of interest and moment is the extraordinary degree of skill exhibited in covering this person from head to foot with most life-like portrayals of animal and other designs, amounting in all to something like three hundred and eighty-eight figures. In addition to the designs there is tattooing of a variegated background, in which the tint is graded to show to the greatest advantage any figure marked thereon.

When stripped the man gave the appearance of being clad in a tightly-woven fabric of rich Turkish material. Between the figures were innumerable little red and blue characters which provided an effective setting. A. W. Franks, who addressed a meeting at the Anthropological Institute, 1872, showed photographs of the tattooed man of Burma, and in the journal for that year an account of

[1] Journal of Anthropological Institute, Vol. II, 1872.

the nature and arrangement of the figures was given. Tabulating the list of designs we get:

	No. of Designs.
Breast as far as waist . .	50
Left arm	51
Right arm	50
Back from neck to waist . .	37
Neck and throat . . .	8
Lower part of body . .	53
Lower extremities . . .	137
Figures on forehead . .	2
Total	388

The designs included snakes, elephants, swans, two crowned sphinxes, eagles, cats, tigers, storks, crocodiles, salamanders, dragons, fishes, gazelles, women with dresses, fruit, leaves, flowers, characters, judged to be ancient Burmese script, the whole work of art being completed after the operators (number unknown) had worked three hours a day for three months.

Writing quite recently (1908), A. T. Sinclair, an American anthropologist who has made a special study of tattooing, says that he saw the celebrated Greek who had been tattooed in Burma. His entire body, except the soles of his feet, was literally covered with devices, some of them minute, but each perfectly accurate and full of detail. There were serpents, lizards, dragons, birds, flowers, and it was only after a close and careful examination that Mr. Sinclair could convince himself that there was no imposture.[1]

Mr. Chamberlain speaks of Japanese designs con-

[1] "American Anthropologist," 1908, Vol. X, p. 372.

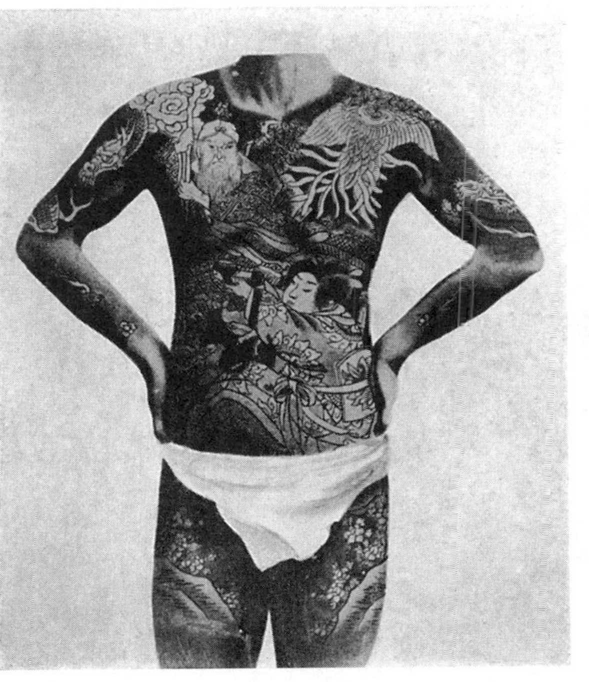

JAPANESE TATTOOING. THE FINEST KNOWN EXAMPLE OF NATURALISTIC WORK IN VIVID COLOURS.

sisting of birds, flowers and landscapes of marvellous finish and beauty, thoroughly Japanese in style and conception.[1] Some of the designs are so microscopic that it is difficult to appreciate their beauty. For outlines and a background the Japanese artist uses sepia, while vermilion makes the details very prominent, as may be seen in the illustrations given in "Die Tatowirung" (W. Joest), whose illustrations are worth describing somewhat fully. The background is a bluish grey which varies in intensity so gradually that a very pleasing piebald effect is produced; and on this, in deeper blue, or vermilion, are birds, flowers, human faces and demons. The human face is that of a Japanese, and it is noticeable that the flatness of the nose and other racial characteristics are much exaggerated. In like manner the ancient Greek sculptors exaggerated in their artistic products, those traits which were held in high esteem.[2] One of Joest's figures shows a huge fish occupying the chest of a man, who also has on each buttock a similar fish in vermilion, each scale being represented with perfect accuracy. The idea of motion is given by the curl of the tail and bending of the pectoral fins. Between the shoulders of the same man is a mythical monster bearing horns, and a terrible expression, while to complete the hideousness, claws are given instead of hands. Another such monstrosity has a widely opened mouth showing enormous canine teeth, and though the conception is weird and fantastic the execution is perfect.

[1] "Things Japanese," B. H. Chamberlain, p. 399.

[2] See also Egyptian sculpture emphasizing long, slim bodies, long feet, full dark eyes,

On what grounds then is it possible to justify the treatment of Japanese art as the acme of excellence? In what particular respects do the designs of the Japanese tattooer surpass those of other people? With regard to technique or mechanical performance, there can be no absolute standard, and no rules which may be of universal application in helping to judge of the excellence of artistic products. Nevertheless, there are two guiding principles for the critic, namely, a consideration of analysis and synthesis.

Respecting analysis, or the elaboration of details, it may be said that the Burmese, Japanese, and Marquesan artists excel all others, but the Maori comes very near to this high standard of excellence, and in his own department of geometric designing and execution is supreme.

Geometric art does not lend itself to such elaboration of detail as may be found in the products of Japanese and Burmese tattooers, who show every feather of a bird, scale of a fish, and marking on the leaf of a plant. The Haidas, and Torres Strait Islanders, it is true, represent the animal form, but there is little attempt at analysis or elaboration of detail. A consideration of the work done on the famous tattooed man of Burma shows, that in arranging for the accommodation of 388 figures on the human body, the Burmese artist exercised an extraordinary amount of synthetic power in adjusting each fragment in its relationship to the whole, before work was commenced. In such power he is at least equalled by the Japanese artist, possibly also by the Maori, who carries out such elaborate facial and thigh designs without any confusion.

In the employment of perspective, and its accompanying idea of distance, the Japanese tattooer possesses supreme skill, for he can give to his scenery, also to human and animal figures, every appearance of solidarity, partly by attention to the laws of perspective, and to some extent by a wise choice of background, which throws the object forward.

In point of coloration, Burmese and Japanese artists may be bracketed at the head of the list, for "Moko," though so excellent in form and general execution, has no colouring beyond a little red ochre in each groove. In Melanesia, Africa, South America, and Australia, it is frequently the custom, not even to insert a little pigment, but to paint the cicatrices on festive occasions.[1] In contrast with the coloration used by other artists, we have in Japan and Burma a most artistic combination of varying shades of blue, red, vermilion, and yellow, and for these countries, it may be said that the background alone is a wonderful work of art, before even a figure is considered. In Japan the artist employs a setting of varying shades of blue, while in Burma the interstices are filled by innumerable alphabetical figures.

This short description of the use of colour includes what an artist would call "values," or the use of light and dark shades in order to give a deceptive effect of solidarity, an effect which is not required in geometric art however elaborate. The Maori and African make no attempt at deceptive solidarity, so to the Japanese is left the honour of having mastered

[1] "Mafulu People of British New Guinea," pp. 41-2, 220.

this question of " values " or light and shade, which he employs so effectvely in the piebald background.

Motion, or what the French would term the " idée plastique," is another factor in art which is inapplicable to a study of geometric designs, and for excellence in representing the flying bird, the human form, the tree blown by the wind, or the swimming fish, the Japanese artist again shows his supremacy, for not even his Burmese rival can compete with him in giving life and activity to a subject. Another term " chic," the artist's slang for imagination, is one which may be used with reference to tattooing, and linked with the use of this term is the entire question of copying directly from nature as opposed to working from memory. Working with geometric patterns, as on the Congo, or in New Zealand, does not imply a mere copying from natural forms, and the African or Maori artist no doubt exercised considerable imaginative power in reproducing and combining his numerous figures. Excellent as some of the cicatrization and Moko may be in point of imagination, it can in no wise compare with the faculty exercised by the Burman who tattooes compound animals, or with the Japanese whose wild imaginative power finds expression in the production of fabulous monsters, such as winged dragons and fearful demons. Some great artists, for instance Michael Angelo, Bocklin, Doré, and Tintoretto, have painted from imagination and memory, and William Morris Hunt, a well-known American artist and critic, always advocated a thorough study of the subject, then painting from memory.

The Japanese and Burmese artists do not

altogether follow this scheme of memory drawing, for the Burmese has his book of patterns, which are submitted to the patient for a selection to be made. Outline drawings are sketched with a brush, most probably from the drawing in the pattern book. The Japanese artist likewise uses an outline drawing and a pattern book. But in all probability there is some reproduction from memory, and a very facile play of imagination, exercised with great freedom from the dictates of social custom. Of course even a Japanese artist is limited by his education and environment, and there are such forms as dragons and demons which are very popular stereotyped designs. But notwithstanding this, there is a high degree of imaginative power and personal initiative in the work of a Japanese tattooer. For knowledge of colour effect, power of analysis and synthesis, perspective, values, motion, imagination, and freedom from convention, we should place his name at the head of a list of tattooers from all parts of the world.

Growth of Æsthetic Sense

Are we justified in considering ornamental tattooing to be the starting-point of the body marking process? and may we say that the origin of such marking was for the purpose of enhancing the natural attraction of one sex for the other? The sexual instinct is of course one of the fundamental traits of human character, and must by no means be left out of reckoning by anyone who seeks to analyse the technique of the body marking process. Probably the sexual instinct had much to do with some early forms of ornamental marking which were undertaken with a view to making the wearer more attractive at dances and other festivities. One feels that the mistake of making ornamental marking the starting-point is that the mentality involved is of too complex a nature. Decorative marks, simple as it is possible for them to be, imply a very definite realization of the importance of self, and further they imply that much freedom of the individual has been evolved. The geometric and other higher forms of the tattooers' art must certainly be given a very late date in the evolution of this particular culture, and that for two reasons: (1) The exceedingly difficult technique which implies a long apprenticeship, and (2) the psychic process involved in the elaboration of such works of art as those of Burma and Japan. The argument, that ancient writers have not spoken of a particular ornament, does not prove that such ornament did not exist, the origin may have been in very remote times. The specialized technique of Japan, Borneo, Marquesas, Samoa, New Zealand and New Guinea is probably due to hypertrophy of design under isolation.

Is there any value in an analogy between the development of a child's mentality and that of a race? In other words, if the development of the individual is an epitome of the evolution of the human family, in the same way that embryology shows the fœtus recapitulating the biological evolution, does intellectual progress from childhood, through adolescence, to adult life, give a digest of man's mental evolution during the course of untold ages? These analogies are perhaps dangerous if pressed too far, but my own twelve years' experience of training children between the ages of seven and sixteen, leads me to believe that the analogy is a sound one if not insisted upon in too great detail. In no aspect of the mental life does this analogy hold more soundly than in the growth of the primary emotions, and their crystallization into permanent tendencies or sentiments.

Fear, anger, jealousy are very early in appearing, and they show much the same strength and tendency to irritable action as in primitive man, who is most unstable, for he may quickly be changed from fear to confidence, or from anger to deference. Few children like to be alone, and Rousseau's system of education, exemplified in his book " Emile " (the name of a youth trained entirely at the hands of a tutor, and without companionship), has been severely criticized on the ground that it ignores a fundamental social tendency which calls for competition, rivalry, and emulation, all of which, under guidance and control, are valuable factors in æsthetic and general education. The sexual instinct and desire for ornaments in order to enhance personal charms comes somewhat late in individual development, and the formulation of æsthetic principles must be looked upon as a late product in human evolution. Apropos of the question of a parallel between artistic products of children and those of primitive races there is interest in studying outline drawings, collected from various Brazilian tribes, with drawing of juveniles. The resemblance in portrayal of human and other figures is remarkable.[1]

Body marking as practised to-day shows three clear stages in æsthetic development. (1) An individual and subjective stage exemplified by crude facial and body designs in brilliant colours, as among Mafulu mountain people of New Guinea, Andamanese, and many Amazonian tribes. (2) Preservation of tattooed designs having an objective value. Such designs among the Haida are well executed, conventional, and persistent because of special totemic significance. (3) Formulation of principles and realization of qualities which make body marking agreeable to all members of a community. There may then be expression of individuality in conformity with general principles of artistic taste as in Japan and Burma.

Under isolation the body marking art in colour and incision has remained rudimentary as with Andamanese, Sakai, and Australians. But in other instances of separation the development of technique has been intricate and distinctive, giving rise to Japanese, Bornean, Samoan, and Marquesan styles. Decorations of the skin, considered without reference to connected belief and ritual, may be arranged in series, the units of which are of gradually ascending difficulty and complexity. From simple markings with paint, technique has passed through a stage of geometric designing, to a period of elaborate workmanship in colour, exhibiting excellencies of constructive and inventive power, combined with perfect

[1] "Anfänge der Kunst im Urwald," Theodor Koch, Grünberg, 1906.

co-ordination of hand and eye. The pricking in of colours, having due regard to perspective, form, and motion, must be regarded as the topmost stair of the flight up which generations of artists have toiled from the remote period in which early palæolithic man resorted to a use of red ochre in order to symbolize the rejuvenating and revivifying power of blood.

CHAPTER V

GEOGRAPHICAL DISTRIBUTION OF TATTOOING

Distribution in Europe—Asia—The Pacific—Africa—American Continents.

THE chief objects to be achieved by a geographical summary are:

1. To determine whether various forms of marking are co-extensive or whether they usually exist independently.
2. To find whether beliefs and practices are general or localized.
3. To discover whether body marking is confined to one sex in any part of the world.

These questions are best answered by summarizing the evidence according to continental areas and their subdivisions.

Europe

Archæological evidence is particularly valuable within this area because of its association with well recognized geological periods and their probable relation to intermittent glaciations. There can be no doubt that red ochre was of great importance to palæolithic man who used it extensively in cave paintings and interments. Of cicatrization in prehistoric times there is no evidence. It seems clear that the Picts tattooed by puncture and that animals were the chief subjects portrayed. "The forms of beasts, birds, and fishes which the Cruithnæ or Picts tattooed on their bodies may have been totem marks; certain marks on faces of Gaulish coins seem to be tattoo marks."[1] The Celts roamed over the southern peninsulas of Europe and probably arrived in Britain 800 B.C.[2]

T. Rice Holmes says: "It is usually inferred from statements in Claudian and Herodian that Picts tattooed, and their testimony is supposed to be strengthened by etymology of names by which Picts were known to Irish and Welsh respectively.[3] Rice Holmes thinks that tattooing by puncture was possibly known among such Gaulish tribes as Ambiani, Baiocasses and Caletes. Professor Donald A. Mackenzie[4] has been good enough to correspond with me on this subject, and his work, "Ancient Man in Britain," summarizes points relating to tattooing and painting the body among peoples with whom the Romans came in contact. Julius Cæsar

[1] "The Religion of the Ancient Kelts," J. A. MacCulloch, 1911, pp. 17, 217.

[2] Saussaye, "Religion of Teutons," Vol. III. Handbook on History of Religions, Jastrow.

[3] T. Rice Holmes, "Ancient Britain and the Invasion of Julius Cæsar," pp. 418-20. Claudian De Bello Gothico, 416-18.

"Venit et extremis legio prætenta Britannis
Quæ Scotto dat frena truci ferroque notatas
Perlegit exanimes Picto moriente figuras."

See also Sir John Rhŷs, "The Welsh People," 1923. "Early Britain," 1904.

[4] "Ancient Man in Britain," p. 136. Pliny Nat. Hist., Vol. XXVII, p. 2, Herodian, Vol. III, p. 14.

mentions painted Britons, A.D. 100-44. Pliny, the elder, natural historian (A.D. 23-79) mentions painting of Ancient Britons. Mackenzie says: "An animal tattooed on one's body evidently afforded protection as did the boar symbol referred to by Tacitus when dealing in "Germania" with the amber collectors."

The extensive use of tattoo marks at the present day by soldiers and sailors, their employment by criminal classes (see Lombroso and Lacassagne), with Sinclair's evidence respecting tattooed symbols in the Balkans, all point to the importance of tattooing as a means of expressing emotions and sentiments. The marking of Picts is historically important in showing the advance of tattoo by puncture to an extreme northerly point of Great Britain before the Christian era. Employment of animal designs has a social and psychological interest in bringing Europe into alignment with many parts of the world where animal forms, in connection with totemism and magical protection, are employed. Miss Harrison[1] notes tattooing of totemic designs in Ancient Greece, and captured Athenians were tattooed on the forehead with the horse of Syracuse.

Asia

Armenian Christians tattoo symbols of the cross.[2] In Persia tattooing is common among lower classes

[1] J. E. Harrison, "Themis," Social Origins of Greek Religion, Cambridge, 1912, pp. 132-3. "Hermes," Vol. XXXVIII, p. 265.

[2] A. T. Sinclair, "American Anthropologist," 1908, Vol. X, p. 361.

in order to avoid the evil eye, and women sometimes use marks as ornament, and for the same reason paint is employed.[1] In Arabia men and women resort to tattooing, the former chiefly to cure rheumatic affections, and this is lawful in spite of Koranic prohibition, but where beauty is the aim the prophet invoked Allah's curse.[2]

The Bedàwy, inhabitants of "bâdia," or great waste land, tattoo.[3] These despised wanderers, who are at once feared and held in contempt by better class Arabs,[4] enable the chain of puncture tattoo marks to be traced without a break from Morocco, through Algeria and Tunis to Egypt. Thence across Arabia, Persia, Bengal, Assam, Southern China, to Japan. Palgrave[5] refers to the Bedouins as less cultivated than true Arabs, pointing out their violation of laws of decorum and courtesy. With advancing civilization tattooing tends to become a contemptible practice. The Koran forbids marking of the body. These facts explain survival among the despised Bedouins of a practice which either failed to attain any hold in Arabia or was largely eliminated by the rise of Islam in the seventh century. Robertson Smith conjectures that in olden times

[1] C. J. Willis, "In the Land of the Lion and the Sun," 1883, p. 323. C. C. Rice, "Persian Women and their Ways," 1923, p. 245.

[2] H. F. Jacob (10 years' residence in Al. Yemen), "Perfumes of Araby," 1915, p. 133.

[3] C. S. Myers, J.A.I., "Contribution to Egyptian Anthropology," 1903, Vol. XXXIII, p. 82. A. T. Sinclair, "American Anthropologist," 1908, Vol. X, p. 361.

[4] C. M. Doughty, "Travels in Arabia Deserta," 1921, Vol. II, p. 537.

[5] "Journey Through Central and Eastern Arabia," 1865, p. 25.

marks were placed not on camels alone, but on the tribesmen. He notes pictorial signs on Arabian rocks, quotes Lucian, and thinks that at an early date the tribal mark was probably a totem mark. [1]

Sir R. F. Burton[2] gives an interesting reference to face gashing in Mecca. " In most families male children forty days old are taken to the Ka'abah, prayed over and carried home. Here the barber draws with a razor three parallel gashes (Mashali) from the external corner of the eye to the mouth." Citizens declare the custom was unknown to their ancestors. The child's body is marked with smaller cuts. Citizens said the custom arose to prevent kidnapping by Persians, and that it is now preserved as a mark of the Holy City. From early accounts of journeys in the Himalayas there is little evidence of tattooing. Marco Polo[3] (1250-1324), in speaking of Yunnan, says: " The men form dark stripes or bands round their arms and legs by puncturing them in the following manner: They have fine needles joined together[4] which they press into the flesh until blood is drawn. They then rub the punctures with a black colouring matter which leaves an indelible mark." To bear these stripes is considered as an ornament and honourable distinction. At Kangigu on route from East Bengal to Burma, Polo found both men and

[1] " Kinship and Marriage in Early Arabia," Cambridge, 1885, pp. 187, 212, 214.

[2] " Personal Narrative of Pilgrimage to Mecca," 1893, Vol. II, p. 234.

[3] Translation, T. Marsden, New York, 1904, pp. 232, 244.

[4] A Burmese instrument of the present day consists of six bamboo splinters united on a median axis.

women with their bodies punctured all over in figures of beasts and birds. There are among them practitioners whose sole employment is to trace out these ornaments. The man or woman who exhibits the greatest profusion of these marks is esteemed the most handsome. In 1270 Burmese tattooing had a technique equal to that of to-day. Marco Polo did not remark on the magical significance of Burmese tattooing, but this aspect has been fully dealt with by Sir J. G. Scott.[1] Watters' edition of Yuan Chwang's Travels in India in A.D. 629-645 mentions "blackening the face," "gashing as a sign of mourning," but I cannot be sure of the people and exact locality.[2] Both politically and topographically access to Tibet has been difficult. Nevertheless, there have been numerous visitors, many of whom have penetrated to Lhasa.[3] W. W. Rockhill says he met a trader who reported having seen in Lhasa devotees from India marked on head, forehead, and sternum with three mystic symbols "Om," "A," "Hum."[4] The Shans[5] tattoo, and their connection with Southern China is important historical evidence of migration of tattoo-

[1] M. Symes, "Religious and Civil Institute of Burmese," 1798, pp. 21, 34. Tattoo marks for criminals, and tattoo marks as a charm against weapons. Scott, under pseudonym "Shway Yoe," in "The Burman, his Life and Notions," 1882, ch. V, pp. 39-47. See also "France and Tonking," London, 1885, p. 348.

[2] T. Watters, Vol. I, p. 41.

[3] See Publications of Hakluyt Society and Sir Clements Markham, relating to journeys of Odoricus, Grueber, Desideri, Bogle, Manning, Huc, and Gabet. Also "Life and Travel in Tartary and Tibet," M. Jones, 1867.

[4] "Diary of a Journey Through Mongolia and Tibet," Washington, 1894, p. 67.

[5] "Shans at Home," Mrs. L. Milne, London, 1910.

ing. Shan tattooing is largely a puberty rite and test of endurance. Sakai and Semang paint and cicatrize marks which are tribal and amuletic.

In India there are:

(*a*) Types of modern tattooing in the Japanese style collected by E. Thurston of the Madras Museum.[1]

(*b*) Religious markings in paint to show adherence to Siva, or Vishnu. Stamping of the Chank and Chakra on girls (Basivis) dedicated to temple service.[2]

(*c*) Branding as a pain cure and child-birth ceremony.[3]

(*d*) Puncture tattooing of primitive Dravidian jungle tribes.

The Agariyas hold that tattooing is a sacred rite by which the body is sanctified. There is a widespread belief that the god Parameswar will not admit to heaven a woman who does not bear the tattooed symbols of his deity. The Agariyas mix pigment with the milk of the patient, but if she is barren or unmarried milk of another woman is used.[4] Tattoo below the stomach is a remedy for barrenness. Women whose children are unhealthy or die young have their own abdomens tattooed. Some women tattoo the conch shell as a sign of coverture, and the

[1] Edgar Thurston, "Ethnographical Notes in South India," Madras, 1906 (many references).

[2] *Ibid.*

[3] *Ibid.*, and W. H. R. Rivers, "Todas of South India," 1906, pp. 313, 576.

[4] I believe this to be a most interesting survival of a prehistoric connection between body marking and fertility rites.

one who wears it does not become a widow in this world or the next. The use of human milk for mixing pigment and the adoption of a conch-shell design are the only instances of their kind that my research has revealed. This tattooing of Dravidian tribes is obviously closely connected with fertility rites, and its relation to immortality is of considerable interest. Some jungle tribes tattoo the elephant (Ganesa god); women often have the design on both arms. " Hansuli " or necklace design is tattooed on a daughter while she sits on her mother's knee. This ensures that they will not be separated in the next world, or at any rate that they shall meet. There are many animal marks probably totemistic in origin, also tattoo marks to resist disease. There is much evidence of the same kind for Bhuyia, Bind, Biyâr (if not tattooed god brands with a torch of grass), Gonds and Dôms.[1] T. C. Hodson relates that Nagas of Assam[2] tattoo men in connection with head-hunting exploits and women for recognition in heaven.

Midway between India and the Malay Peninsula lie the Andaman Islands inhabited by a negrito people probably akin to the Semang, Aetas, and New Guinea pygmies. All these negritoes paint and scarify, and the Andamanese retain legends of a divine origin of colours which are applied to denote

[1] "Tribes and Castes of North-West Provinces and Oudh," W. Crookes, Calcutta, 1896, four volumes. Vol. I, p. 22, par. 9 (Agariyas). See index Vol. IV for many references throughout the four volumes. Risley, "People of India," Plate XXXV, Dôms.

[2] "Descriptive Ethnology of Bengal," T. Dalton, Calcutta, 1872. "Naga Tribes of Manipur," 1911, pp. 30, 31, 77, 94, 159.

emotions of pain and pleasure. Scarification among Andamanese was at one time accompanied by ritual and restrictions on food.[1]

Tattooing by puncture survives in China only as a punishment, but unless the investigator visits one of the remote parts of the empire to which such criminals are exiled, he would never see persons thus marked. "Tattooing is not practised among the Chinese to any great extent as a means of decorating the person. I have seen a few men with dots pricked on arms and hands, but they had lived with foreigners or travelled abroad." The Chinese have, however, a word "chen-hua," to draw with a needle to prick a pattern.[2] Bazin de Malpière gives several hundred coloured plates dealing with Chinese life in many localities and social phases. Mandarins, criminals, merchants, and craftsmen are all represented, but tattoo marks are absent.[3] So far back as 575 B.C. the Wu on the Yang-tse-Kiang and Shanghai coasts tattooed their bodies in order, according to some legends, that they might frighten dangerous fish. The year 842 B.C. may be considered the first accurate date in Chinese history, and at this time central China knew nothing of the "tattooed barbarians" south of the Yang-tse.[4] Professor Parker tells me that the

[1] E. H. Man, "Andaman Islands," J.A.I., 1883, pp. 304, 334. A. de Quatrefage, "Les Pygmies," London, 1895, p. 121 (Starr's translation). A. R. Brown, "The Andaman Islanders," 1921, p. 275. H. H. Risley, "People of India," 1915, Plate XXIII. G. E. Dobson, "Andaman Islands," 1874, p. 465.

[2] W. W. Rockhill, "Diary of a Journey Through Mongolia and Tibet" in 1892, Washington, 1894, p. 58.

[3] Bazin de Malpière. Two volumes. Paris, 1825.

[4] E. H. Parker, "Ancient China Simplified," 1908, pp. 5, 159, 163, 170.

Chinese have never tattooed, but branding criminals was the practice in ancient times, and perhaps is occasionally carried out now.

The most ancient Chinese histories say that some of the earliest members of what was afterwards the Chou Dynasty 1100-300 B.C., either tattooed their bodies or emigrated among the tattooers. But the Chinese orthodox have never tattooed. Professor Parker has travelled widely over China, Indo-China, Siam, and Burma, but has never seen real Chinese tattooed.[1] Chamberlain, in discussing relations between China and Japan, states that a Chinese writer of the early Christian era asserts that the men of Japan all tattooed their faces and ornamented their bodies with designs, difference or rank being indicated by the position and size of the patterns. But from the dawn of history down to the Middle Ages tattooing seems to have been held in contempt among Japanese upper classes.[2] There was intercourse between the tattooed Wu of South-East China and Japan as early as 473 B.C., so there may have been borrowing of patterns and beliefs. The first trustworthy date in Japanese history is A.D 461, about the time when the gradual spread of Chinese culture filtering in through Korea had suggested the keeping of records.[3] If technique be any criterion of antiquity one must look to Japan for early, perhaps the earliest attempts at this form of corporal ornament. There is no evidence of ritual and taboo in connection with Japanese work; the striking point

[1] Personal communication.
[2] B. H. Chamberlain, "Things Japanese," 1898, p. 380.
[3] *Ibid.*, p. 380.

about which is the colour, life and motion.[1] The Ainu to the north of Yezo, also in the Kuriles, tattoo their women. The marking is a puberty rite, indispensable to marriage, had a divine origin, and gives access to heaven.[2] The Ainu are of Caucasian affinities, and preceded the Japanese to whom they may have given knowledge of tattooing, the technique of which was developed with patience, accuracy and skill characteristic of the Japanese, while ritual was wholly neglected. Tattooing, chiefly in the form of a marriage mark for women, and dots for prowess in killing Russians, are noted among the Chukchee of far North-East Siberia.[3]

To the south of Japan lies Formosa where tattooing by puncture is closely connected with prowess in head-hunting. Carried out by a priestess, it is a bond between bride and bridegroom. Tattooing among Taiyal seems to have the greatest importance, indicating social significance of the individual in the tribe. At the tattooing ceremony children are formally accepted as members of the tribe.[4]

In Borneo tattooing is definitely connected with head-hunting, marks being given for prowess. Women of the Kayan and Klemantan are elaborately tattooed with accompanying sacrifice of fowl, food taboos and many other restrictions. The marks also guarantee

[1] W. Joest, "Die Tatowirung," Berlin, 1887, coloured plates.

[2] G. Batchelor, "Ainu and their Folk-Lore," London, 1892, pp. 20-5.

[3] Bogoras, "Jesup Expedition to North Pacific," Vol. VIII.

[4] Janet B. Montgomery McGovern, "Among Head-Hunters of Formosa," 1922, pp. 111, 160, 188, 190. J. W. Davidson, "Island of Formosa," 1903, pp. 106, 109, 565, 572, etc.

certain privileges in heaven.[1] Sumatra and Java appear to have escaped the influence of tattoo by puncture, or the practice may have been completely suppressed by centuries of Muhammadan influence. In the Philippines negritoes scarify themselves with their own sharpened teeth. The Bisaya are most elaborately tattooed, a practice having a long, if not honourable connection with head-hunting.[2]

The Pacific

In South-East New Guinea tattooing is a puberty rite for women. There are definite stages with appropriate designs, food taboos and other restrictions. The Koita have a distinctive tattoo mark for homicides. Mafulu mountain people are addicted to elaborate painting. Papuans scarify, but there is a present-day migration of tattoo by puncture from South-East to West.[3] The islanders of Torres Strait scarify with animal forms.[4]

In the Solomons, New Britain, New Ireland, New Pommern, New Hebrides, New Caledonia,

[1] C. Hose and W. McDougall, "Pagan Tribes of Borneo," London, 1912, two volumes. Bock Carl, "Head-Hunters of Borneo," 1881, pp. 66, 130, 132, 139, 189. C. Hose in "People of All Nations," Vol. II, p. 803. O. Rutter, "British North Borneo," 1922, p. 335.

[2] A. L. Kroeber, "People of Philippines," New York, 1919. Handbook 8, American Mus. Nat. Hist. A. B. Meyer, "Distribution of Negritoes," Dresden, 1899.

[3] Seligman, Capt. F. R. Barton, R. W. Williamson, J. H. Holmes, W. Beaver.

[4] Reports Cambridge Expedition Torres Strait, 1898, Vol. V. Totemism.

and Fiji tattooing by puncture is accompanied by scar marking, often by burning. Tattoo proper is found in Hawaii, Samoa, Tonga, Hervey Islands, Austral Islands, Society Islands, Marquesas, Paumotus, and Easter Island, where it was noted at an early date by Roggeveen (1722). Wherever tattooing exists in the vast area mentioned from Hawaii to Samoa, from the Paumotus to the Carolines, it is definitely associated with the puberty of women and their marriageability, and there are usually accompanying taboos and rites. This region is so essential a factor in migrations that perhaps it is better reserved [1] for discussion in relation to the origin and distribution of the tattooing practice. In New Zealand " Moko " or tattooing in grooves traced as elaborate spirals is a unique specialization. Designs were essential for women who had an elaborate chin tattoo. Marks for men were tribal, heraldic, and personal; and in the tattooing of chiefs there were elaborate restrictions, precautions, and rites.[2]

Australia

Throughout Australia various kinds of paint are employed in connection with totemic ceremonies, trial by ordeal, rain making, and other magical practices. Travellers are not unanimous with regard to the import of scarification, which is of a crude

[1] See this work, Ch. VI, pp. 328 *et seq.*

[2] Robley, " Moko," London, 1896. Elsdon Best, " Articles on Maori Race," Wellington, 1918. J. Cowan, " Maoris of New Zealand," Wellington, 1910.

kind; but a consensus of opinion regards the marks as tribal and sub-tribal, while the scarification itself is in some cases definitely associated with puberty rites for boys. The Urabunna, a decadent people, preserve their simple scarifications made in imitation of the marks on the bell bird, also a clear account of the legendary origin.[1] Tasmanians scarified and used red ochre.[2]

Africa

Apart from Morocco, Algeria, Tunis, and Egypt, where puncture tattoo prevails to-day as amuletic, therapeutic, and ornamental in function, Africa is a country where scarification with painting is of almost uninterrupted sequence. From the Limpopo to the Niger and Guardafui to the mouth of the Congo, cicatrization by cutting or irritation with caustic juices is the rule. The most elaborate examples of scarification are from the Mid-Congo region where the patterns are intricate, varied, and correctly overlapped. As the technique advances tribal marks become confused and desire for ornament is the sole purpose. Secret societies have special incised marks, and there are scarified designs to attract women, keloids to barter for food in heaven (Ekoi people), also other sporadic and unusual functions of cicatrization. The evidence makes clear that children were in early days, and as recently as twenty years ago in some districts, marked in

[1] This work, p. 175.

[2] Bonwick, "Daily Life and Origin of Tasmanians."

infancy with the mother's designs. Henri Junod, for the Ba Thonga, and Turner for coloured mine labourers of South Africa, show how important are taboo and ritual in the making of scars during puberty rites of girls. Young women of the Bargesu commence and complete their own scarification by wearing and using for several years a hooked iron ring (Roscoe). The question of body marking in ancient Egypt is more fittingly considered in concluding remarks relating to the origin and antiquity of these practices.

North America

The cultural home of the Eskimo is generally held to be Alaska, whence the tribes have spread to Hudson Bay and Greenland.[1] Various authorities, Boas,[2] Rink, Steffansohn, Cranz, make clear that tattooing by drawing a thread, previously blackened with soot, under the skin, is practised in all tribes. Tattooed designs are of two kinds—a chin mark for women, denoting puberty and marriageability, and an honorific mark for successful whalers. Rasmussen has completed a three years' investigation, 1921-4, of all Eskimo tribes, and further information may be forthcoming respecting body marks. Bogoras

[1] David Cranz, "History of Greenland," London, 1767, Vol. I, p. 138. Boas, "Central Eskimo," A.B.E., 1888, p. 561. A.B.E., 9th report, 1887-8, p. 140. People of Kadiak paint the face before an important undertaking such as crossing an arm of the sea, or following the sea otter.

[2] Reports Jesup Expedition to North Pacific, Part VIII, and "Memoir American Mus. Nat. Hist.," 1904-9, p. 254.

mentions tattoo marks of the Chukchee made for the same purpose as those of the Eskimo, so providing a link between the Asiatic and European sides. Cicatrization has a vogue among tribes of North American Indians chiefly in connection with the sweat bath ceremony which usually accompanies initiatory rites for boys. Parallel incisions were sometimes made on the cheeks of Maya people in Yucatan. A small figure in red ware showing these marks is pictured in a report of the "Königliche Museum zu Berlin."[1] The Mayas painted the body and face in red and tattooed by incision. The marks were honorific signs. Heads were artificially deformed.[2] The Güetares of Costa Rica tattooed the arms with designs representing animals, principally the jaguar.[3] Diego de Landa says that tattoo by puncture was a sign of bravery, and those who were not tattooed were mocked.[4]

Father Bernardino de Sahagun was one of the earliest Spanish missionaries to Mexico, and author of books relating to religion, manners, and customs of ancient Mexicans. Sahagun composed his famous "Historia de la Cosas de la Nuera España," chiefly in the native language known as Nahuatl. Apparently body paint was extensively used in ancient Mexico. Sahagun states that in the month of Toxcatl the priests with a stone knife made scars on children of

[1] Volume containing reports, 1889-1894, Band 1-3, Tafeln, 1.

[2] H. Beuchat, "Manuel d'Archæologie Americaine," Paris, 1912, p. 454.

[3] *Ibid.*, p. 536.

[4] "Collection de Documents dans les Langues Indigènes de l'Amerique Ancienne," Vol. III. "Relagion de Las Cosas de Yucatan," 1864, p. 121.

both sexes, on the breast, stomach, middle of arms, and wrists. The Otomi women made on their breasts and arms designs in a blue colour by means of small instruments which fixed the colour in the skin.[1] Tattoo by puncture was usually given to women at marriage, and stamping of the face with coloured designs of animals was common.[2] Probably the custom of tattoo by puncture was of long standing since representations of this marking are often seen on the faces of monumental figures.[3] Lewis Spence[4] summarizes the evidence, showing how an Aztec youth chosen for sacrifice to Tezcatlipocâ was painted black. In honour of the god Xipe faces were painted with stripes of red and yellow.[5] When a boy dedicated to Quetzalcoatl completed the second year of his novitiate the Superior of the institution made a small incision on the youth's breast which, like the collar given at presentation, was a mark of service.[6]

Painting and puncture tattoo are of general distribution throughout North America. The former is connected with rites of the medicine men, war, ceremonial dances, also with tribal and clan marks which are sometimes painted on the face after death to ensure recognition in heaven by predeceased clansmen.[7] There is painting of twins and their

[1] "Mexican Archæology," T. A. Joyce, p. 151.

[2] *Ibid.*, p. 150.

[3] *Ibid.*, p. 295.

[4] "Gods of Mexico," 1923, p. 96.

[5] *Ibid.*, p. 205.

[6] *Ibid.*, p. 137. See also Lord Kingsborough's monumental work on Mexican antiquities, nine volumes, 1831.

[7] A.B.E., 1918-9. "Death Paint," pp. 144-6, 204, 228, 249.

parents with ceremonial observance.[1] We have already discussed in full the dedication of Pawnee children to the sky god, the painting of the child with symbolic designs being attended with much ceremonial and song. Puncture tattoo is largely connected with totemic devices, and of many instances perhaps the Haida provide the best examples. Tattooing and painting were known throughout the Greater and Lesser Antilles, whither fled from South America the Arawaks pursued by more warlike Caribs.[2] By all authorities the importance of tribal and clan painting is mentioned. J. G. Bourke[3] says of the Moquis: "Each clan or gens in sending representatives to foot races or dramatic dances will have them marked with totemic or gentile emblems such as the eagle, or conventional representations on the breast and back."

South America

With regard to South America there is positive proof that the Inca or pre-Inca civilization acquired a high technical skill in puncture tattooing, but the objects and ceremonies, if such existed, are at present unknown. Excellent pictorial representations of painted and tattooed Inca designs are shown in a plate dealing with dried human remains from Peru.[4]

[1] A.B.E., 1916-7, pp. 58, 343, 679.

[2] *Ibid.*, 1915-6, pp. 230-2.

[3] "Snake Dance of Moquis of Arizona," New York, 1884, p. 229.

[4] "Necropolis of Ancon," Reiss and Stübel, Vol. I, Plate XXIX, translation by A. H. Keane. See this work, pp. 315-16.

The descriptive text says: "Of the many mummies taken from their coverings on the spot, a great number betray clear traces of painting limited, however, to the arms and hands or to larger surfaces on the upper part of the body. There are stars and darts whose motives reappear also on the material of garments. Professor Virchou's examination has shown that there is here no question of a superficial painting only, but that colouring matter permeates the tissues. Joyce, quoting early Spanish historians, Garcilasso and Cieza de Leon, states that there were, when the Spaniards arrived, people along the coast who punctured their faces with sharp-pointed stones. Men tattooed themselves with designs extending from the root of the ear to the chin.[1]

Designs of tattoo figured by Reiss and Stübel show the marks to be symmetrical, the technique advanced, and the recipients to be of several ages from eight years to adult stage, possibly also of both sexes. Archæological evidence of the Chibcha civilization of Colombia includes pattern blocks used to stamp clothing, possibly also the body. Truxillo ware in the British Museum shows a tattooed pattern round the outline of the lower jaw on a human face ornamenting the jar.

Tattooing, painting, and cicatrization are all common in the Amazon region and along its affluents. Semicircular black patches are common across the middle of the face covering the bottom of the nose and the mouth. Crossed lines are found on the back and breast, stripes down the arms and legs.

[1] T. A. Joyce, "South American Archæology," London, 1912, p. 61, 132.

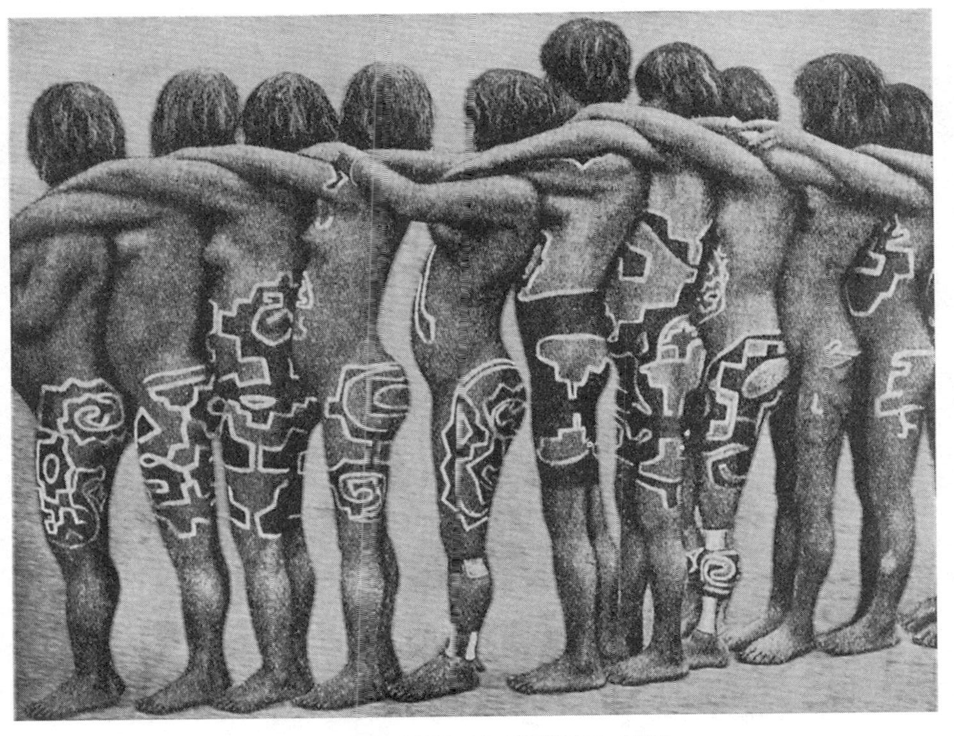

SNAKE DANCE OF AMAZONIAN GIRLS

(These girls are specially trained and fed for this strenuous exercise.)

In Brazil tattooing is characterized by straight lines and patches; there are no graceful curves. The nearest approach to elegance of design among Tucunas of the Upper Amazon consists of a scroll-like mark on each cheek proceeding from the corners of the mouth. The taste, as far as form is concerned, would seem to be far less refined than that of the Tahitian and New Zealander.[1] Examples of elaborate painting for dancing ceremonies are given in "People of All Nations," the pattern for the snake dance, where each girl is painted with a section of the complete design, being exceptionally attractive.[2] Tattoo is said to be used as an indication of tribe and rank.[3] Tattoo is little resorted to by Lengua Indians of the Chaco, but facial painting is common.[4] Excellent photographs by Paul Ehnenreich show scarification under the eyes of Karaya women, the marks being complete incised circles.[5] When describing the Tobas who wander over the Central and Southern Chaco, Guido Boggiani pictures an unbalanced, but well executed cheek design for women of Central South America.[6] C. F. P. Martius notes characteristic Brazilian tattoo designs and remarks on the utility of these in assisting quick

[1] H. W. Bates, "Naturalist on River Amazon," p. 223, edited 1915.

[2] "People of All Nations," edited by J. A. Hammerton, London, Fleetway House, E.C.4, Vol. I, p. 503.

[3] *Ibid.*, Vol. I, p. 507.

[4] W. B. Grubb, "An Unknown People in an Unknown Land," p. 71.

[5] "Anthrop. Studien Urbewohner Brasiliens," 1897, p. 95, Tafeln. XXI.

[6] "Viaggi d'un artista nell' America Meridionale," Rome, 1895, p. 165, Fig. 78. This work, p. 253.

distinction between friends and foes.[1] Young girls are tattooed by the mother, boys by the father.[2] Men of the Patamona tribe, Guiana, slash the breast, arms, and legs, then rub acrid juice into the wounds in order to give success in hunting.[3] The Antipas tattoo to a limited extent, the limbs being marked with simple designs such as the cross, circle, and wavy lines. Up de Graff sees no signs of external influence and thinks the practice indigenous. He notes the ready adoption of designs, for example, the tattooing of letters L. L. F. from cigarette packets.[4]

Seclusion of girls at puberty is certainly a custom of South American aborigines, and among the Tobas, a tribe of the Southern and Central Chaco, puberty is announced by a few tattooed lines on the arms and scars under the breasts.[5] W. B. Grubb, who spent many years as a missionary in the Paraguayan Chaco, states that at first menstruation girls are secluded in a hammock in the roof of the hut with face to the wall. The patient remains thus for three days, the hair is cut, a silence taboo is imposed, and no food is given. Following this there is abstention from fish and meat for a year, during which the only permissible occupations are weaving and spinning.[6]

The fullest account of tattooing in South America

[1] "Beitrage zur Ethnographie, etc., Brasiliens," 1867, p. 55.
[2] *Ibid.*, p. 510.
[3] Leo. E. Miller, "In the Wilds of South America," 1919, p. 186.
[4] Fritz W. Up de Graff, "Head-Hunters of the Amazon," London, 1923, p. 190-1.
[5] Colonel G. E. Church, "Aborigines of South America," 1912, pp. 115, 245, etc.
[6] W. B. Grubb, "In the Paraguan Chaco," London, 1904, p. 60.

is given by Dobrizhoffer,[1] a missionary, who spent eighteen years among the Abipoines, an equestrian people of Paraguay, about the middle of the eighteenth century. " They (Abipoines) mark their faces in various ways, some of which are common to both sexes, others peculiar to women. They prick their skin with a sharp thorn and scatter fresh ashes on the wound. They all wear the form of a cross impressed on their foreheads and two small lines at the corner of each eye extending towards the ears, besides four transverse lines at the root of the nose between the eyebrows, as a national mark. What these figures denote I cannot tell. . . ." At puberty girls are tattooed at intervals, meanwhile they are shut up for several days in their father's hut. Food restrictions are imposed.

Accounts relating to body marking of the Fuegians are important because they complete the establishment of an unbroken chain of geographical evidence which shows extension of the practice of puncture tattoo from Point Barrow in Alaska to Cape Horn.[2]

" Many people of both sexes were painted with white, red, and brown colours in different parts of the body, and had also various dotted lines pricked on their faces."[3] The Fuegians, like the Andamanese, have various colours and designs to denote emotional states. The natives of Tierra del Fuego have special paintings of the face for different bonds of friendship,

[1] Martin Dobrizhoffer, " The Abipoines," London, 1822, three volumes, see Vol. II, p. 19-22.

[2] S. Parkinson, " Journal of a Voyage to the South Seas," London, 1773, p. 8.

[3] P. Hyades and J. Deniker, " Mission Scientifique du Cap Horn," 1891, Tome VII, p. 350, Plate XV.

likewise for ceremonial visits. Colours applied to the face convey news of the death of a relative and the manner in which he died. Women paint their faces as an ornament chiefly with red, white, and black.

Summary of Chapter V

The foregoing survey makes clear that the practices of painting, scarifying, and tattooing are co-existent and co-extensive. There is no geographical limit to the practices of painting and scarifying, and the only check on adoption of puncture tattooing appears to have been the existence of a skin too dark to allow the tattoo marks to show. Consequently Bantu, Negritoes, Australians, and Papuans resort chiefly to scarification and painting. Scarification, which reaches its acme of excellence in the Congo region, is therapeutic, ornamental and tribal.

Painting is most elaborate in Australia, Africa, and South America, where it is definitely allied with magical acts of medicine men, totemic ceremonies, recognition in heaven, personal ornament, and expression of changing emotional states.

The beliefs and practices associated with tattooing by puncture are more numerous and important than those associated with other body marking practices. Probably scarification, originally therapeutic, borrowed from both painting and tattooing. Painting originally in prehistoric times probably had its magical, ornamental, and social aspects which were deliberately transferred to the more permanent puncture tattoo.

With regard to association of body marking customs with sex the evidence is clear. Both sexes scarify, paint, and tattoo. Painting is more important for men than it is for women, because of the essential part played by the practice in all magical ceremonies conducted by the medicine man.

The Ainu tattoo their women only, but this restriction is exceptional. All the earliest archæological evidence from Egypt demonstrates the paramount importance of tattooing and painting of women. The whole world over, tattooing of women at puberty is the most remarkable and constant feature of the body marking art. On the whole the evidence suggests transfer of puncture tattoo from women to men.

Decline of belief and ritual, likewise the transfer of associated ideas from one technique to another, have been too numerous and complex to justify dogmatism. The conclusions advanced in Chapter VI cannot be regarded as resting on an irrefutable demonstration, but rather as strong probabilities suggested by the evidence as a whole.

CHAPTER VI

HISTORICAL DISTRIBUTION OF TATTOOING

Prehistoric body marking—Tattooing among civilizations of antiquity—Dateable evidence—Places of probable origin and hypothetical lines of migration.

A SURVEY of the social and psychological importance of painting, tattooing, and scarifying in relation to the geographical distribution of these practices should now be followed by discussion relating to problems of origin, chronological sequence, and lines of migration.

The origin of body marking calls for comment with regard to circumstances, locality, and period, all of which points may conveniently be dealt with in relation to:

(1) Prehistoric times.
(2) Sumer and Babylon.
(3) China and Japan.
(4) The Aryans.
(5) Civilizations of Peru, Yucatan, and Mexico.
(6) Egypt.

(1) *Painting.*—Of the three varieties of body marking, namely, painting, scarifying, and tattooing by puncture the first is probably most ancient. Colours

were extensively employed in the cave paintings of palæolithic man in Europe and elsewhere. Osborne[1] has summarized the instances of association of red ochre with Cro-Magnon burials, Moorhead [2] deals with prehistoric " Red Paint People of Maine," Sollas[3] describes the " Red Lady of Paviland," found near Swansea, while works of Buckland,[4] Dechelette, Lartet, and Christy[5] establish use of red ochre in palæolithic times. Use of red paints had a vogue in Egypt which will be considered in some detail. Employment of red and other pigments by Negritoes, such as the Andamenese and Semang, who represent outliers of very ancient migrations, have been described; so also have the efforts of Australians and North Americans to obtain red ochre from long distances. The Andamanese still retain legends of the divine origin of colours, and there is a strong case for regarding use of red ochre as the first stage of the body marking process.

Primitive hunters doubtless noticed the departure of movement and animation as the blood ebbed from a wounded animal or human being. The uses of blood from human and other sacrifice for fertilizing land have been too well collated to require amplifying; and association of red earth with interments, or the rubbing of human bones with this colouring matter, must be regarded as the earliest known

[1] " Men of Old Stone Age," H. F. Osborne, 1916, p. 304.

[2] W. K. Moorhead, " American Anthropologist," 1913, Vol. XV, p. 43.

[3] " Ancient Hunters," 1924, and J.A.I., 1913, Vol. XLIII, p. 364.

[4] " Reliquiæ Diluvianæ," London, 1823, pp. 82 *et seq.*

[5] " Revue Archæologique," 1907, p. 38.

attempt to vitalize by symbolically applying the life-giving fluid.

(2) *Scarifying.*—The primitive medicine man is invariably concerned with removing a foreign substance from his patient. Pain is widely regarded as the result of introducing into a victim some object which occasions a disorder, and scarifying may rightly be regarded as having its origin in an attempt to let out a demon or object. Scars due to cutting, burning, and cupping no doubt became ornamental, especially when colouring matter was in the first instances accidentally introduced. Cicatrization probably borrowed much ritual and belief from painting and tattooing where the processes came into contact. But ritual connected with scarifying is very slight compared with that associated with the other processes, and Rivers' lines in "Medicine, Magic, and Religion" may be extended to areas other than Polynesia. "In Polynesia the letting of blood by means of gashes and scarification as a therapeutic practice, is especially characteristic of the Western Islands, for example Samoa. The common distribution of the therapeutic and religious forms of blood letting in the Pacific suggests that there is a definite connection between the two. It is highly probable that the medical practice introduced into the highly religious atmosphere of Polynesia has come to form part of religious ceremonial."[1]

(3) *Tattooing.*—Various interrupted dark mark-

[1] Rivers, *loc. cit.*, p. 99. See also G. Turner, "Samoa," 1884, p. 55, etc., and W. Mariner, "Tonga Islands," 1817, Vol. II, pp. 223, 243-4.

ings on a white or red background, given to dolls of female form, described more fully in succeeding paragraphs, suggest that tattooing by puncture was practised before the commencement of dateable periods. The very ingenious invention of making small separate punctures, possibly with pygmy flint implements, and introducing coloured matter I regard as a deliberate attempt of some thoughtful individual seeking consciously to impart a more enduring symbol of vitality than that afforded by mere surface painting with red ochre. Observation of human skin, especially on the backs of hands, shows small circular depressions and rugæ which intersecting gives lozenge-shaped patterns; and by these dots and rhomboids the early artist may have been guided; his efforts in pricking and colouring being an accentuation of outlines and depressions already provided by nature.

There can be no doubt that painting, scarifying, and probably tattooing had definite purpose and a wide distribution before the dawn of history. Possibly these practices migrated with early cultures of cave painting, flaking weapons in the widely distributed ovoid and lanceolate forms, and manufacturing of pygmy flints.

These general considerations of the inception of body marking processes lead to a more detailed consideration of their development in technique, ritual and belief in several great centres of civilization from the dawn of history onwards to the period when they were described, firstly by navigators and travellers, later by trained ethnologists.

Babylon.—There is no evidence to show that

tattooing or painting were ever practised in Babylonia and Assyria, though cosmetics and eye paints were employed.[1]

The Far East.—The fact has already been noted that although the Northern Chinese have never tattooed, the practice was common to the south of the Yang-Tse, probably before 1100 B.C. The fisher folk who tattooed were in relationships with Japan long before the commencement of reliable, dateable, Japanese history. The Japanese themselves tattooed in the middle of the fifth century A.D., and probably the custom was existent long before that date. Chamberlain quotes a Chinese historian who says that early in the Christian era the men of Japan tattooed their faces, and ornamented their bodies with designs, difference of rank being indicated by the position and size of the patterns.[2] Evidently tattooing in Japan was not always a practice confined to the lower orders as is the case to-day.

Japanese technique, with which no other style can compare in colour, form, motion, or light and shade of background, may indicate a long period of development. On the contrary, the Japanese are skilled artisans with exceptional ability to imitate with patience and perseverance. Consequently when interest in tattooing had been aroused technical skill might quickly be acquired. The appearance of the dragon in most Japanese designs may substantiate a claim to great antiquity, for the dragon is said to be

[1] "Life and Customs of Babylonians and Assyrians," A. H. Sayce, 1900, p. 105, and personal communication Mr. Sidney Smith, British Museum.

[2] B. H. Chamberlain, "Things Japanese," 1898, p. 380.

a composite beast with a long history.[1] This composite creature originally expressed divine power of life-giving, but ultimately became the embodiment of evil. It is possible that the Japanese borrowed from the Ainu the art of tattooing, rejected all beliefs connected therewith, and concentrated only on the technology of the craft, for of ritual and allied belief in association with Japanese tattooing there is no trace.

Clearly in dealing with the Far East we are in a region of surmise, where historical facts are few, and archæological evidence meagre. Body marking of all kinds has been avoided in China with the exception of puncture tattooing at the mouth of the Yang-Tse noted as early as 1100 B.C. Tattooing in Japan was practised as early as 500 B.C., but there is no evidence of belief or ritual connected therewith by Chinese or Japanese. Among the Ainu only women tattoo, but the extant beliefs in divine origin of these marks, and their necessity as a preparation for marriage and recognition in heaven, bring the Far East into agreement with all other centres where tattooing is practised. The Ainu are regarded as an outlier of the Alpine Race.[2] Their origin and migrations are unknown; but their presence in Japan antedated the arrival of the Koreans. Tenacious retention of beliefs by the Ainu, in connection with tattooing, suggests that they are the original sponsors of that craft in Japan, and as the Ainu are an ancient immigrant stock, the evidence is opposed to an

[1] "Evolution of the Dragon," 1919, p. 60.

[2] A. C. Haddon, "Wanderings of Peoples," Cambridge, 1912, p. 33.

assumption of the origin of tattooing by the Japanese.

Aryans.—Aryan-speaking peoples wandered so widely that there would be great interest in learning of body marking practices among them. There is, however, no such evidence, and my own negative research on this point is supported by Professor A. A. Macdonell,[1] who states that during forty years of reading he has found no indication that the Aryan invaders tattooed or had a word for tattooing, neither did they scarify. In India tattooing is practised only by Dravidian peoples, and it is important to note that these retain beliefs in the efficacy of tattoo marks for recognition in heaven, and as a prophylactic against disease and sterility.[2]

American Continents.—The task of assigning dates to archæological evidence from Peru, Colombia, Yucatan, and Mexico is difficult, even for experts. Consequently great caution in drawing deductions from the presence of tattooed bodies or their representation in art is demanded. Tattooing and painting were well advanced in the Inca civilization of A.D. 1100, and a consideration of dried human remains from the Necropolis of Ancon, which probably dates from the eleventh century, suggests a long period for development of technique during the pre-Inca period. The Incas painted the faces of their dead with red pigment.

Pottery from Colombia, which may be dated just prior to the Christian era, or perhaps very early A.D.,

[1] Personal communication.

[2] "Tribes and Castes of North-West Provinces and Oudh," W. Crookes, Calcutta, 1896, Vol. I, p. 22, etc.

shows painted or tattooed markings on human faces; it is impossible to be certain of the technique.

There is definite archæological evidence of painting, tattooing, and scarifying in Maya, Toltec and

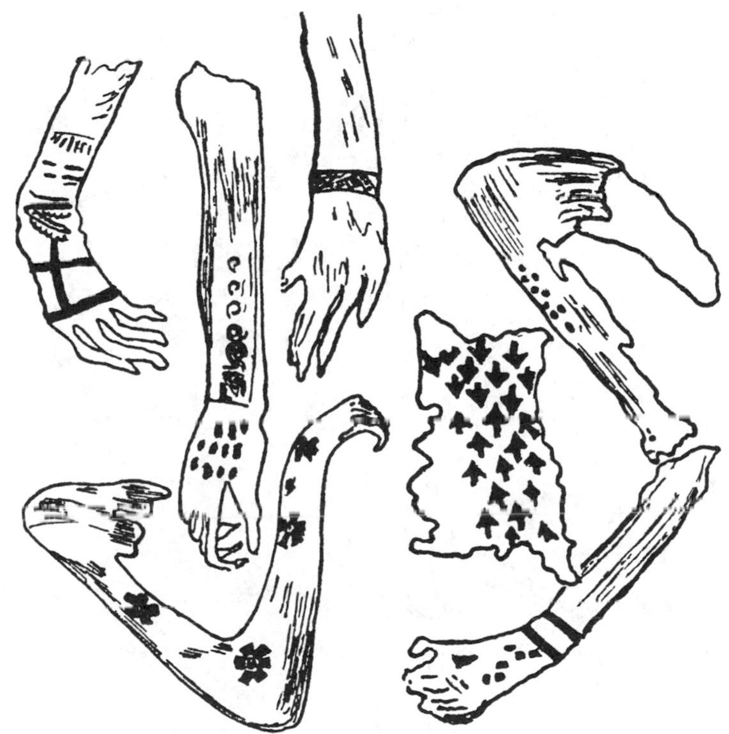

Tattoo on Skin of Mummies found in the Necropolis of Ancon, Peru.

Aztec civilizations. The former may be dated A.D. 200-800, and the latter from A.D. 1100 to 1519. The late dating of these American finds will be seen to have an important bearing on a probable migration of puncture tattooing through the Pacific, and its introduction into the New World. In Yucatan and

Mexico tattooing was regarded as a mark of distinction. Cicatrization was practised when dedicating male novices to service of a deity, and the use of pigments had a wide observance in relation to

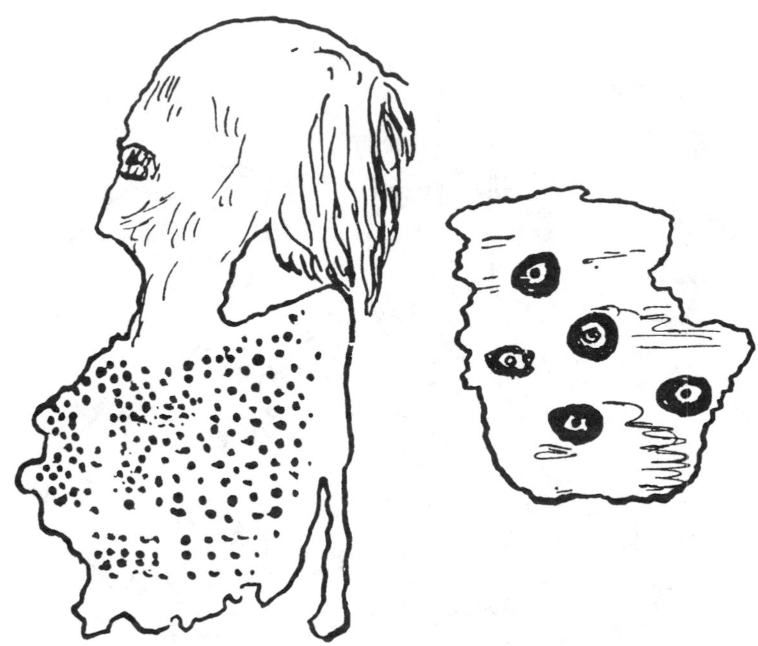

Tattoo on Skin of Mummies found in the Necropolis of Ancon, Peru.

religious festivals, and the decoration of youths who were eventually sacrificed not merely to the gods, but as gods themselves.[1]

Lewis Spence[2] thinks the civilizations of the

[1] T. A. Joyce, "South American Archæology," London, 1912, pp. 61, 132, etc. Reiss and Stübel, "Necropolis of Ancon," Vol. I, Plate XXIX. See scheme of dating American antiquities in Burlington Fine Arts Club Catalogue, London, 1920.

[2] "Gods of Mexico," 1923, "Mythologies of Ancient Mexico and Peru," 1905.

Americas indigenous but admits persistent legends of culture bringers. Duckworth says of the origin of man, " It is important to notice that time after time the attempts made to demonstrate the early origin of man in the American continents have resulted in failure."[1] Probably it is true that the " New World " was racially and culturally developed by migration from the " Old World." What is known of tattooing and painting in their social and religious aspects in American civilizations of antiquity is certainly consonant with theories of migration of culture from the Pacific to the western shores of the New World.

Egypt.—Branding, cicatrizing, painting, and tattooing by puncture all require consideration in relation to this country, but painting and tattooing are by far the most important of these practices.

Branding.—On the stelæ outside Abydos cemetery are the lines, " As for him whom anyone shall find within these stelæ, whether a craftsman or a priest at his business, he shall be branded " (Reign of Neferhotep).[2]

Ramses III, speaking of the Libyan wars, says: " I carried away those whom my sword spared—branded and made into slaves impressed with my name; their wives and their children were made likewise."[3]

Cicatrization.—Fouquet, describing the unwrapping of the mummy of the Theban priestess, Lady Ament, of the Eleventh Dynasty, speaks of white and

[1] " Prehistoric Man," Cambridge, 1912, p. 55.

[2] " Ancient Records of Egypt," J. H. Breasted, five volumes, 1907, Vol. I, par. 770.

[3] *Ibid.*, Vol. IV, par. 405, p. 201.

blue ante mortem cicatrices on abdomen and elsewhere. He concludes that she had been treated for chronic pelvis peritonitis in a manner still practised among the Fellahin of the present day.[1]

Tattooing and Painting.—In examining specimens of body marking applied to small female figures of prehistoric period there can be no positive distinction between tattoo and paint, though the former is strongly suggested. In the British Museum (sixth Egyptian Room) are several female figurines of the First and Second Dynasties. No. 32141 is a bone figure of a woman with inlaid lapis lazuli eyes. Covering the abdomen and pubes are a large number of dark, circular, separated marks which represent paint or tattoo, and a similar decoration occurs on Fig. 32144, a female dwarf of the Archaic period.[2]

Sir Flinders Petrie says: "The earliest human figures are found in the second stage of the prehistoric age immediately after the white lined pottery. They are of ivory, limestone, slate, pottery, or stick and paste. Such figures did not continue to be made after the middle of the prehistoric civilization. Some of the limestone cement figures have tattoo marks painted on the stone, others are of the armless form seated and clearly of steatopygous Bushman type."[3]

With regard to such figures in the Ashmolean

[1] Fouquet, quoted by C. S. Myers, J.A.I., Vol. XXXIII, 1903, p. 84. See Fouquet, "Le Tatouage Medical en Egypte dans l'Antiquite," "Archives d'Anthrop. Criminelle," Tome XIII, 1899, p. 270.

[2] This work, p. 108.

[3] "The Arts and Crafts of Ancient Egypt," 1909, p. 29, Fig. 16. See also "Primitive Art in Egypt," Jean Capart, 1905, p. 161, and De Morgan's "Recherches sur les Origines de l'Egypte," 1896, Vol. II, p. 52, etc.

Museum, Oxford, Mr. E. T. Leeds has been good enough to write to me: "The steatopygous (so-called) figures here being made of clay have had a red slip laid on the surface as in the case of figurines of animals of similar fabric. Over the red slip in some cases can be detected black painted marks, which certainly suggest tattooing, as in the case of the head-

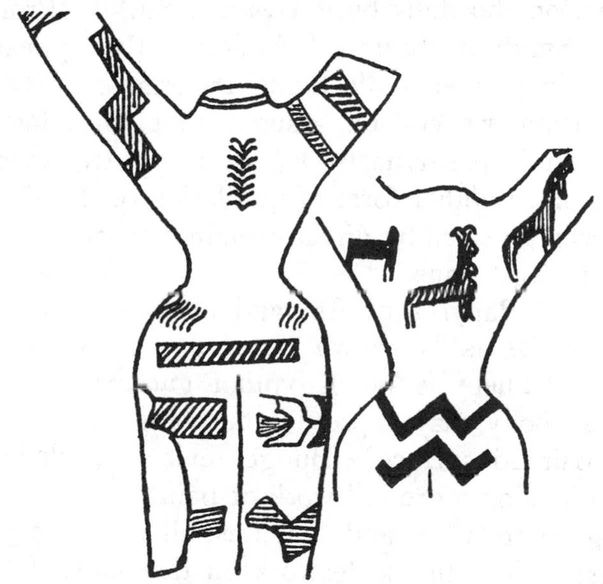

Egyptian Female Figures, *circa* 3000 B.C. The Corporal Marks are painted or tattooed.

less figure of whitish clay covered with painted black marks. Both come from the finds at Naquada and Ballas. These figures date from considerably before 3000 B.C. According to illustrations given in reports of Naquada and Ballas excavations, seated female figures of the "Great Mother" type are coloured red, a very interesting point in connection with the hypothesis that body marking originated in the use of red ochre to symbolize revitalizing by blood.[1]

"In course of archæological surveys of Nubia Mr. Firth found a number of bodies of Nubians of the time of the Middle Empire (2000 B.C.) with definite scarring, and the patterns pricked on the skin of these desiccated bodies were identical with those painted on the dolls buried with them."[2] Professor Elliot Smith continues: "Although the appearance of certain painted dolls found in archaic graves has led certain writers to assume that tattooing was customary in pre-dynastic Egypt no positive evidence of this or any other form of mutilation of the skin has ever been revealed by direct examination of the bodies of proto-Egyptians."[3]

In the Papyrus of Ani and elsewhere the entire body of Osiris is shown covered with scale work pattern. There is no Egyptian garment like this, and the body may represent tattooing or scratching on a painted surface. Budge reviews evidence for scratchings on a ground work of paint also cicatrizing among negro tribes and Hamites, all of which points suggest "That the scale work on the body of Osiris represents a design made by tattoo, paint, or cicatrix."[4]

Capart states that Egyptians of the classical

[1] "Naquada and Ballas," M. F. Petrie and J. E. Quibell, 1896, p. 34.

[2] "Ancient Egyptians and Origins of Civilization," G. Elliot Smith, 1923, p. 63.

[3] *Ibid.*, p. 63.

[4] "Osiris and the Egyptian Resurrection," Sir W. Budge, 1911, Vol, I, p. 324.

TATTOOED SKIN, AND DOLL WITH CORRESPONDING MARKINGS, FROM A MIDDLE NUBIAN CEMETERY, 1300 B.C.

period tattooed themselves occasionally on the breast and arms with names or representations of divinities, but the practice appears to be confined to the second Theban Empire. " I do not remember having met with examples outside Amenophis IV and his Queen, who bore the names of the god Aten tattooed upon breast and arms." [1]

Figures of a group of Libyans depicted on the tomb of Seti I, 1330 B.C., reveal tattoo marks, one of which is clearly the symbol of the goddess Neith.[2] This adoption of the symbol relating to Neith is of extreme importance owing to the antiquity of this goddess. Net or Neith is one of the oldest of all Egyptian goddesses, and there is evidence that her worship was widespread even in pre-dynastic times. In addition to minor functions, such as patroness of hunting, Neith was the personification of a form of primeval watery mass out of which sprang the sun god, Re.[3]

Even in the First Dynasty the cult of Neith had acquired age and tradition. In the Fourth Dynasty she was thought to be at once the mother and daughter of the sun god, Re. Neith possessed the power to conceive and bring forth daily a new sun god by use of divine and magical formulæ. Among early titles of Neith is "Apt-Uat," that is, opener of the ways, for she was believed to have a function in connection with dressing the dead and so assisting in their preservation.[4] "The doctrine of

[1] "Primitive Art in Egypt," 1905, p. 32.

[2] This work, p. 105.

[3] "The Gods of the Egyptians," E. A. Wallis Budge, London, 1904, Vol. I, p. 30.

[4] *Ibid.*, Vol. I, pp. 450 *et seq.*

parthenogenesis was well known in Egypt in connection with the goddess Neith of Saïs."[1] "Mena of the First Dynasty (4000 B.C.) visited Saïs to make offerings at the shrine of Neith, the protecting goddess of his royal mother."[2]

The Libyans, a fair-skinned people, of whom Kabyles and Berbers are thought to be modern representatives, lived to the west of Lower Egypt. Dr. C. S. Myers notes the peculiar distribution of tattooing among modern Egyptians, the practice being most common in western areas adjoining ancient Libya.[3] The tattooing of names "Aten" on King Amenophis IV and his Queen;[4] the figures on the tomb of Seti I, 1350 B.C.; and the marked dolls accompanying fragments of human skin similarly tattooed all occur at a time when Libyan influence was strong.

A most common tattooed design in modern Egypt is a rayed disc which appears to represent the sun. Many patterns include three dots arranged in a triangle, which was part of the hieroglyphic sign for eye paint. "The simpler and more purely geometrical patterns of Modern Egyptian tattooing are akin to those which prevail throughout North Africa, while the more complex, for example, the minarets and lion with a sword, have been derived from an Eastern source."[5]

[1] "The Gods of the Egyptians," Vol. II, p. 220.

[2] "A Short History of Ancient Egypt," P. E. Newberry and J. Garstang, London, 1907, p. 20.

[3] C. S. Myers, "Contributions to Egyptian Anthropology," "Tattooing," J.A.I., 1913, Vol. XXXIII, p. 85.

[4] De Morgan, "Recherches sur les Origines de l'Egypt," Paris, 1897, p. 222.

[5] C. S. Myers, *loc. cit.*, p. 89.

Paint, curative and cosmetic, was widely used in pre-dynastic Egypt. " In the rituals there are frequent allusions to green paint as early as the Pyramid texts, and belief in the protective and curative virtues of the paint was such, even at that time, that the painted eye was called the sound or healthy eye."[1] The earliest female figurines are reddened. Painting of stone statues with red ochre to make them life-like was in vogue in Egypt before 3000 B.C.; wherever the conception of human beings dwelling in stones, whether carved or not, was adopted, the Egyptian practice of applying red paint also came into vogue.[2] The face of the mummy of Ramses V was painted red, and there were red bandages among the wrappings of Siptah.[3] The mummies of many priests of the Twenty-first Dynasty were given red facial paint. All of these facts must be remembered in connection with those already collated relating to varied use of colour symbolism throughout the world. The Egyptian was concerned with perfecting mechanical means of imparting life, and painting was one of many methods which kept the body alive in the under world. Widespread ideas of tattoo and paint marks securing admittance to and recognition in heaven, are, I think, a development of the idea of red paint having a vitalizing power or potence in preventing desiccation of the body.

[1] Sir Gaston Maspero, " Revue de l'Histoire des Religions," 1897, Vol. XXXV, p. 297.

[2] Elliot Smith, " Migrations of Early Culture," p. 27.

[3] " Bulletin de L'Institut Egyptien," 1907-8, Tome I, pp. 49, 62, etc.

The world over, tattooing, painting, and scarifying are regarded as an essential accompaniment of the puberty, marriage, and fertility of women. From no other country have we an example of a female figure sometimes designated "Great Mother," marked with designs exactly like those on human skin, interred therewith. This instance, combined with the reddening of female figures, and the apparently tattooed designs on female figures from Naquada and Ballas, suggest that in Egypt from pre-dynastic times to 2000 B.C. body marking had a definite association with problems of fecundity and other aspects of fertility cults. If this surmise be correct, and such conceptions spread in company with other factors, one can understand the food taboos, seclusion, and other rites accompanying puberty of women the world over. A prehistoric alliance of tattooing with a cult of fertility either in Egypt or elsewhere would explain why the Naga girls must stay at home, and a Motu girl must parade the centre street of the village only during the period of her tattooing. The idea is probably avoidance of cultivated ground. The Kayan girl must not dig or draw water during tattooing operations; dreaming of floods causes the operation to be abandoned, possibly because in remote times flooding of the land, a prime factor in fertilization, was a sacred act connected with fertility cults. We had to note certain Dravidian jungle tribes mixing tattooers' pigments with human milk, and there was one instance of tattooing the conch-shell design as a guarantee that the woman would never be without husband. All these points are comprehensible if we may ally tattooing at an early stage of its history with the

"Mother Cult," and with regard to Egypt there is justification for so doing.

These facts relating to tattooing and painting in Egypt are so important that they should be briefly summarized:

(1) The occurrence in pre-dynastic times, of corpulent female figurines covered with red ochre on which darker marks appear. (These antedate 4000 B.C. Palæolithic European sites furnish similar examples.)
(2) Bone female figurines of the First and Second Dynasties with dark circular markings on abdomen and pubes.
(3) Female figurines from Naquada and Ballas (3000 B.C.) The painted or tattooed designs are those of antelope and regular zigzag patterns. The antelope may be a totemic emblem, and the zigzag, which later became the hieroglyphic sign for water, was possibly used to indicate fertility and rejuvenation.
(4) Tattooed skin showing lozenge-shaped patterns identical with those on an accompanying female figurine (2000 B.C.).
(5) Symbols of the goddess Neith tattooed on figures of Libyans on the tomb of Seti I (1300 B.C.).
(6) Tattooing of Amenophis and his Queen with the name of the god Aten.
(7) Use of red facial death paint and reddening of statues to give life.

All these examples connect body marking in

Egypt with women and the fertility cult they symbolized, while the importance of body marking in relation to social status and religious belief is indicated.

From no other civilization is there such ancient and definite evidence of body marking. Egypt no doubt was indebted to a prehistoric idea of the technique and cultural value of body marking. But in the Nile Valley, as the foregoing instances show, the art of painting and tattooing became incorporated with a complex of social and religious usages and beliefs of a kind fundamental in human society. Such a fact is made the basis of the following section dealing with probable lines of dispersal.

Migration.—The earliest recorded tattoo marks, namely those shown on preserved skin accompanying similarly marked dolls from Egypt, date back to 2000 B.C. Egypt was in communication with Crete, Greece, Assyria, Persia, Arabia, and the Sudan at various times between that date and the Christian era. Hence the practice of tattooing had time to make its way to Scotland by the Picts, and across Arabia, and Persia, into Southern China where the first records of the practice are of date 1100 B.C. Tattooing was general among Japanese several centuries before the Christian era, but for the Ainu, an outlier of the Alpine race, who preserve legends of divine origin of tattooing, there is no dateable evidence. From the Japanese islands tattooing may well have had an easy transit to Kamschatka and Northern Siberia where the Chukchee have adopted puncture marking. Southward from Japan tattooing migrated, in strong association with head hunting, through Formosa, the Philippines, Micronesia, and Borneo. The Shans are a tattooing people whose original home was in Suthern China about 2000 B.C.[1] In the thirteenth century B.C. they were in full occupation of the Yung Chang Plain, from whence they made a succession of migrations into the Irawaddi Valley, making contact with and conquest over the Burmese,[2] with whom tattooing is highly developed in technique and magical belief. " It can be conclusively shown that the dominant race of Tsu of various cognate tribes were the Tai, the Shan's name for themselves.[3]

The Polynesians undoubtedly played a most important rôle in the distribution of tattooing in association with religious beliefs and fertility rites, while they developed the practice on its heraldic side most elaborately in New Zealand. Christian states that in the Marquesas, tattooed signs have a decisive and arbitrary character, highly suggestive of a hieroglyphic system, which can be interpreted only by the Tuhunas or priests now very few in number.[4] Percy S. Smith [5] believes that the original Polynesian stock can be traced to India from which emigration commenced 450 B.C. Cowan[6] gives photographs showing Maoris of Semitic type, and it may be that the Polynesians came from as far west as the

[1] M. Terrien de Lacouperie, " The Cradle of the Shan Race."

[2] " To the Alps of Chinese Tibet," J. W. and C. J. Gregory, 1923, p. 62.

[3] " Shans at Home," Mrs. Leslie Milne, London, 1910, p. 2 of Historical Preface by Wilbur.

[4] " Eastern Pacific Islands," p. 93.

[5] " Hawaiki," London, 1910.

[6] " Maoris of New Zealand," Wellington, 1910.

Persian Gulf. Tattooing has been shown to exist among Dravidian tribes of Bengal and Oudh, where the operation is connected with beliefs regarding entry to heaven, and fertility of women. Possibly the Polynesians appropriated and amplified these beliefs during their journey into the Pacific. Of Polynesian residence in Java for a century, dating from 65 B.C. onward, there is no evidence so far as tattooing is concerned. But Java has for six centuries been under Muhammadan influence which is opposed to body marking on the strength of Koranic prohibition. In A.D. 600 the Polynesians were living in Tonga and Samoa, still strongholds of the tattooing operation, and in journeying thither the migrating streams touched Borneo, South-East New Guinea, and the Bismark Archipelago. In these areas tattooing is strongly associated with taboo and ritual in the preparation of girls for marriage, and in the Bismark Archipelago and Solomon Islands tattooing exists in conjunction with painting and scarification by burning. Hawaii was first settled by the Polynesians in A.D. 650 though the islands had been reached from Borneo in A.D. 450. The Marquesas were reached twenty-five years later. The latter islands developed an elaborate tattoo associated with heraldry, social status, and possibly religious symbols. New Zealand was visited in A.D 850, and was occupied about the middle of the fourteenth century.[1] Here a special Moko tattoo was developed with peculiar patterns for women, tribal, family and heraldic devices, and these were associated with taboo and ritual. The Polynesians

[1] "Hawaiki," Percy S. Smith, Auckland, 1921, p. 283.

carried tattooing operations as far east as the Paumotus and Easter Island. From the writings of Beechy[1] (1825) and Roggeveen[2] (1722) it became evident that the tattoo of women was in the form of dark blue breeches like those of the Maori females. The technique of tattooing was evidently considered important in Easter Island, for at one time the Araki or chief inspected the tattooed. Those who were artistically marked were sent to stand on one hill, those who were badly tattooed were sent to stand on another where they were laughed at.[3]

Distribution of tattooing in the Pacific shows a close correspondence with that of pearl fisheries. Mr. Perry postulates the transit of a complex culture from early dynastic Egypt through the Pacific to America. The culture carriers he terms the "Children of the Sun," who were responsible for the conveyance of such essential arts of civilization as building in stone, irrigation, and on the non-material side sun worship and dual organization. Perry notes the quest of these people for life-giving substances which include pearl-shell. Assuming the validity of this hypothesis, the conveyors of the "Archaic Civilization" may have been responsible for distribution of tattooing over the pearl and pearl-shell producing area.

Through Polynesian migrations assisted by pearl fishing, or other movements, tattooing traversed the entire Pacific area covering the region from the atolls of the Paumotus to the Gilberts, and from Hawaii

1 "Narrative of a Voyage in the Pacific."

2 See "Voyage of Gonzalez," Hakluyt Society, Series II, Vol. XIII, pp. 3-26.

3 Scoresby Routledge, "The Mystery of Easter Island."

to Samoa, the last named generally being regarded as a base of Polynesian migrations. An observer with a residence of twenty years in Fiji points out the importance of ritual in connection with the tattooing of women. There are various restrictions including fasting. The tattooer prays to spirits of the dead to alleviate pain, and of the two operators one is a supervisory " wise woman." [1] Such information is completely in agreement with what we know of tattooing in all other parts of the Pacific. Brewster's reference to his informant's statement that there was tattooing in Fiji before the arrival of the Polynesians is startling, and on account of its disagreement with all other information would require cautious acceptance.

The passage of tattooing into the American continents merits careful consideration. Lewis Spence says: " Origins of religions in Mexico and Peru could not have been of any other than an indigenous nature." [2] But at once he adds that there are persistent legends, similar among Mexicans and Peruvians, relating to white and bearded culture bringers. An indigenous origin for these American civilizations has, of course, been seriously questioned.[3] Red face painting of Peruvian mummies, the blue puncture tattooing of these, ceremonial scarifying and painting in Aztec religious rites, Maya and Aztec puncture tattooing, all harmonize in belief and ritual with similar practices in many parts of the Old World, as already described. To treat such as spontaneous

[1] " The Hill Tribes of Fiji," A. B. Brewster, 1922, pp. 83, 185-6.
[2] " Mythologies of Ancient Mexico," p. 77.
[3] G. Elliot Smith, " Migrations of Early Culture."

origins, and lightly to dismiss legends of culture bringers, is too facile a method of dealing with an important and intricate problem.

An opponent of the theory of Polynesian introduction of tattooing into America might suggest the entrance of the practice into the Americans continents at the north-west extremity of Alaska. Here Eskimo tribes, who chin-tattoo their women, give honorific marks to successful whalers, and paint the face red when engaged in dangerous hunting of the sea otter or crossing a treacherous arm of the sea, may have derived body marking from the Chukchee on the opposite side of Behring Strait. The tattooing of blue marks spread with other aspects of Eskimo culture, and was known in Greenland in the time of David Cranz (1750). But tattooing practices, likewise painting, play such an important part in the tribal life of North America that it is difficult to think that such an extensive variety of technique, ritual and taboo was introduced by the Eskimo, who themselves retain only two uses for tattooing, and these without accompanying ritual.

For a hypothetical introduction of puncture tattooing into America by Polynesians it may be said that distances from Hawaii to Vancouver, or to San Francisco, are 2,400 and 2,100 miles respectively. The journeys from Easter Island to the coasts of Peru or Chili are almost exactly the same as those involved for the more northerly route from Hawaii to California. Winds and currents are adverse to the journey by both routes, and so far as distance is concerned, there is nothing to favour northern or southern arrival. The Polynesians were in the

Marquesas and Easter Island about the latter end of the seventh century A.D. The Inca Empire was founded about A.D. 1100, prior to which there was a pre-Inca civilization of unknown date, which leaves a reasonably long period for transit and development of tattooing, such as is described by early Spanish conquistadores. Maya civilization was probably flourishing in the seventh century A.D. The year 1376, not much more than a century before the Spanish Conquest of Mexico, is perhaps the earliest reliable date which can be given to any aspect of Aztec civilization. Tattooing and painting, with cicatrization, in Yucatan are described in Spanish codices of the late fifteenth and early sixteenth centuries, and archæological evidence indicates the existence of body marking several centuries prior to Spanish intrusion. The Polynesian arrival at Hawaii in A.D. 450 was followed by colonization of the islands two centuries later, a time sequence which probably allows opportunity for the introduction of puncture tattooing to the Pacific coasts, and subsequent inland transit to the culture centres of the east of North America. A voyage from Hawaii to the coast of North America involves a distance of over 2,000 miles, but such has on occasions been accomplished in a small open boat, notably by Captain Bligh when sent adrift by the mutineers of the *Bounty*. Introduction of tattooing to the Pacific coast does not necessarily involve a large landing. A few artistically tattooed navigators might soon communicate a practice which, on account of its attractiveness, and the migratory habits of the Plains Indians would rapidly cross the continent.

Migrations from Easter Island to Peru are probable. Megalithic monuments are prominent in Easter Island, and Hiram Bingham[1] points out by description and photographs, that Captain Cook's account of stone ruin on this island is strictly applicable to the dry-built, well-fitting megalithic structures of Upper Peru. In view of the great antiquity of puncture tattooing, its geographical, social, and psychological association with other cultural factors, and the known tendency of cultures to travel in a group complex, there is strong evidence to suggest the entry of tattooing into South America from islands of the Eastern Pacific.

Summary

The archæological and ethnological evidence indicate that the oldest forms of body marking, namely, painting and scarifying, had a wide distribution before the historical period. Tasmanians, whose southerly migrations were very ancient, employed both forms of technique. So also do all negrito peoples of the Andamans, Philippines, Celebes, and New Guinea. Probably these simpler forms of body marking travelled with the art of cave painting and flaking of simple palæolithic forms of implements which are so widely distributed. Archæological evidence from Egypt with regard to puncture tattoo is the oldest, most abundant, and most important of any discovered. In addition to this the known

[1] "Across South America," London, 1911, p. 276.

existence of tattooing in Egypt as early as 2000 B.C., probably earlier than 4000 B.C., gives a chronological starting point which, supplemented by dateable Polynesian migrations, renders the introduction of puncture tattoo into America by Polynesian incursions highly probable. On the social and psychological side it may be said that tattooing in Archaic Egypt was associated with a fertility cult, ideas of heaven, and social status, all of which points are essentials of the beliefs, ritual, and practice of tattooing in all parts of the world.

Against this idea of cultural development of tattooing in Egypt, a hypothesis supported by palpable archæological evidence, the following points should be weighed:

1. That by far the most elaborate tattooing technique is developed in Japan.
2. That archæological excavations in the Far East (where tattooing was known to exist in South-East China about 1100 B.C.) are insignificant compared with the thorough research of Egyptian explorers. Hence excavations in China and Japan may change the historical outlook of this complex body marking problem.
3. If painting and tattooing were as important in Egypt as the archæological evidence would suggest, is it not strange that Egyptian texts make no reference to the necessity for tattooing—not even an injunction to tattoo women at puberty, perhaps the most important aspect of the tattooing craft?

Perhaps in our pre-dynastic and dynastic evidence of body marks on female figures and mummy skin we have a reminder of a one-time important procedure, discarded before dynastic times, after being passed to a Semitic people of the Persian Gulf or Northern India, who, under the name of Polynesians, amplified original beliefs and disseminated them over wide areas.

INDEX

NOTE

The following terms are those under which references to body marking may be indexed in English, German, French, Italian and Spanish works.

English.
Tattooing or (Tatuing).
Cicatrization.
Keloids.
Scarification.
Tribal Marks.
Painting.
Personal Ornament.

German.
Tätowirung.
Einschnittung (Scarification).
Körperbemalung (Body painting).
Körperschmuck (Body ornament).
Narbe tätowirung (Scar tattooing).
Brandnarbung (Burnt scars).
Ziernarben (Ornamental scars).

French.
Le Tatouage.
Peinture Corporelle.

Italian.
Tatuaggio.

Spanish.
Pintada.

A

G

H

I

J

K

L

M

N

O

P

Q

R

S